TEACHINGS OF
GURDJIEFF

TEACHINGS OF GURDJIEFF

A
Pupil's Journal

*An Account
of Some Years With
G. I. Gurdjieff and A. R. Orage
in New York and
at Fontainebleau-Avon*

by

C. S. NOTT

SAMUEL WEISER INC.

First Published in the United States of America, 1962
by Samuel Weiser Inc.
740 Broadway, New York, N.Y. 10003

Reprinted 1969, 1971 and 1974
Reprinted and first published
as a paperback 1978

ISBN 0-87728-106-8 (c)
ISBN 0-87728-395-8 (p)

Printed in Great Britain

CONTENTS

PLATES

PREFACE

IT IS NOW over thirty-five years since I first came in touch with the Gurdjieff system. This journal, begun in 1924, is a partial record of my early years of work (1923 to 1928) with G. I. Gurdjieff and A. R. Orage. It is not an exposition of the system, but a relation of my own experience of some of the acts and sayings of these two men, compiled from diaries and hundreds of pages of notes. It is sequential rather than chronological; many talks were repeated, sometimes at long intervals, and from different aspects and in different forms.

In compiling this journal I have had in mind the increasing number of people who are becoming interested in the ideas of George Ivanovitch Gurdjieff. Those who are unacquainted with his teaching may find some of the terms and expressions used confusing; at the same time there is much that will interest many who are dissatisfied with our present way of existence. Some of them may wish to read Gurdjieff's own Book *Beelzebub's Tales to his Grandson: an Objective Impartial Criticism of the Life of Man*.

When I first met Gurdjieff and Orage I was immature, naïve, and restless, with no knowledge of real ideas; and I can never be grateful enough to Gurdjieff for his infinite patience in those early years, and to the older pupils around him for their guidance, especially A. R. Orage, Dr Stjoernval, and Thomas de Hartmann, who later became my close friends and, as it were, elder brothers. I am no longer young; in my varied existence I have experienced almost all that ordinary life has to offer—both what is called good and what is called bad. And I can see now that whatever I have been able to achieve for my own being and understanding, whatever of reality I have been able to cognize and comprehend, I owe to Gurdjieff and his system and method. They have given me a centre of gravity and a real aim, and with Paul I can say 'Thanks be to God for his unspeakable gift'.

Cosmology and cosmogony, the creation and maintenance of the universe, the laws of Three and Seven, the causes of man's degeneration and the means for his redemption, eschatology—the four last things: detailed explanations of all these may be found in Gurdjieff's book *All and Everything* (Beelzebub's Tales to His Grandson), an objective work of art of the first magnitude. P. D. Ouspensky's *In Search of the Miraculous; Fragments of an Unknown Teaching*, while not in the category of objective art, is nevertheless a masterpiece of objective reporting of Gurdjieff's talks in Russia. As an introduction to Gurdjieff's system it can never be equalled. But while study of the *Fragments* gives knowledge alone—though of a high order—study of *Beelzebub's Tales* gives both knowledge and 'understanding'.

Briefly, the Gurdjieff system comprises writings; sacred dances, movements, and exercises; music; and the inner teaching. Gurdjieff's writings are arranged in three series: The first, *Beelzebub's Tales*; the second, *Meetings with Remarkable Men*; the third, *Life is Real Only When 'I Am'*. The first was published in 1950, the second is available in French though not in English, the third has not been published; some of the music has been published.

Gurdjieff collected a large number of sacred dances, folk-dances, and exercises in the Near and Far East; and he himself composed many dances and movements, a number of them based on the symbol of the enneagram. He also composed and collected a great many pieces of music, which were harmonized under his supervision by Mr de Hartmann. Many of these dances and musical compositions are objective art.

A knowledge of the theory of the system may be acquired from books; and indeed every serious enquirer should read *Beelzebub's Tales* and *Fragments of an Unknown Teaching*. But the inner teaching, which includes practical work—the Method—can be imparted only to special groups by teachers who have themselves been through long periods of intensive work.

The first part of the present book consists chiefly of accounts of work with Gurdjieff; the second of Orage's commentary in the New York group; while the third is a kind of sequel to and result of the first two.

C. S. NOTT

PROLOGUE

EVEN WHEN quite a young child in the Hertfordshire village where I was brought up, there often seemed to me to be something strange and even absurd in the behaviour of grown-up people; their attitude to one another in public, and what they said about each other in private, did not agree. As I grew up I became more aware of the difference between life as I thought it ought to be and as it actually was. In time, of course, I had to begin to accept it. 'Perhaps,' I wondered, 'it may be not life, not the grown-ups, but I that am wrong.' Yet something in me would not entirely accept this. As a boy, I imagined that there must be some place where I should be content; that I would find satisfaction in a job, or in a religion other than that of the Methodist chapel. I loved my home and my parents, yet I was seldom satisfied. Whether because of something in my heredity or of the influence of the planets at my conception and birth, or a mixture of these, I do not know; but an inner restlessness and dissatisfaction with what I happened to be doing on the one hand, or with circumstances on the other, gave me no inner peace; there was always the unformulated question 'What is life for?'

At the age of six I bought my first book; its title, oddly enough, was *Johnny's Search*.

I left school at the age of thirteen, having learnt literally nothing— for I read and wrote without having been taught—and went from one job to another, always asking what life was for. At the age of eighteen, I wandered to Tasmania, then to New Zealand, Australia, and Canada, working on sheep-stations and farms, and at other physical jobs. In 1914, when I was living on a small island off the coast of British Columbia, the first World War broke out. I joined up at once, to become one of the millions of youths and young men who were swept up in that collective catastrophe; and in 1917 I was invalided out of the trenches in France. It was then that I began to think seriously about the meaning of life.

Although I had had a religious upbringing and as a youth had been a Sunday-school teacher and lay preacher (literally a 'God-fearing' young man), organized religion had now no content for me, nor could it give me a satisfying answer to the questions that arose in me as a consequence of the disillusionment resulting from the war, in which, it seemed, one's life or death often depended on the whim of some vain, stupid man who happened to be in authority. The stupidity and absurdity of so much of ordinary life was as nothing compared with the colossal stupidities of war, when thousands lost their lives through someone's vanity, or pride. I used to ask myself, 'Why must men suffer like this? Why do the politicians and papers pour out lies? Why is life lived in an atmosphere of lies?' I met only one man, George Bernard Shaw, with whom I had several talks, who was ready to admit that the war was a ghastly business, and that there was something strangely wrong with men's attitude to war and to life in general. To him it was as if we were living in a lunatic asylum.

There must, I felt, be someone, or some teaching, that could give a clear answer to my questions. And one day, in the last year of the war, the conviction came that I should find this teacher or teaching; but that I should have to search, and the most likely place to find one or the other would be in the Far East. After the armistice I set off, and for two years worked my way round the world, visiting America, Japan, China, Malaya, Burma, India, Egypt, and Italy; but though I had many interesting experiences, met men and religions of all kinds, and saw many wonderful sights, I did not discover either the teacher or the teaching that in my inner being I felt would satisfy me.

I returned to England better in health, though still suffering from the effects of trench-fever and shell-fire. Financial success now came to me through business relations with Vienna, where I spent the best part of a year. Money came easily; and I was able to live as a young 'man about town'. Also I 'took up' social reform and became a resident of Toynbee Hall. There, an opportunity came to work with a relief mission in Russia, in the Ukraine. Here, with the peasants, I spent one of the most interesting years of my life, for the disease of Communism had not yet come to the district where I was. Returning to England, I soon found myself in the literary and bookish world, and moving in the 'highest society'. Everything that an ambitious young man could ask for came my way, including a public career, backed by people with family, money, and influence. In a sense it was satisfying, but the satisfaction was accompanied by a profound dissatisfaction. I seemed to be heading for a blind alley. I felt that all my experiences were as nothing, a mere background. I must find the Magic Book of the Russian fairy-tales, the Magic Ring, the Golden Bough; something that would give me a clue to the meaning of life.

At this time I came across a sonnet of Barnabe Barnes which described my inner state. So vivid was the impression it made that I must have read it a hundred times. It is from *Parthenophil and Parthenophe* (1593):

> Ah, sweet Content! Where is thy mild abode?
> Is it with Shepherds, and light-hearted Swains
> Which sing upon the downs, and pipe abroad
> Tending their flocks and cattle on the plains?
>
> Ah, sweet Content! Where dost thou safely rest?
> In heaven, with angels, which the praises sing
> Of him that made, and rules at His behest
> The minds and hearts of every living thing?
>
> Ah, sweet Content! Where doth thine harbour hold?
> Is it in churches, with religious men,
> Which please the gods with prayers manifold,
> And in their studies meditate it then?
>
> Whether thou dost in heaven or earth appear,
> Be where thou wilt, Thou wilt not harbour here!

Suddenly—and unreasonably as it seemed—I gave up my life in England. Actually I was constrained by something within me, something which had been set going by a chance conversation; and in October 1923 I sailed for New York, where I got work in a bookshop, with the idea of eventually starting one there myself. The shop 'The Sunwise Turn', was a kind of cultural centre, which attracted the young writers, artists, poets, and musicians of the time. My week-ends I spent with intellectual friends at Croton on Hudson, discussing and disputing about how the world ought to be run. My situation and inner state repeated themselves as they had been in London.

Meeting so many people and absorbing so many new impressions, I forgot that I had been looking for a teaching, a new way. But wherever we go, whatever we do, we carry on our backs Sinbad's 'old man of the sea'. Though we may forget him for a time, he never lets go, for he is part of ourselves.

So, after some three months of the ceaseless round of the social, cultural, and business activity of New York, I again began to experience the inner emptiness. And it was then that through the apparently chance appearance of an Englishman, A. R. Orage, everything became changed for me.

I

NEW YORK AND
FONTAINEBLEAU 1923-5

AT THE END of December 1923 Orage, arriving in New York from
Fontainebleau with a Dr Stjoernval, asked permission to give a talk, in
the shop where I worked, on the ideas of G. I. Gurdjieff and his Institute.
In London Orage had owned and edited the *New Age*, which Shaw
called the best magazine of literature and ideas England had produced
since the eighteenth century. I had met Orage but once. Dr Stjoernval
was a physician who had worked with Gurdjieff in Russia, and with his
wife had accompanied him to France.

A meeting was arranged, and on the appointed evening the shop was
crowded with an audience of well-dressed, intellectual-looking men
and women. I will give the substance of Orage's talk; it is clear and
concise, and forms a basis for what follows in this Journal.

'The Institute for the Harmonious Development of Man, at Fontainebleau,' said Orage, 'which is based on the system of G. I. Gurdjieff,
is really a continuation of the society called the "Seekers after Truth",
which was founded in 1895 by a group of doctors, archaeologists,
scientists, priests, painters, and so on, whose aim was to collaborate in
the study of so-called supernatural phenomena, in which each of them
was interested from a particular point of view. The members of the
Society went on expeditions to Persia, Afghanistan, Turkestan, Tibet,
India, and other countries, investigating ancient records and all kinds of
phenomena. There were great difficulties, and some lost their lives
through accident, others died, and some gave up the work. Eventually,
with a small number of survivors, Mr Gurdjieff arrived in Russia in
1913. Their first stay was at Tashkent. From here they went to Moscow
with the idea of arranging and putting to use the vast amount of

material that had been collected. In Moscow Mr Gurdjieff gave a series of talks, with the result that a number of scientists, musicians, doctors, engineers, and writers became interested. Preparations were made to start an Institute for the purpose of training pupils. But the outbreak of the first World War, followed by the revolution in 1917, made it impossible to continue the work there.

'Mr Gurdjieff decided to leave Russia. He and a group of pupils made a hazardous and difficult journey over the mountains to Tiflis, and there he carried out his plan of forming the Institute for the Harmonious Development of Man. More pupils joined. Later he found it necessary to go on to Constantinople, where, after many difficulties, the work of the Institute was continued. As time went on Mr Gurdjieff came to the conclusion that Europe would be more suitable for his aim. They went to Germany for a short time, and finally arrived in Paris. A demonstration of sacred dances and movements was given there, but although many French came, few showed interest. After a good deal of searching for a permanent place, the Château du Prieuré (or Château des Basses-Loges) at Fontainebleau-Avon was found and purchased in 1922, and here the Institute was established.'

At this point questions were asked. After answering them, Orage continued:

'Pupils are divided into two categories: those who are interested mainly in the theory of the system, and those who are not only interested in the theory, but also wish to work and be trained in the method.

'The system of training is based on the following conclusions: The life of our time has become so complex that man has deviated from his original type—a type that should have become dependent upon his surroundings: the country where he was born, the environment in which he was brought up, and the culture in which he was nurtured. These conditions should have marked out for a man his path of development and the normal type which he should have arrived at; but our civilization, with its almost unlimited means of influencing a man, has made it almost impossible for him to live in the conditions which should be normal to him. While civilization has opened up for man new horizons in knowledge and science and has raised his material standard of living, thereby widening his world-perception, it has, instead of lifting him to a higher level all round, only developed certain faculties to the detriment of others; some it has completely destroyed. Our civilization has taken away from man the natural and essential

2

qualities of his inherited type, but it has not given him what was needed for the harmonious development of a new type, so that civilization, instead of producing an individually whole man adapted to the nature and surroundings in which he finds himself and which really were responsible for his creation, has produced a being out of his element, incapable of living a full life, and at the same time a stranger to that inner life which should by rights be his.

'It is upon this that the psychological system of Mr Gurdjieff takes its stand. The system proves by experiment that the world-perception of a man of our time and his way of living are not the conscious expression of himself as a complete whole; but, on the contrary, are the unconscious manifestation of only one of the three parts of him.

'From this aspect our psychic life (as we perceive the world and express our perception of it) is not a whole, a whole that acts as a repository for our perceptions and a source of our expressions. On the contrary, it is divided into three separate entities, which have almost nothing in common, being different both in their substance and their function.

'These three separate and quite distinct parts—sources of the intellectual, emotional, and instinctive-moving life of man, each taken in the sense of the whole set of functions proper to it—are called by the Gurdjieff system the thinking centre, the instinctive-moving centre, and the emotional centre.

'Each truly conscious perception and expression of a man must be the result of simultaneous and co-ordinated working of all three centres, each of which must take its part in the whole task; that is to say, it must supply its quota of associations. A complete apperception in any given case is possible only if all three centres work together. But because of the many and varied influences which disturb and affect modern man, the working of the centres is almost always unconnected, with the result that his intellectual, emotional, and moving-instinctive functions fail to complete and correct one another; they travel along different paths, they rarely meet, and so his moments of real consciousness are very few.

'The three centres do not co-ordinate for this reason: there are, so to speak, three different men in a single individual; the first man only thinks, the second only feels, and the third lives only by his instincts and moving functions; so we have, as it were, a logical man, an emotional man, and a physical man. These three in one never understand each other; not only that, but consciously, and even unconsciously, they

3

interfere with one another, with each other's plans and intentions and work; and yet each of them at the moment when he is in action speaks with authority, and says "I".

'If we observe the working of the centres, we shall see how contradictory they are, how divided, and it will be obvious that man cannot be master of himself because he himself cannot control the work of his centres. He does not know even which of his centres will begin to function next. We do not notice this because we are under the illusion that there is a kind of unity of our various "I"s.

'If we will observe correctly the manifestations of the psyche of a modern man, it will be clearly seen that he never acts on his own initiative and for reasons within himself, but, by his actions, only expresses the changes that are brought about in his mechanism by causes outside him. He does not think: something in him thinks; he does not act: something acts through him; he does not create: something in him creates; he does not accomplish: something is accomplished through him.

'This becomes clear when we are able to understand the processes of perception of external and internal influences by each centre, by which responsive actions are brought about.

'The centres of a newly-born child may be compared to blank gramophone records upon which, from the first day or first hours, impressions of both the inner and outer world become inscribed. The recorded impressions are preserved in each of the three centres in the same order (often absurd) and in the same relation in which they were first received. The processes of thinking, reasoning, judgement, memory, and imagination are the result exclusively of the impressions recorded, which combine and associate in different ways under the influence of chance shocks. The records, whose contents thus become the centre of association, are set in motion with varying degrees of intensity by these same shocks. Another shock, or one of a different intensity, sets another record going and evokes still another association and consequently another train of thoughts, feelings, acts; and no centre can add anything of itself to the combinations formed in the other centres. The result is that a man's world-perception is the result of only part of his being, or, to put it another way, man has three different modes of processes of perception, which either have little contact with each other, or make contact by chance, and only partially. Therefore every conclusion a man comes to, every judgement, is the work of only one part of his make-up, the expression of only a small portion of the

4

material he has stored up; hence his judgements and conclusions are always partial, and consequently false.

'From all that has been said we can see that the first step in a man's balanced development is to show him how to be able to introduce, from the beginning, the work of the three centres into his psychic functions. When the three centres are able to work with equal intensity at the same time, then the three main wheels of the human machine will run smoothly and will not interfere with one another. They will not work as now, haphazardly, but function at their best in their separate capacities; also as regards the degree of consciousness which it is possible for a man to attain, but which in ordinary life he never reaches.

'It must not be forgotten that the degree of development possible for each centre differs with every man; so also do the impressions registered differ. Therefore the teaching and training of each person in the work must be strictly individual.

'In course of time the functional disorders to which the human machine is liable in ordinary conditions increase; and the machine can only be made to run smoothly after a long and determined struggle with the defects which have arisen in it. A man is unable to carry on this struggle alone and by his own efforts. Nor can he profit by the many methods of self-training and personal development in vogue (whether produced at home or imported from the Orient) which recommend indiscriminately methods and exercises—such as physical exercises, exercises in meditation, concentration, and breathing; systems of diet and fasting, induced experiences, and so on. These methods are prescribed for everyone, with no regard for individual needs and abilities, and take no account of personal peculiarities. Not only are they useless, they may even be dangerous; those who attempt to repair a defective machine without all-round and deep understanding may bring about certain changes, but these changes will cause other changes which an inexperienced person can neither foresee nor guard against. The human machine is always in mechanical equilibrium, whether it is running smoothly or not; therefore any change brought about in one place is bound to bring about a change in another place, and it is absolutely necessary that this should be foreseen and allowed for.

'To avoid unexpected and undesirable consequences it is important, when a man begins to work on himself, that he submit to the discipline imposed by the special and strictly individual methods employed by the Institute. We may say that one of the purposes is the development of new processes which will change and regulate the old ones. In other words, in this work we have to develop new faculties, which cannot be attained in the conditions of the daily life we see around us; and a man can neither develop them unaided, nor by practising any general method.

'Only when every particular of man's organic and psychic condition as well as his upbringing and all the circumstances of his life are taken into account is the use of strictly individualized methods of training of this kind possible. To determine and prescribe for these conditions accurately a long period of time is necessary. The chief reason for this is that man from his earliest days, as a result of his upbringing, acquires an external mask and presents an external type that has nothing in common with his real type. As a man grows older this mask grows thicker, and at last he is unable to see himself because of the mask.

'To discover the particulars of an individual—what is real behind the mask—it is necessary to uncover the features and faculties of his type. For this his mask has to be destroyed; and this is a question of time. Only when the mask has been destroyed can we study and observe the man himself, that is, his real type.

'Those of you who are interested are invited to attend further talks, the time and place of which will be announced shortly.'

He then gave a short description of life at the Prieuré, and the kind of work that was done there, and ended by asking for questions. Of these there were a great many, but I could not follow them, though the audience seemed deeply interested and there was some discussion. For me the talk had little meaning. I was unable to grasp a single one of the ideas; perhaps they were too novel for me. It might have ended there, and the system have been just another straw in the wind, but the next day Orage came into the shop, and when I was introduced, he asked me what impression I had got. I said, 'None at all. I could not get the hang of it.' 'Never mind,' he replied, 'Gurdjieff is arriving in a week's time with forty pupils to give demonstrations of sacred dances and exercises. Why don't you come?' Since dancing had always interested me, I agreed.

At this first meeting with Orage it was as if I had always known him. Rather, it was as if I were meeting someone whom I had known intimately and had liked, and from whom I had been separated for a very long time.

The first demonstration was given at Leslie Hall, and all seats were free. The hall was filled with what are called 'interesting' people, that

TO KNOW—TO UNDERSTAND—TO BE

The Science
of the Harmonious Development of Man
according to the method
of
G.I. GURDJIEFF.

Representation of a design for the programme of the Institute, 1923.

is, those who read, wrote, painted, or composed, or just talked about such things.

I found Orage behind the scenes swinging a little girl by her hands and talking to a man and woman, obviously her parents. When they moved away he told me that the man was a policeman in civilian dress, sent to ensure that no 'erotic' dances were shown.

I took my seat in the audience. A long time passed, and we became restless. Then, about nine o'clock, Orage mounted the platform, and after asking for silence, said: 'The demonstration this evening will consist chiefly of various movements of the human body taken from the art of the Ancient East—examples of sacred gymnastics, sacred dances, and religious ceremonies preserved in certain temples in Turkestan, Tibet, Afghanistan, Kafiristan, Chitral, and other places. Mr Gurdjieff, with other members of the "Seekers after Truth", carried out over many years in the Near and Far East a series of investigations which prove that in the Orient certain dances have not lost the deep significance—religious and scientific in the real sense—which they had in the remote past. Sacred dances and posture and movements in series have always been one of the vital subjects taught in esoteric schools in the East. They have a double aim: to convey a certain kind of knowledge, and to be a means for acquiring an harmonious state of being. The farthest limits of one's endurance are reached through the combination of non-natural and non-habitual movements, and by performing them a new quality of sensing is obtained, a new quality of concentration and attention and a new direction of the mind—all for a certain definite aim. Dancing still has quite a different meaning in the East from what we give it in the West. In ancient times the dance was a branch of real art, and served the purposes of higher knowledge and religion. A person who specialized in a subject communicated his knowledge through works of art, particularly dances, as we spread knowledge through books. Among the early Christians dancing in churches was an important part of the ritual. The ancient sacred dance is not only a medium for an aesthetic experience, but a book, as it were, or script, containing a definite piece of knowledge. But it is a book which not everyone who would can read. A detailed study of sacred dances and special movements and postures over many years has proved their importance in the work of the harmonious development of man; the parallel development of all his powers—one of the principal aims of Mr Gurdjieff. Exercises and sacred gymnastics are used in his system as one of the means for educating the student's moral

8

force, for developing his will, patience, capacity for thought, concentration and attention, hearing, sight, sense of touch, and so on.

'Tonight's programme will consist chiefly of group dances. In the Institute they precede individual movements, more complicated, and most of which are solo dances. In addition to the movements we shall give a demonstration of "Supernatural Phenomena", one of the subjects studied at the Gurdjieff School, a short explanation of which will be given later. The audience is asked not to applaud.'

After another long pause Mr de Hartmann came in with a small orchestra. Thomas de Hartmann, an aristocrat of the old school, had been a page at the Tsar's court, but had given up court life to devote his time to music. He was a brilliant pianist and composer. In his ballet, 'The Pink Flower', one of the first that Diaghileff produced in Moscow, Nijinsky first danced in public. Mme de Hartmann in her twenties had been a rising young opera singer. They met Gurdjieff in Moscow, and when the revolution came, literally left all and followed him over the mountains to Tiflis.

I was struck by the way Mr de Hartmann sat at the piano during the long pause. While the orchestra fidgeted and we, the audience, whispered tensely among ourselves, looking round to see who was there, Hartmann sat quite still, relaxed yet taking everything in.

At last the pupils came on to the stage and stood in lines. They were dressed in white tunics and trousers, the women's tunics long, the men's short. The women's hair was bound with gold fillets; not so the men's. In the Oriental dances which followed, both men and women wore appropriate and gorgeous costumes designed by Gurdjieff and based on those that were still worn in the East at the beginning of the century, some of which I myself had seen there.

At the command 'ruki storn' (or ruki v storonu) the pupils stretched their arms straight out to the sides; the music began, and, keeping the arms out, they beat out complicated rhythms with their feet. They kept this up, with arms outstretched, for fifteen minutes or more. There followed a 'machine group' in which the movements seemed to represent the working of machines or parts of a machine—single pupils or groups of two or three performing different movements, yet as a harmonious whole.

A group of the first six obligatory exercises was followed by a second six—'obligatory' because pupils were obliged to go through a course of them before they were allowed to perform the dances and the more complicated movements. These were called 'gymnastic

9

exercises' but were totally different from what I knew as gymnastics. Of the first six, three were from the Temple of Medicine at Sari in Tibet, and three from an esoteric school, The Seers, in Kafiristan. The effect on me of these exercises, the movements and the music, was electrifying. It was as if I had seen them before; they were new yet familiar, and I longed with all my feelings and instincts to do them myself.

These were followed by a large group, The Initiation of a Priestess, a fragment of a mystery called The Truth Seekers. As it proceeded, with movements, postures, gestures, and dances, it was as if all present were taking part in a religious ceremony. The music moved me profoundly, as indeed it did the rest of the audience; the change in the atmosphere of the hall could be sensed and felt. Gurdjieff's wife took the part of the priestess in this group.

After this came a series of Dervish dances in appropriate costumes. They comprised the Ho Yah Dervish dance from Chian (Ho Yah—O Thou Living God); a Big Prayer from an order of monks who call themselves They who Tolerate Freedom and whom the people call They Who Have Renounced; the Camel Step from Afghanistan; the ritual movements of the Veiled Monks of the Lakum order; a funeral ceremony for a dead dervish in the Subari Monastery in Thershzas; also dances of the Warrior Dervishes and the ritual movements of the Whirling Dervishes.

The Dervish dances were performed by the men pupils, although in some of them one or two women had minor parts. The rhythms and movements were vigorous, strong, and positive—masculine. One had a picture, so to speak, of man as the really active force.

Next came a demonstration of a pilgrimage. We were told that 'In Asia, especially in Central Asia, unusual pilgrimages are undertaken by people who have made a vow to compel themselves to suffer for a blessing received or hoped for. They travel to a holy place in an unusual or painful manner, such as turning somersaults, walking backwards, or on their knees. We shall show you a form of pilgrimage which is common in Caucasia and Turkestan. It is called "Measuring the way by one's length". The way is sometimes very long, up to eight hundred miles. The pilgrim proceeds from his home to the holy place in any kind of weather, perhaps carrying a pack of a hundred pounds, and often holding a fragile object, a gift for the shrine. Though such a pilgrimage often causes wounds which, according to Western ideas, ought to result in blood-poisoning, observers have never been able to discover any cases in which the wounds were not healed the next day.'

Two or three pupils came to the platform and knelt, then stretched themselves out flat. They then drew up their legs under them and stood on the spot their fingers had touched, and repeated the movements round the stage. It is said that the famous Sufi saint, Rabia, who, 'although a woman, was the crown of men', made a pilgrimage in this way from her home to Mecca, a distance of some hundreds of miles.

The Pythia was a fragment of a ceremony performed in the sanctuaries of Hudarika in Chitral. It was described as the magnetic sleep of the priestess who, on the eve of the new year, foretells the events the members of the sanctuary will see during the year to come.

The women's dances were said to be a few preparatory exercises for the novices of various convents and some movements belonging to their ritual. I had seen something similar in Northern India and in China, but never in East or West had I seen anything to compare with the loveliness, the grace, the charm of these. The names were given as The Sacred Goose, The Lost Loves, The Prayer, The Waltz, and so on. While the dervish dances had expressed the active qualities of manliness and masculinity, the women's dances expressed the passive qualities of womanliness—tenderness and feminity. The music, too, with its lovely melodies, had a deep appealing quality.

The crowning point of the evening for me came during the series of movements called the Big Seven or the Big Group. It was from a religious order seated near Mount Ararat, the Aisors, a Christian sect tinged with Sufism. The series of movements was based on a very ancient symbol, the Enneagram, mathematically constructed like the movements of the order of the Pure Essenes, which was founded hundreds of years before Christ.

All through the evening thoughts and feelings had been stirring within me, reminding me by association of vivid emotional experiences—of dances of men and women I had seen in India and China; of the incredibly sweet singing of women in temples; of the drums; of the Taj Mahal, the Sphinx, and the Pyramids; the images of Buddha; the singing of choirs and the pealing of the organ in old cathedrals at Easter; all that had most deeply touched me in religion, music, and art had been gradually waking. Now the music of the Big Group began in a slow and solemn measure, almost of warning. As it proceeded, rising and falling in waves of sound, a sense of joy pervaded my feelings; at the same time my mind was fixed on the complicated movements of the pupils. But with the feeling of joy was blended a sense, not of sadness, but of deep seriousness. It was as if it were saying something to me and I was trying to understand—a script that I was trying to decipher. Then, as the music swelled to a triumphant crescendo, a light broke. 'This,' I felt, 'is what I have always been searching for. Here is what I went to the ends of the earth to find. Here is the end of my search!' It was a clear conviction, without a particle of doubt, and from that time to this, never has any doubt assailed me.

During the interval, after the Big Group, I did not feel like talking. People no longer idly chattered; their talk was subdued. Also they were a little bewildered, since the movements fitted into no category of dancing known to them.

After the interval Orage came back to the platform and began to talk about the 'Stop' exercise. He said:

'In this exercise the pupil, on the command "Stop!" must arrest all movement. The command may be given anywhere, at any time. Whatever the pupil may be doing, whether during work, rest, or at meals, he must stop instantly. The tension of his muscles must be maintained, his facial expression, his smile, his gaze, remain fixed and in the same state as when the command caught him. The resulting postures are used by beginners for mental work, to quicken intellectual work while developing the will. The *Stop* exercise gives no new postures; it is simply an interrupted movement. Generally, we change our posture so unconsciously that we do not notice what positions we assume between postures. With the *Stop* exercise the transition between two postures is cut in two. The body, arrested by a sudden command, is forced to stop in a position in which it has never stopped before. This enables a man to observe himself better. He can see himself in a new light; he can sense differently and feel himself differently, and so break through the vicious circle of his automatism.

'The arbitrariness of our movements is an illusion. Psychological analysis and the study of the psychomotor functions as laid down by the Gurdjieff system show that every one of our movements, voluntary or involuntary, is an unconscious transition from one automatic posture to another automatic posture—the man takes from among the postures open to him those that accord with his personality; and the number of his postures is very small. All our postures are mechanical. We do not realize how closely linked together are our three functions;

moving, emotional, and mental. They depend on one another; they result from one another; they are in constant reciprocal action. When one changes, the others change. The posture of your body corresponds with your feelings and your thoughts. A change in your feelings will produce a corresponding change in your mental attitude, and in your physical posture. So that if we wish to change our habits of feeling and our habitual forms of thinking, we must first change our habits of posture. But in ordinary life it is impossible for us to acquire new physical postures; the automatism of the thinking process and habitual movements would prevent it. Not only are the thinking, feeling, and moving processes in man bound together, so to speak, but each and all three of them are compelled to work in the closed circle of automatic habitual postures. The Institute's method of preparing a man for harmonious development is to help him free himself from automatism. The *Stop* exercise helps in this. The physical body being maintained in an unaccustomed position, the subtler bodies of emotion and thought can stretch into another shape.

'It is important to remember that an external command is necessary in order to bring the will into operation, without which a man could not keep the transitional posture. A man cannot order himself to stop, because the combined postures of the three functions are too heavy for the will to move. But coming from the outside the command "Stop" plays the role of the mental and emotional functions, whose state generally determines the physical posture; and so the physical posture, not being in the state of habitual slavery to the mental and emotional postures, is weakened, and in turn weakens the other postures; this enables our will for a brief moment to rule our functions.'

At this point Gurdjieff came on to the stage, and I was able to observe him closely. He was wearing a dark lounge suit and a black trilby hat: a very powerful man physically, yet as light on his feet as a tiger. He looked at the audience with a half smile, and took us all in with a glance of his piercing dark eyes. He fitted into no type that I had known: certainly not the 'mystic' type, or yogi, or philosopher, or 'master'; he might have been a man who made archaeological expeditions in Central Asia.

The pupils having gathered at one side of the stage, Gurdjieff threw something into the air, and the pupils ran to catch it. He shouted 'Stop!' As if by magic the group became like statues in various attitudes. A minute or so passed. 'Davolna,' said Gurdjieff, and everyone relaxed and walked off. The exercise was done several times.

13

After this came the Chorovods—the folk and country dances, Mme de Hartmann coming on to the platform before each dance to give a few words of explanation. She began by saying:

'Almost all the peoples of Asia have their own dances. The Institute has collected over two hundred of them. The first we shall show, which is usually danced by young girls, comes from the region of Kumurhana in Turkey, though its origin lies in ancient Greece, and the postures of the dancers resemble very strikingly the designs on ancient urns and vases.' They actually did so, and the lilting melody might have been played on the pipes of Pan. This was followed by a harvest dance, of men and girls round a woman, from the oasis of Kerie.

The dance of the Tikins of Transcaspia was from the Festival of Carpets. It was a custom of the Tikins from various districts to bring the carpets woven during the year to a certain town and to celebrate. The carpets were combed and then pressed, so that only the fine fibres of the wool were seen. The ways of pressing were many and various. In Khorassan, for example, camel races were run over the spread-out carpets. In Persia they were laid out on the streets for people, camels, and donkeys to walk over. Among the Tikins, whose carpets are considered to be the finest, they were spread out and trodden in time to music.

After the folk dances came the Manual Labours. Mme de Hartmann said:

'These exercises form part of the rhythmical work of the Institute, that is, manual labour performed rhythmically. This was common in the East, where music was played during various kinds of manual work in order to increase production. It was to the accompaniment of music that many of the colossal constructions of the Ancient East were erected, as is known from inscriptions. The custom is still kept up at the source of the Pianje and in the oasis of Kerie and other places. When work in the fields is no longer possible, the villagers assemble in the largest building during the winter evenings and work at various tasks to the sound of music. Observations made at the Gurdjieff Institute of work done by groups to rhythmical music show that productivity increases from five to twenty times, compared with that of people working alone. We will now show three groups:

1. Combing wool and spinning thread;
2. Sewing shoes and knitting stockings;
3. Carpet weaving.'

14

The work movements, done to music and a sort of humming by the pupils, particularly interested me, for in a glove factory in Devonshire I had watched the girls working: one sang a folk song while the rest accompanied her with a sort of low humming. In Japan and China I used to watch the coolies doing monotonous tasks, hauling on ropes, driving piles, while singing in chorus; they really enjoyed the work. And I could not help comparing it with the way I used to toil, in New Zealand, for weeks on end, digging post-holes and undergoing other drudgery, suffering unbelievable boredom. Work rhythms were used in every part of the world up to fifty years ago—even in England. In ships the shanties went out with steam. In Germany, before the first World War, music was experimented with in factories; and in England radio music has been tried. But in neither case has it resulted in increased production; the rhythm is missing. In my father's factory the work was done by hand, and whenever the girls began to sing together spontaneously more and better work was done. Now all this seems to have disappeared under planning and automation. Human rhythm in work, which is an instinctive and emotional thing, has been superseded by the non-human rhythm of the machine and the conveyor belt. A deep instinctive need is left unsatisfied, and this leads to a craving for abnormalities, and even crime.

After the second interval came the last part of the programme, the 'tricks', 'half-tricks', and 'real supernatural phenomena'. Orage said:

'We shall now present some of the so-called "supernatural phenomena" also studied at the Institute. Mr Gurdjieff puts all such phenomena into three categories: tricks, semi-tricks, and real supernatural phenomena. Tricks are done artificially, the performer pretending that they result from some source of natural force; semi-tricks are not produced by sleight of hand, such as finding a hidden object blindfold; the third category, real phenomena, has as its basis laws which official science does not explain.

'As an example, let us take the well-known one of finding a hidden object. Something is hidden without the knowledge of a person who, though blindfolded, finds it, through holding the hand of a member of the audience. The audience believes that the finder reads the thoughts of the other person. It is deceived. A phenomenon really takes place without any trick on the part of the performer, but it has nothing in common with transmission of thought. It is done through the reflection on our muscular system of our emotional experiences. Since there is a muscular reaction to every small vibration of the physical body, either by relaxation or contraction, it is possible with much practice to sense the most feeble vibrations, and these occur in the most stolid, even when the person is specially trying to subdue them. The hand which the blindfolded person holds responds unconsciously to its owner's knowledge of the hiding-place; its slight, almost imperceptible changes are a language which the medium interprets—consciously if he is versed in the secret, instinctively if he is ignorant of the law—and which leads him to guess where the object is hidden.

'Similar phenomena, produced through laws different from those to which they are ascribed and at the same time not artificial in their essence, Gurdjieff calls semi-tricks.

'The third class of phenomena comprises those having as the basis of their manifestation laws unexplained by official science: real supernatural phenomena. This has nothing to do with spiritualism, ghosts, and so forth. It is experiment in the reaction of a lower force to the impact of a higher force; or the reaction of pupils at a lower level to something given out from a higher level. The study of this class of phenomena is organized in the Institute very seriously and in full accordance with the methods of Western science. Not all members or pupils are admitted to it. Three conditions are necessary. The first is a wide and deep knowledge in some special branch; the second is a naturally persevering and sceptical mind; the third and most important is the necessary preliminary assurance of the future trustworthiness of the pupil, to ensure that he will not abuse the knowledge he may thus acquire for the pursuit of egoistic aims.

'As regards the tricks, their study is considered necessary both for the future investigators of genuine phenomena and for every pupil of the Institute; not only will their cognizance free a man from many superstitions, but it will also introduce in him a capacity for a critical observation indispensable to the study of real phenomena, which requires a perfectly impartial attitude and a judgement not burdened by pre-established beliefs.

'Among the present pupils there are some who have worked for a long time and are already acquainted with these phenomena. There are also young pupils who are far from understanding them. Yet all take part in the experiments.

'The phenomena tonight will be given as if all were genuine, though in reality they will consist of the three kinds—tricks, half-tricks, and true supernatural phenomena. But their classification we shall leave to your discernment.'

16

'The first,' continued Orage, 'is an exercise in memorizing, in remembering words. Some of the pupils will now go among you and collect words, which may be in any language. Although we can remember and repeat up to four hundred words at one sitting, we shall, in order not to weary you, take only forty. This is enough to give an idea of the possibility of developing the memory within a very short time. It must be pointed out that in the Gurdjieff system teaching is seldom direct, but almost always indirect. It must be borne in mind that all the exercises are designed for the development of quickness of mind and attention, which again have as their aim the fundamental one of the harmonious development of the pupil. No special exercises are given for the development of memory; the results are obtained through general work and exercises which assist the development of the whole man.'

About forty words were collected from the audience and read out once to the pupils on the stage, who then began to repeat them; and, as far as I could tell, most of them repeated them correctly, although many of the words were very strange. Then Mme de Hartmann, sitting among the audience, said, 'Now if you will give me some numbers I will transmit them, by suggestion, to the pupils.' She faced the pupils, who were on the stage, and in a few minutes they began to repeat the numbers which had been given.

She continued, 'The next exercise will be in the transmission of the names or shapes of objects at a distance by representation. We ask you to show or to name to the pupil who is sitting among you some object which you have on your person. The name or shape of it will then be guessed by the pupils on the stage.'

I had on my watch chain a small, rare greenstone 'Tiki', which I had acquired in New Zealand. I showed it to her, and the pupils gave a recognizable description of it.

When this was finished Mr de Hartmann said, 'Now I ask you to suggest to the same pupil the name of any opera that ever existed in any part of the earth. She will transfer it to me and I shall play an extract from it. Meanwhile I ask those of you in the front row to keep very quiet.' He then played extracts from a number of operas, some of which I had never heard of.

All this time the attention of the audience was drawn to the stage. They were completely mystified. Now Mr de Salzmann came on with an easel and large sheets of white paper, and Mme de Hartmann again sat in the audience. Orage said, 'We ask you to suggest, in the same way, any creature, from the tiniest microbe to the largest beast, existing or prehistoric—fish, flesh, or fowl—to the pupil sitting with you. She will transmit it to the artist on the stage, and he will draw it.' Mr de Salzmann then sketched the animals, etc., with surprising rapidity and exactness. With this the evening's demonstration, which had lasted nearly four hours, came to an end.

The tricks and half-tricks completely baffled me. As a 'show' they were much more difficult than many I had seen done by professionals. I might have thought that the pupils had been through courses of magic; but I was a little relieved, and rather astonished, to see among the pupils two who had been fellow-members with me of the 1917 Club in London. All the same, it seemed like magic; and, as I was to discover, it was magic—but real magic.

As we were getting up to go I remembered that there had been no demonstration of 'real phenomena', and I wondered why. It was not until very much later, after much study, that I realized there had indeed been a very definite demonstration of real phenomena.

During the days that followed I could think of nothing but the dances and the music; and I was somewhat bewildered by the feeling that I had found that for which I had sought so long. My mind went back to Christian in the *Pilgrim's Progress from this World to the Next*, as was natural enough, for my family had been brought up on John Bunyan and the Bible; and my mother's people came from the Bunyan country. When I was a child it was as if his characters lived in the next village. I knew the book almost by heart and, thinking it over, there came to me the following passage:

> Now I saw in my dream that the highway up which Christian was to go was fenced on either side with a wall, and that wall was called Salvation. Up this way therefore did burdened Christian run, not without great difficulty, because of the load on his back. He ran thus till he came to a place somewhat ascending, and upon that place stood a cross, and a little below, in the bottom, a sepulchre. So I saw in my dream, that just as Christian came up with the cross, his burden loosed from off his shoulders, and fell from off his back, and began to tumble, and so continued to do, till it came to the mouth of the sepulchre, where it fell in, and I saw it no more. Then was Christian glad and lightsome, and said, with a merry heart, 'He hath given me rest by his sorrow and life by his death.' Then he stood awhile to look and wonder; for it was very surprising to him that the sight of the cross should ease him of his burden. He looked therefore, and looked again, even till the springs that were in his head sent the waters down his cheeks.

18

1. New York, January, 1924.

2. Château du Prieuré or Château des Basses Loges, Fontainebleau-Avon, looking south.

I had come to the end of my quest. Yes, but the pilgrimage had just begun.

For a day and a half the New York papers gave a good deal of space to the demonstration. One of the baser sort of Sunday papers devoted two pages to it with pictures and fantastic captions. An article was headed, 'The Great Harmonizer tunes up'. Another, giving a supposed description of life at the Prieuré, told how the pupils would gather on the great lawn at midnight and begin a wild dance, and at its height Gurdjieff himself would appear walking among them and calling out, 'Dance! Dance! Dance to Freedom!' There are always journalists who will drag the noblest ideas in the mire to provide a sensation for the Sunday reader.

But the sensational articles did not prevent the succeeding demonstrations from being packed to capacity by really thoughtful people. Everywhere, among people who were 'doing things', as they say, or discussing anything, the subject of conversation became 'Have you seen the Gurdjieff dances?' Some said the pupils were hypnotized; others that they were browbeaten, because they never smiled; others complained because they could not fit the dances into a category, so that they could label them and write articles about them or about the 'system'. No one was having the satisfaction of explaining to others what it was all about. This annoyed some of the intelligentsia, who would have sneered had it not been for the high standing of Gurdjieff's older pupils. Orage had an international literary reputation; of Mr de Salzmann, Gordon Craig had said that he understood more about stage lighting and stage sets than anyone in the Western world. De Hartmann was a musician of the first rank, and Dr Stjoernval had a high reputation in Russia as an alienist. Also, three of the young women pupils— English, Armenian, and Montenegrin—were numbered among the best dancers in Europe. As some said: 'There must be something in a system which constrains such varied talents to follow Gurdjieff'. On the other hand, a man from London, reader of the *New Age*, said to me: 'Isn't it a pity to see a man with Orage's reputation and gifts giving up his literary life in London to follow a charlatan!' A lady, speaking to me about the demonstration, said: 'I understand that Mr Gurdjieff lives in the forest at Fontainebleau with Katherine Mansfield, and that they call themselves "The Forest Lovers".'

My first personal contact with Gurdjieff took place a day or two after the demonstration. I had been talking to Jane Heap, who had come to the shop where I worked. She, with Margaret Anderson, was editing and publishing the *Little Review*—which if not the equivalent in America of the *New Age* in England, was similar in its aims. A few minutes after she had gone, Orage and Dr Stjoernval came in. At once I sensed that I was a mere youth in the presence of these adult men. Very soon I made another and more striking comparison; Gurdjieff arrived, very impressive in a black coat with an astrakhan collar and wearing an astrakhan cap. With a twinkle in his eyes he began to joke with the others. Then he walked round, and I found him standing beside me. I looked up, and was struck by the expression of his eyes, with the depths of understanding and compassion in them. He radiated tremendous power and 'being' such as I had never in all my travels met in any man, and I sensed that, compared with him, both Dr Stjoernval and Orage were as young men to an elder.

I was a little uneasy, and, as was my habit, tried to make conversation. Picking up a copy of Ouspensky's *Tertium Organum*, which I had tried in vain to read, I said, 'Have you read this, Mr Gurdjieff?' He made a gesture with his hand and said, 'Very difficult.' I thought he meant it was difficult for him. I then said, 'Mr Gurdjieff, I should like, if you have room, to go and work at your Institute.' He replied, 'Room enough. But also necessary to think about life. Many young men at Institute study for life. One will be engineer. He study to get paper. Very necessary in life have paper.'

He summed me up at a glance as a youth immersed in dreams—thought dreams, feeling dreams, dreams of women, a youth to whom the idea of living in a community, relieved of responsibility, seemed very desirable; to one part of me, at any rate. This was the only occasion on which I tried to talk books with Gurdjieff.

I was disappointed that only one of my friends among the intellectuals from Croton showed interest in the ideas of the Institute. The exception was Boardman Robinson, the artist. The 'Left' was vaguely hostile. But the Left is always opposed to ideas which have as their aim the changing of the inner state of man. They want to change outer conditions, results. 'Change the form of government and all will be well.' 'The best is yet to be.' Happiness, for them, is in the future. But as Pope says:

> Hope springs eternal in the human breast;
> Man never *is*, but always *to be* blest.

20

I speak of this because up to this time I had lived among the 'intelligentsia' and believed as they did; and was on the way to becoming a fossilized intellectual, identified with outworn ideas.

Almost every evening Gurdjieff met groups of people. He did not give lectures in the ordinary way, but informal talks consisting chiefly of questions and answers. Once, at a meeting in Jane Heap's apartment, I was having difficulty in keeping my attention on the talk; it wandered continually to a good-looking young woman sitting not far from me, and I had a shock when, in answer to someone's question, Gurdjieff began to speak about sleep and attention. Indicating me, he said, 'This young man, for example, has no attention, he is more than three-quarters asleep.' I woke from my daydream and began to take notice.

Someone asked him: 'How can we gain attention?'

He said: (I shall not attempt, except on occasion, to reproduce his broken English) 'In general, few people have attention. It is possible to divide one's attention into two or three parts. In this work you must try to gain attention. Only when you have gained attention can you begin to observe yourself and know yourself. You must start on small things.'

'What small things can we start on?'

Gurdjieff: 'You have nervous, restless movements which make people think you are a booby and have no authority over yourself. The first thing is to see these movements and stop them. If you work in a group this may help; even your family can help. Then you can stop these restless movements. Make this your aim, then afterwards perhaps you can gain attention. This is an example of *doing*. Everyone, when he begins in this work, wishes to do big things. If you start on big things you will never do anything. Start on small things first. If you wish to play melodies and begin to play them without much practice you will never be able to play real melodies, and those you play will make people suffer so that they will hate you. It is the same with psychological things. To gain anything real, long practice and much work is necessary. First try to do small things. If you aim at big things first you will never *do* anything or *be* anything. And your actions will irritate people and cause them to hate you.'

About the middle of January 1924, at a meeting in the O'Neil Studio, I arrived to find a number of people already sitting around; they were people who were comfortably off and interested in contemporary art, music, and ideas. The meeting was timed for nine, but it was almost ten before we saw Gurdjieff. He came in from another room, wearing a grey suit and an old pair of carpet slippers and holding a large baked potato. Everybody became frigidly silent. He sat on the edge of the low platform facing us and began to eat. He seemed to be playing a part— that of a benevolent, middle-aged gentleman at a party. He made a joke, and the rather tense atmosphere disappeared in a peal of laughter. After a few remarks his expression changed, and he said, 'Perhaps someone have question?'

The first question was: 'Would you explain about the Law of Three?'

Gurdjieff said: 'Take a simple thing—bread. You have flour, you have water. You mix. A third thing is necessary—heat, then have bread. So in everything. Three forces, three principles are necessary. Then you have result.'

Another said, 'It seems rather a silly question to ask, but what would you say is the difference between men and women?'

Gurdjieff: 'In general, men have minds more developed; women, feelings more developed. Men are logical, women are not logical. Men should learn to feel more, women to think more. You must think, feel, and sense a thing before it can become real to you.

'About sensing, you do not know what "sensing" is. You often mistake sensing for feeling and feeling for sensing. You must learn to know when you are thinking, when you are feeling, and when you are sensing. Three processes necessary, and much work is necessary for understanding.'

Question: 'What is suffering? I don't mean physical pain, but suffering that weighs on the feelings and on the mind. Perhaps I mean emotional and mental suffering, when often there is no apparent reason for it.'

Gurdjieff: 'There are different kinds of suffering. In general, everyone suffers. But most of your suffering is mechanical. There are two rivers of life. In the first river suffering is passive and unconscious. In the second river suffering is "voluntary", which is very different and of great value. All suffering has cause and consequence. Most of your suffering now is because of your corns or because someone treads on them. To get to the second river you must leave everything behind.'

Question: 'Can you tell us what place love has in your system?'

Gurdjieff: 'With ordinary love goes hate. I love this, I hate that. Today I love you, next week, or next hour, or next minute, I hate you. He who can really love can *be*; he who can be, can *do*; he who can do, *is*. To know about real love one must forget all about love and must look for direction. As we are we cannot love. We love because something in ourselves combines with another's emanations; this starts pleasant associations, perhaps because of chemico-physical emanations from instinctive centre, emotional centre, or intellectual centre; or it may be from influences of external form; or from feelings—I love you because you love me, or because you don't love me; suggestions of others; sense of superiority; from pity; and for many other reasons, subjective and egoistic. We allow ourselves to be influenced. We project our feelings on others. Anger begets anger. We receive what we give. Everything attracts or repels. There is the love of sex, which is ordinarily known as "love" between men and women—when this disappears a man and a woman no longer "love" each other. There is love of feeling, which evokes the opposite and makes people suffer. Later, we will talk about conscious love.'

In answer to another question he said: 'All life needs love. Cows give more milk and hens more eggs when their keepers love them. Different people sowing seeds get different results. Strong men can wither plants through hate, and even destroy other people. Begin by loving plants and animals, then perhaps you will learn to love people.'

'Yes,' said the questioner, 'but what is love? We talk about it all the time, but when I ask myself I know that I don't know. Perhaps wishing a person well, wishing their good, is loving them. But do I know what is good for people? Even for my own children—sometimes when I have struggled for something for their good, as I thought, it has turned out not to be good.'

Gurdjieff: 'When you know that you don't know, it is already a great deal. You come to groups and we will later on speak about this.'

Question: 'Why is it that men are so often attracted to women who make them suffer? And women, of course, by men in the same way?'

Gurdjieff: 'Think over what I said about love of feeling.'

At the meetings I always had a feeling of pleasure while listening to Gurdjieff, and I felt as if already I was 'on the way' and able to 'do', and that henceforth I would be quite different; but by the next day I had slipped back into the old ways. I knew in my essence that what he was saying was the truth I had so long been waiting to hear; but, by myself, in life, I began to have some idea of the difficulty of *doing* anything. Though I 'felt' it was the truth, I did not 'understand'.

I spoke to Orage about the difficulty I had in remembering what was said at the meetings and the difficulty of doing anything. He said, 'The time has not come yet for you to "do". It is necessary to ponder everything that Gurdjieff says, to learn and prepare yourself.' I asked, 'What is pondering?' He replied, 'From one aspect it is thinking with the thinking part of each centre—mental, emotional, and moving. In the New Testament it says, "Mary pondered all these things in her heart". It means to go over them, weigh them.' When I began to try to ponder I realized that I had never 'pondered'. I had only milled over something with part of my emotions. So, remembering what Gurdjieff had said about me I began to recall what I had heard about sleep; 'Awake, thou that sleepest!' says the prophet, 'Now is Christ risen from the dead and become the firstfruits of them that slept,' says Paul. According to the Sufis, the Christ that rose in the body of Jesus rode into Jerusalem on the Ass of Desire. In the *Mahabharata*, one of the great heroes is called 'Conqueror of Sleep'. The Greeks spoke of the body as the 'Tomb of the Soul'; and in the Orthodox Church they sing at Easter, 'Christ is risen from the dead. He has conquered death by death, and given life to those that were in the tomb'. The idea is echoed in poetry. The Tudor poet wrote:

> All this night shrill chanticleer,
> Day's proclaiming trumpeter,
> Claps his wings and loudly cries
> 'Mortals! Mortals! Wake! Arise!'

The crowing of the cock—to me one of the sweetest sounds in nature —is often associated with waking. Prudentius said, 'At the crowing of the cock Christ arose from the underworld'. And Peter, when the cock crew, 'remembered' himself.

The idea is found in fairy tales. There is the *Sleeping Beauty*. In each one of us is a sleeping something, waiting to be awakened by the kiss of real teaching. Some nursery rhymes also convey the idea; 'Little Boy Blue' who is 'under a haystack fast asleep'. The Sufi poet Attar, in *The Conference of the Birds*, speaks of 'the sleep that fills your life'.

The talks and demonstrations began to give me a taste of how deep in sleep I was. The first intimation that something was indeed beginning to make an impression on my subconscious, beginning to change in me, came in a dream.

Ever since November 1917, when I was invalided out of the front line trenches on the Somme, I had been troubled by a dream which recurred every few nights. In the dream I was again in the Army, going into action, to what seemed certain death; often I was shot and woke as I fell. Always the events were accompanied by a feeling of astonishment, mixed with dejection, despair, and regret that I should have allowed myself once more to get into that terrible situation from which there was no escape. All the feelings of fear, hopelessness, and despair were compressed into the few seconds before I woke. The dream was so much more real than reality that two or three minutes passed before I came to, with an enormous sense of relief. A long and expensive course of psycho-analysis had produced no lasting effect; so long as I was with the analyst I was free, for I transferred my suffering to him. When I left him, the fear returned. One result of the analysis was that I discovered that dreams are caused as often by fear and apprehension, money and stomach, as by sex. Ordinary psycho-analysis is like taking a piece of bent steel and twisting it straight; when it is released it usually twists back again. A process of re-tempering is necessary. The Gurdjieff system, it seemed, was a technique for re-tempering.

After a few weeks of going to meetings and demonstrations, the dream of which I speak recurred. I was in the Army, filled with depression, despondency, and self-reproach for having let myself be caught again in that intolerable situation from which there seemed no escape. We were marching into action to be slaughtered. In war—and in our waking state—nature generally provides buffers between the emotions of fear and the prospect of painful wounds, suffering, and death; but in dreams the buffers are removed, and I, in my dreams, suffered a realization of what war really is. Now, in the dream, something began to change, and I found myself withdrawn from the Army. I was on a high place; it was dark, but in the gloom I could discern the army, below, marching away without me and a feeling of enormous relief possessed me. Behind me was a glow of light in which I could dimly see the forms of two men. I looked round and saw Gurdjieff and Orage, and I heard one say: 'A way of escape?' Then I woke.

The recurring dream never quite left me, but little by little it became less troublesome, and there was always a way out; and in time it was accompanied by only a feeling of vague unrest. Perhaps I did not want to forget it entirely; perhaps I wanted to remember the state of sleep I was in when I offered myself as a sacrifice to Moloch, Kali, Shiva the Destroyer, Mars, or whatever name men give to the force of destruction.

There were further demonstrations of the movements and dances—

at the Neighborhood Playhouse, the Church of St Mark's-in-the-Bowery, and Carnegie Hall. At the Neighborhood Playhouse was read what became 'From the Author' in *Beelzebub's Tales*, in which he speaks about the 'River of Life'; and it was here, at the end of one of the demonstrations, as the pupils were leaving the platform, that Gurdjieff called one of the young women, a beautiful and accomplished dancer, and in a voice that most could hear, rebuked her. He said: 'You spoil my work. You dance for yourself, not for me.' As she began to defend herself he made a gesture with his hand and walked away. I was rather shocked, but it brought home to me the connexion between the Gurdjieff system and the Christian idea of doing all for the glory of God—the idea of working for one's own inner being and for the glory of God.

In February I accompanied Orage to Boston, where he was to make arrangements for a demonstration and the possible formation of a group. I hoped that I should be of use, for I knew important people in Boston and Cambridge, Mass. When I found myself in Cambridge in 1919, I had the idea of taking a degree in English literature and psychology; but, suffering as I was from the disillusionment and restlessness caused by the war, I found it difficult to study. Sitting one day in the Widener Library, the idea came to me concerning psychology that it would take three years to master one school, and that there were several schools, each specializing in only one aspect of man's psyche. To study all the well-known schools and so get a complete view of man would take years. Would I then know very much more about myself and other men? Something seemed to tell me that I would not; and so with the academic study of literature. Culture, as an end in itself, no longer interested me. I gave up the idea of studying at Harvard and continued my pilgrimage round the world. But I had formed a friendship with Charles Townsend Copeland which was renewed at this, my second visit to America. He was a professor and a public figure, but also a warm human being. I told Orage that I thought he might be very useful. 'I doubt it,' he said. 'I've met only one professor interested in real ideas, the Frenchman, Professor Denis Saurat. Even business men are more likely to be interested than professors, scholars, or writers.'

None of the 'important people' I talked to showed the least interest in Gurdjieff, who was regarded as just another eccentric philosopher from Europe.

My stay in Boston with Orage gave me opportunities of talking to him and getting to know him. In answer to a question I asked about the purpose of Gurdjieff's visit to America, he said, 'The demonstrations, the meetings and talks, are a kind of net thrown out. Of the hundreds of people who see and hear, only a few, in a state of dissatisfaction with themselves and with life, will feel that we have something they are looking for. It does not necessarily mean that these few will be "unhappy" people. They may be leading an active life, be well off and comfortably situated, but they will feel that there is something else besides the round of ordinary existence. In other words, there are certain people who possess a magnetic centre, or the beginnings of one; these are the people who have the possibility of working on themselves. The rest of humanity, not feeling the need, will do nothing. We are, in fact, offering people an opportunity of having a purpose in life, of using their suffering—the dissatisfactions they feel—for their own good. How many will take it? We shall see.'

'Were you in a state of dissatisfaction with yourself and life when you met Gurdjieff?' I asked.

'Indeed I was. I was already beginning to be disillusioned with the purely literary and cultural life when I met Ouspensky, who came to see me before 1914. It was becoming more and more difficult for me to force myself to write the notes of the week in the *New Age*. It had been a profound disappointment to me to realize that my intellectual life, with which was associated all that was highest and best in Western culture, was leading me nowhere. As they used to say, "I had not found God".'

'Then you knew Ouspensky before he met Gurdjieff?'

'Yes. I corresponded with Ouspensky when he was a journalist in Russia, and he came to see me when he was on his way to Russia from the East in 1914. When the revolution broke out there, I put him in touch with Mr F. S. Pinder, who was the British Government representative in Ekaterinodar. Ouspensky was stranded and Pinder gave him a job on his staff. The Government wouldn't pay his salary, and I believe Pinder paid that out of his own pocket. When Ouspensky arrived in England for the second time he came to see me. I got in touch with some writers, doctors, psychologists and others, and meetings were held in Lady Rothermere's studio in St John's Wood. Ouspensky had found what I was looking for. But, after Gurdjieff's first visit to Ouspensky's group, I *knew* that Gurdjieff was the teacher.

'Eventually, I sold the *New Age*, gave up my literary life and Ouspensky's groups, and went to Fontainebleau. My first weeks at the

Prieuré were weeks of real suffering. I was told to dig, and as I had had no real exercise for years I suffered so much physically that I would go back to my room, a sort of cell, and literally cry with fatigue. No one, not even Gurdjieff, came near me. I asked myself, "Is this what I have given up my whole life for? At least I had something then. Now what have I?" When I was in the very depths of despair, feeling that I could go on no longer, I vowed to make extra effort, and just then something changed in me. Soon, I began to enjoy the hard labour, and a week later Gurdjieff came to me and said, "Now, Orage, I think you dig enough. Let us go to café and drink coffee." From that moment things began to change. This was my first initiation. The former things had passed away.'

Thus Orage, who, through his paper, the *New Age*, had been the focal point of all that was best in all branches of contemporary thought of that period; for whose paper men like Chesterton, Belloc, Shaw, Wells, and Arnold Bennett were glad to write for nothing; of whom T. S. Eliot said that he was the best literary critic of his time.

I learnt from Orage that Gurdjieff, on his last visit to Ouspensky in London, had taken F. S. Pinder with him to interpret. Ouspensky had disagreed with some of Pinder's interpretations, but Gurdjieff insisted. He thought Ouspensky was too intellectual, with too much theory and too little practical work. Eventually only Orage and Pinder and a few others were left of the English pupils at the Prieuré; the rest returned to London. Among the Ouspensky pupils was a Mr J. G. Bennett, who was there for a few odd days; he did not meet Gurdjieff again until shortly before his death in 1949. Mr Rowland Kenney, who had been editor of the *Daily Herald* during its first year in 1912, and his wife were also at the Prieuré for a time.

Orage said that he was grateful to Ouspensky for being the means of his meeting Gurdjieff, as 'it was only then that I began to distinguish between knowledge and understanding'. Orage added: 'Ouspensky for me represented knowledge—great knowledge; Gurdjieff, understanding—though of course Gurdjieff had all the knowledge too.'

F. S. Pinder, who also had no doubt of Gurdjieff as the teacher, was a civil engineer. After he met Ouspensky at Ekaterinodar he was imprisoned by the Bolsheviks and sentenced to death. During his imprisonment he perfected his Russian. Ultimately he was released and after the war was awarded the O.B.E. It is interesting to me, by the way, that these three, Orage, Pinder, and Kenney, remarkable men in the real meaning of the word, men of understanding, had received, like myself, their 'lack of education' as they expressed it, in elementary or Board Schools, now Council Schools.

It is a great blessing when a man can have the friendship of men older and in some respects wiser than himself; a friendship based on something essential and on a common and fundamental aim. Friendship with women and love of them can go on at the same time, but can never be a substitute. I count myself fortunate to have had these three as friends: 'as iron sharpeneth iron . . .'

Another conversation with Orage in Boston began with my saying: 'Are you going to start esoteric groups in New York? If so, I should like to become a pupil.'

'No,' he replied. 'Not esoteric, nor even mesoteric. These are very far from us. If we can start an outer exoteric group, we shall do well.'

'But isn't the Prieuré an esoteric school?'

'It is. Probably the only one in the Western world today; but a man may live at the Prieuré and be quite unaware of it. You get from the Prieuré just as much as you give in work on yourself—that is, according to real effort. There are people living there now to whom the place is no more than a *maison de santé*.'

'It seems,' I said, 'that you and I have started at opposite ends. I have done almost every kind of physical work and earned my living at many kinds of jobs; I've travelled or lived in twenty different countries, but I have never used my mind. As a sheep before its shearers is dumb, so am I before intellectuals—inarticulate. Physical work or business for me is easy, but to use my mind, difficult. I cannot think things out—I only feel.'

' Well,' he replied, 'I think I can say that I know more about current intellectual ideas than most men, but when I began to work with Gurdjieff I soon realized that I understood almost nothing. I had to begin all over again. In this system we all, as it were, start from scratch. At the same time, my background as an editor can be very useful in this work.' He added, 'You, you know, think with your feelings. You must learn to think with your mind. One of the aims of this work is to enable a man to sense, feel, and think simultaneously. We are all abnormal in that we are undeveloped in one or more of our centres. That is why Gurdjieff calls his school "The Institute for the Harmonious Development of Man".'

'Is it true that we are all abnormal?' I asked. 'Take Bernard Shaw for example. I've met him several times. I should have thought that he was normal.'

29

'I have known the Shaws well for many years,' said Orage. 'I was with them the day before they were married. Shaw feels with his mind, and he lacks what is called "emotional understanding". On one occasion Shaw and I were dining together with a woman friend, and the talk turned on emotion and intellect. The woman said to him: "But, you know, Shaw, you lack emotional understanding". "What do you mean?" he said. "Of course I have emotional understanding." "Oh, no," she said, "Orage has it, but you haven't." Shaw was annoyed, for he could not see that this was true. Later, when he left, she said "Poor old Shaw. He was a bit hurt. His trouble is that his brains have gone to his head."'

'I'm disappointed,' I said, 'that none of my friends in Cambridge or Boston are interested either in the Gurdjieff ideas or in seeing a demonstration of the dances. When I was at Harvard in 1919 it seemed to me that the life of the cultured people in Cambridge was perhaps the best that could be found—comparable to the cultured life of eighteenth-century England, before the dark ages of the nineteenth and twentieth centuries.'

'I agree,' said Orage, 'but, according to Gurdjieff, the inner development of individual man does not depend on culture, though culture may provide a background. On the contrary, culture depends on developed individual man, or rather a group of men working together. The flowerings and blossomings of culture which occur from time to time in history, apparently for no reason—the building of the Gothic cathedrals, the Renaissance, Shakespeare's plays—are examples of the results of a group of men working consciously. Another thing, you cannot convince anyone of the soundness of Gurdjieff's system by intellectual argument. And we do not wish to convince people or make converts. We offer a means of help to those who feel the need of it. Those that are whole, you know, have no need of a physician. Gurdjieff says that the Prieuré is a repair shop for broken-down motor-cars.'

I returned to New York in the state of wanting to take an active part in the dances and groups, but something held me back. There was, as they say, a struggle between two parts of me. One part said: 'Make an effort. Do it.' The other part said, 'Wait. You don't know what you may be letting yourself in for.' Really it was a mixture of fear, timidity, and inertia that held me back: fear that I might have to give up something I cherished—certain vague things I clung to. So instead of taking an active part in the classes of movements, I merely watched. Being what I was, I could do no other. 'A machine can only behave as a machine.' I was chiefly afraid that I might be prevented from gratifying my precious whim: that of starting a bookshop in New York.

Whims, desires, arise usually from causes unknown to us, some legitimate, some not. The non-legitimate—those which are harmful—have to be repressed; the harmless ought to be satisfied, or they may give us no peace.

'Satisfy your harmless whims but don't cultivate them,' Orage said. 'In this work you are not required to give up anything. Things and associations will drop away of themselves when you are no longer identified with them. After all, you have to do something for a living; why not a bookshop?' 'I want to go to the Prieuré, too,' I said. 'Well, why not do both? Spend the summer at the Institute and then come back and start your business. But, tell me, why do you want to be a bookseller?'

'Because I'm fond of books.'

'To become a bookseller because you are fond of books is, to my mind, rather like becoming a butcher because you are fond of animals.'

There was another problem. In Russia I had met a young American woman. We had parted, gone our respective ways, and met again in New York. We had had a great deal in common and we became engaged, but already our common interests seemed weakening. She was becoming resentful of my interest in the Gurdjieff system, and after the first demonstration refused to go to the meetings any more. She complained that Gurdjieff was against the Russian revolution and that already I was losing my interest in the things we had both worked for —'Social reform and the good of others'. When I told her I was planning to go to the Prieuré, and asked her to come, she said, 'No, you will have to choose between Gurdjieff and me.' I told Orage, who said, 'A man I knew in London was in a similar situation. He was in love with a woman. In time something cropped up which he very much wished to do. It meant a great deal to him. When he told the woman she began to raise objections. The more they discussed it the harder she pleaded with him not to do it—at last with tears in her eyes. Now, he no longer resisted. And no sooner did he tell her that he had given up his plans than she despised him for his weakness. Their relationship eventually came to an end. He never forgave himself; and he had to make great efforts to carry out his original, though now modified, plans.' This made a deep impression on me. For, although Orage did not know, he could have been relating an event in my own life of a few years before. I, too, had never forgiven myself; and, but for the intervention of Orage, I might have repeated my mistake.

'You must remember,' Orage continued, 'that American women, more than any others, are spoilt. Of course, all women want their own way, but one of the tragedies of American life is that women have succeeded in getting it to the extent of dominating the men. The passive force has become the active. One of the consequences is the enormous number of divorces here compared with Europe. Gurdjieff blames men for the deterioration in the status of women in America. The strange thing is that Americans regard it as a sign of "progress".

'Even the peasant women of Central Europe instinctively understand the art of love better than a great many sophisticated American women—or English women, for that matter. Women fail to grow up inwardly because their men remain children. Women wish to be dominated, in the right way; but it takes a *man* to dominate a woman. European men have had thousands of years in which to become relatively adult. Americans, instead of going on where Europeans left off, have returned to childhood—or at least, adolescence. But while it is one of their great drawbacks it is also one of their possibilities. It is possible to do something with children. Gurdjieff says that Americans have more possibilities for good than any other nation, but that they are so at the mercy of wrong ideals brought from Europe and eventually distorted—they have come to power and money so easily—that their civilization may decay and rot long before it is ripe. In a real civilization woman understands her function and has no wish to be other than a woman.'

I told my young mistress that I had chosen to go to Fontainebleau.

During this winter, when every few days I encountered a new experience, there occurred the meeting with a 'wise' woman. I heard about her through a friend, on whose suggestion I sent to her my full name and date of birth and a fee. In a few days there came back four closely written sheets of paper about my essential characteristics and possibilities, good and bad; and even an outline of the types of circumstances I should be likely to meet. Some of the things she told me about myself were extraordinary—possibilities of good and evil that I never even suspected. She also outlined the characteristics of people I had not yet met, but who later became part of my life.

She lived in a small town in northern New York State and I went to see her. A quiet, sympathetic little woman, she was of the type of 'wise woman' that I had met in villages in Russia, for in old Russia every village had its wise woman, one who was endowed to an unusual extent with the subconscious wisdom of the race, to whom the peasants would go for advice and to talk over their problems. She was not a medium in the usual spiritualist sense. I asked her how she knew so much about me, whom she had never either seen or heard of. She said, 'I don't know. I take your paper in my hands, I do some calculations, then I sit at the typewriter and put myself in a certain state, and it just comes to me. At first I used to tell people what I thought was going to happen to them, but this depends on many things and I was often wrong, so I stopped it. Now I just do character; and I feel that I can help people by telling them of their possibilities, both good and bad.'

She could tell things about a person by writing only when she was alone; not by talking, but by using the gift called—or rather, miscalled—by spiritualists, psychometry. It almost seems as if the film of our life were made at our birth and presented to us, and that certain people in certain states can see bits of it ahead. If we are told about our 'future' we put our subjective interpretation on it, and waste energy hoping for the expected good and fearing the expected bad.

We became friends, and I took her to one of the demonstrations. 'This,' she said, 'is the real thing. Mr Gurdjieff is a man who understands the meaning of true religion. He is a man who has seen God.'

It is not enough to say 'Know thyself' and it is always a shock to be told about one's dark side, for we do not wish to see it.

'Gurdjieff's system provides a technique,' said Orage. 'You can be told of your faults for years, but unless you make the right kind of effort yourself, you will remain the same. His system has a method not taught in books, by which you can learn little by little how to make this effort to know yourself, but you must be prepared to work for a long time—for years, perhaps—and there will be long periods when nothing seems to happen and nothing in oneself seems to change.'

Gurdjieff took his pupils first to Boston and then to Chicago, where demonstrations and talks were given. From all this effort the subsequent results were small; the seeds fell on stony ground. On their return to New York a final demonstration was given in Carnegie Hall. There had been trouble with the Musicians' Union over the orchestra; the union insisting on extra players being employed, including a pianist. So Gurdjieff dispensed with the lot and Mr de Hartmann alone played the music on a concert grand piano. This last demonstration was the only one in New York at which seats were sold. Since a number of the audience were sitting in far-away cheaper seats and some of the expensive ones were empty, Gurdjieff invited the people in the cheaper seats to come nearer and fill the dearer ones, which they did. The programme was very long, lasting nearly four hours, yet few people left before the end; needless to say they did not stay out of politeness! All the dances and movements were performed, and also the tricks and half-tricks. Except for the lecture-talk which was read at the Neighborhood Playhouse and which was eventually added to *Beelzebub's Tales*, all the explanations were read.

I remember this particular evening because of something which later astonished me. With me was a rich young woman who had come more in the hope of seeing Orage than the demonstration. After the performance she suggested asking Gurdjieff to take coffee with us. Surprisingly, he agreed. Leaving all the important people in Carnegie Hall, he led us to Child's in Columbus Circle across the way. I was struck by the way he crossed the road through the traffic, not in the nervous, tense way most people do, but as if he was sensing with the whole of his presence, completely aware of what he was doing, like a wise elephant I had seen making his way in a difficult part of a forest in Burma.

While we drank coffee, Gurdjieff spoke of the difficulties he encountered in getting money for his work. 'People will pay anything for trivial things,' he said, 'but for something they really need, even in ordinary life, they will not pay.' I asked him some questions, only because I thought I ought to say something, and he answered so that 'seeing I should not see, and hearing I should not understand'. Also, conditioned as I was by a religious upbringing to believe that 'salvation was free for all', a feeling arose in me that Gurdjieff's teaching ought to be imparted for nothing, and that such a man should have no difficulty in getting all the money he needed. So, although I could have given him a few hundred dollars, which would have been useful to him then, I refrained; and this was for me one of the many things which later became a 'reminding factor', as he called it, for remorse of conscience.

Gurdjieff had set Orage a big task—that of raising enough money for his stay in America. Orage did not mind being poor, but his family had suffered much from poverty when he was a boy and he hated it. Equally he hated having to slave for money and almost as

34

much he disliked asking for money for any purposes—even one not his own. Gurdjieff had arrived in New York with forty people and with no money; at the same time he insisted that the first demonstrations should be free. So Orage had to use his assets to the limit —his charm, his persuasiveness, his fame as an editor. However, Americans are open-handed people and really love to give to something that touches them, and that with no expectation of material reward, or even the publicity usually so dear to them. Money flowed in.

Orage said, 'We are naïve about money according to Gurdjieff, both as individuals and nations we are hypnotized by ideas of money, ideas that have existed for ages. Thousands of people are being made bankrupt and hundreds of thousands are being thrown out of work in England now (1924) because the Financial dictator, Montagu Norman, says that the monetary system must not be changed. Each age has its superstitions, in each age men and women are sacrificed to false gods, false ideals.

'Gurdjieff says that the attitude to finance is all part of the dream state that we live in. If men could wake up it would very soon be changed. Gurdjieff's attitude to money is different from that of anyone I have met. He needs money for his aim. Nothing important can be done without money. At least one of Jesus' preaching trips was financed by rich women. Gurdjieff may appear to be throwing money about, but he calculates and uses it for certain non-personal ends. A few days ago a man gave him a cheque for one hundred dollars for 'his great work', implying by his manner that he was conferring a favour. Gurdjieff thanked him profusely and invited him to dinner the next day at a restaurant. There were ten of us at the meal. When the waiter brought the bill Gurdjieff disputed it, saying that he had forgotten to charge for something or other, and the waiter took the bill away. When he returned, Gurdjieff looked at it, paid it, gave the waiter a good tip and placed the bill on the table so that the donor could see it. I was sitting next to him. It came to just one hundred dollars.'

Someone asked: 'What place has freewill in your system?'

'Ordinary man,' Gurdjieff replied, 'has no will, he does nothing of himself. What is regarded as will is merely a strong desire. A strong man has strong desires; a weak man, weak desires. Man is pulled this way and that way by his desires, his wants. He has no real *wish*, but many wants. A man may have many desires, but one may predominate, and he devotes his life to accomplishing this desire—he sacrifices

35

everything; and people say he has a strong will. Only a man who has an "I" can have will. When man has an "I" he can be master of himself, then he has will that is free—not a want or desire, subject to everything around him, which can change with food, people, climate, sex. Real will comes with conscious wish, by doing things voluntarily. But you must work for years, for centuries, perhaps. We have a Master in us, but this Master is asleep. He must wake up and control all these little masters in us. Very often what is called will is an adjustment between willingness and unwillingness. For example, the mind wants something, the feelings do not want it. If the mind in this case is stronger than the feelings, man obeys his mind. If the two are more or less equal the result is conflict, hesitation, dilly-dallying. This is what is called free will in ordinary man. He is ruled now by the mind, now by the feelings, now by the body—still more often by the sex centre.'

After the meeting someone asked Orage: 'Does the system provide a technique for obtaining free will, and is there a clear statement or description of the system in print?'

Orage replied, 'There are two parts to this question. First, there is a definite technique or method for practical work on oneself. There is also a theoretical side as taught by Ouspensky in London. At the Prieuré both are taught, but for new people the work is mostly practical. Gurdjieff says that both the practical method and the theory are taught little by little, they are given out in bits and pieces which have to be fitted in and stuck together. "But you must make paste," he says, "without paste nothing will stick." Will, and the acquiring of will, is a great mystery. No one has ever seen will, but we can see its manifestation in those who have it. Gurdjieff, for example, has tremendous will. It is the power to *do*.'

'Well,' asked another, 'how would you put into words the technique by which will may be acquired?'

'First of all,' said Orage, 'you must know that wrong will can be acquired. For example, a man wishes to have power over people for his own material ends. After a time something crystallizes in him, but wrong crystallization. The method can be summed up in the following phrase: voluntary suffering and conscious labour. Voluntary suffering is compelling oneself to bear the unpleasing manifestations of others; conscious labour is the effort to sense, remember, and observe oneself. It is the doing of small things consciously; the effort made against the inertia and mechanism of the organism; not for personal gain or profit, not for exercise, health, sport, pleasure, or science; and

36

not out of pique, or like and dislike. Self-remembering never becomes a habit. It is always the result of a conscious effort, very small to begin with, but it increases with doing. A moment of self-remembering is a moment of consciousness, that is, of self-consciousness—not in the ordinary sense, but a consciousness of the real Self, which is "I", together with an awareness of the organism—the body, the feelings and thoughts.'

A woman novelist said to Gurdjieff at one meeting: 'I sometimes feel that I am more conscious when I am writing. Is this so or do I imagine it?' He replied: 'You live in dreams and you write about your dreams. Much better for you if you were to scrub one floor consciously than to write a hundred books as you do now.'

About self-remembering, he said, 'A man cannot remember himself because he tries to do so with his mind—at least, in the beginning. Self-remembering begins with self-sensing. It must be done through the instinctive-moving centre and the emotional centre. Mind alone does not constitute a human being any more than the driver is the whole equipage. The centre of gravity of change is in the moving and emotional centres, but these are concerned only with the present; the mind looks ahead. The wish to change, to be what one ought to be, must be in our emotional centre, and the ability to *do* in our body. The feelings may be strong, but the body is lazy, sunk in inertia. Mind must learn the language of the body and feelings, and this is done by correct observation of self. One of the benefits of self-remembering is that one has the possibility of making fewer mistakes in life. But for complete self-remembering all the centres must work simultaneously; and they must be artificially stimulated; the mental centre from the outside, the other two from inside. You must distinguish between sensation, emotions, and thoughts; and say to each sensation, emotion, and thought, "Remind me to remember you", and for this you must have an "I". And you must begin by separating inner things from outer, to separate "I" from "It". It is similar to what I said about internal and external considering.'

Someone said, 'I'm not very clear about what you mean by considering.'

Gurdjieff replied, 'I will give you a simple example. Although I am accustomed to sitting with my legs crossed under me, I consider the opinion of the people here and sit as they do, with my legs down. This is external considering.

'As regards inner considering. Someone looks at me, as I think, disapprovingly. This starts corresponding associations in my feelings; if I am too weak to refrain from reacting, I am annoyed with him. I consider internally, and show that I am annoyed. This is how we usually live; we manifest outside what we feel inside.

'We should try to draw a line between the inner and the outer impacts. Externally, we should sometimes consider even more than we do now; be more polite to people than we usually are, for example. It can be said that what until now has been outside should be inside; and what was inside should be outside. Unfortunately, we always react. But why should I be annoyed or hurt if someone looks at me disapprovingly?—or if he doesn't look at me, doesn't notice me? It may be that he himself is the slave of someone else's opinion; perhaps he is an automaton, a parrot repeating another's words. Perhaps someone has trod on his corns. And tomorrow he may change. If he is weak, and I am annoyed with him, I am even weaker; and by considering, making a mountain out of a molehill and getting into a state of resentment, I may spoil my relations with other people.

'It must be understood very clearly and established as a principle that you must not let yourselves become slaves to other people's opinions; you must be free from those around you. And when you become free inside you *will* be free of them.

'At times, it may be necessary for you to pretend to be annoyed; and it does not follow that if someone slaps you on one cheek you should always offer the other. It is necessary sometimes to answer back in such a way that the other will forget his grandmother. But you must not consider internally. On the other hand, if you are free inside it may happen that if someone slaps you on one cheek it is better to offer the other cheek. It depends on the other person's type; and sometimes a man will not forget such a lesson in a hundred years. Sometimes one should retaliate, other times not. A man can choose only when he is free inside. An ordinary man cannot choose, cannot sum up the situation quickly and impartially, for with him his external is his internal. It is necessary to work on oneself, to learn to be unbiased, to sort out and analyse each situation as if one were another person; only then can one be just. To be just at the moment of action is a hundred times more valuable than to be just afterwards. And only when you can be really impartial as regards yourself will you be able to be impartial towards others.

'A very great deal is necessary for this. Free will is not to be had for the asking, nor can it be bought in a shop. Impartial action is the basis of inner freedom, the first step towards free will.'

At another meeting the question was asked, 'Is it necessary to suffer all the time to keep conscience open?'

'As I have already told you,' said Gurdjieff, 'there are very many kinds of suffering. This also is a stick with two ends. One kind of suffering leads to the angel, the other to the devil. Man is a very complicated machine. By the side of every good road there runs a corresponding bad one. One thing is always side by side with another. Where there is little good there is little bad; where there is much good there is also much bad; where there is a strong positive there will be a strong negative. But where there is much bad it does not mean that there will be also much good. With suffering it is easy to find oneself on the wrong road. Suffering easily becomes transformed into pleasure. Many people love their suffering. You are hit once—you are hurt. The second time you are hit you feel it less. The fifth you already wish to be hit. One must not fall asleep but always be alert. One must know what is necessary at each moment, or one may stumble off the path into the ditch.'

Another question: 'What part does conscience play in the acquiring of an "I"?'

'In the beginning,' replied Gurdjieff, 'conscience helps in that it saves time. He who has conscience can be calm; he who has calm has time which he can use for work. Later, conscience serves another purpose. With an ordinary man most of his time is occupied with considering; one association stops, another begins. He goes out in the morning glad, in a few minutes he becomes sad, another few minutes and he is resentful or angry—he is at the mercy of hundreds of useless associations; the machine works all the time. The energy collected during sleep sets our daytime associations flowing. All day the expenditure goes on in us. Our store of energy is sufficient for our ordinary mechanical life, but not for work on ourselves. If, for example, we compare the energy that is expended by a 15-watt electric bulb, the energy expended by active work corresponds to a 100-watt bulb, which very quickly consumes the available current. If we use our store of energy in useless associations—anxiety, resentment, worry, and so on—we shall have only enough energy, say, for the morning, and none for the rest of the day; and without energy man is only a lump of flesh. What we have to do is to learn to spend our energy economically. Nature formed us so that we could have enough energy to do both kinds of work, ordinary life-work and work on ourselves. But we have forgotten how to work normally, hence the waste of energy. The energy produced by our dynamo and stored in our battery is used up by our movements, emotions, sensations, and manifestations. We spend it not only on what is necessary but on what is unnecessary. For example, when you sit and talk you need energy for this, but you gesticulate as well. This may be necessary for emphasis; but no energy is needed for the legs and other muscles, yet all the time you sit tensed up. You cannot help this, even if you know it. Your mind has no power to give orders. A long period of exercises is needed to free oneself from unnecessary tensions. However, the body does not use as much energy as associations do. All the time we have thousands of useless thoughts, feelings, and experiences, pleasant and unpleasant; and they all take place without "I".

'The energy used in conscious work is converted for future use; that used unconsciously is lost for ever.'

Question: 'How can we economize energy?'

'To learn this a long time is needed. You cannot begin by trying to economize energy of the emotions. Begin by what is easier—energy in the body; when you have learnt this you will have acquired a taste which will serve as a key.'

Question: 'Do we use less energy when we are lying down?'

'When you are lying down you have fewer external impacts, but you may spend much more energy in mental associations. You may spend less energy in walking than in sitting, because the legs move by momentum and need to be pushed only from time to time. When a car is running in low gear, it uses more energy than when in top gear, when a great part of the motion is by momentum. When you are lying down, a prey to associations, you are in low gear, so to speak. In the same way, the expenditure of energy of a given muscle may be different.'

At another meeting he was asked: 'What is the attitude of your system to morality?'

'Morality,' he replied, 'can be subjective or objective. Objective morality is the same for all men everywhere. Subjective morality is different in different countries and at different periods. Everyone defines subjective morality differently. What one person calls "good" is called by another "bad", and vice versa. Subjective morality is also a stick with two ends; it can be turned this way and that. From the time when men appeared on the earth, from the time of Adam, there began to be formed in us with the help of God, of Nature, and our surroundings, an organ whose function is conscience. Every man has this organ, and whoever is guided by his conscience lives according to the precepts of the inner voice. But man lives according to the whim of subjective conscience, which, like subjective morality, is different everywhere.

'Objective conscience is not a stick with two ends, it is a realization of what is good and bad formed in us through the ages. But it happens that this organ, for many reasons, is covered by a kind of crust, which can only be broken by intense suffering; then conscience speaks. But after a time man calms down, and again the organ is covered up. In ordinary circumstances a strong shock is needed for the organ to be uncovered. For example, a man's mother dies, and he begins to hear the voice of conscience. To love, honour, and cherish one's mother is the duty of every man. But man is seldom a good son. When his mother dies he remembers how he behaved towards her and he begins to suffer from remorse. Man is also a great swine, and like a swine he soon forgets; conscience sinks down again and he begins to live in his usual automatic way. He who has no conscience cannot be truly moral.

'Another example. I may know what I ought not to do, but from weakness I cannot refrain. For instance, the doctor tells me that coffee is bad for me. I think about it, but only when I do not feel a craving for coffee do I agree with him and refrain from drinking it. It is the same with everything; only when a man is full can he be moral. You should forget about morality. Present talk about morality is empty—pouring from the empty into the void. Your aim is to be Christians in the real sense; but to be able to be a Christian you must be able to *do*. And at present you cannot. When you are able to *do*, you will be able to become Christians.

'External morality is different everywhere, and in this one should behave like others. As they say: "When in Rome do as the Romans do"; this is external morality. For inner morality you must be able to *do*!'

*   *   *

In April I sailed for London. As I watched the receding outline of the towers of New York I reviewed the experiences and events of the past six months. In life one sometimes goes through emotional deserts, arid tracts where nothing happens. At other times experiences and impressions crowd in. Sometimes one is in an oasis, at others in a jungle among wild animals. In a few months, weeks, or days even, one can live years. In my present case I had been living in a land of plenty of emotional and mental experiences.

It was strange that I should have found a teacher and teaching in New York of all places, for I had not expected to find anything of inner value there. On my first visit in 1919, though I had liked the people, the city, as a place for living, had repelled me. I had the same feeling about it on this my second visit; and it is still a city more foreign to me than any other world-capital, even Peking. Yet though I still dislike it as a city, I never think of it but with a feeling of thankfulness, for I owe so much of good to it. As Gurdjieff used to say, 'Every stick has two ends, a good end and a bad end.'

New York is a city of fear and, like all big cities, a centre of tension. A big city is a kind of dynamo which sucks the energy from millions of human beings, whom nature causes to herd together in certain parts of the planet in enormous numbers, like ants and termites in their colossal hills—all doubtless for a cosmic purpose. The termites, who have sacrificed their sight, their sex, and their liberty to the State, no doubt point with pride to the size of their towns, as some New Yorkers and Londoners boast of their cities as the largest in the world.

One can say that France and England stand in relation to America as ancient Greece did to young Rome. For hundreds of years after Rome became a great power, Greece continued to have an enormous influence over her, and on the new groups of peoples that arose in Europe.

As soon as I arrived in London I wrote to the Prieuré asking if I might go and work there. In the meantime I arranged my business affairs.

Although part of me still wished to go to the Institute at Fontainebleau, another part still held back. When no reply came, this other part began to offer all kinds of reasons for not going. Then there was timidity, fear of the unknown and the unfamiliar. Ought I not to be attending to my business instead of spending my time on something which, after all, might turn out to be only another cult? For a week or two this struggle between 'Yes' and 'No' went on, and then at last something in me, or the grace of God, impelled me to go.

I arrived at Fontainebleau and took a fiacre. As the horse trotted down the road my emotions were stirred as though by a spoon; and everything was so strongly imprinted on my receiving apparatuses that the impressions are as clear today as then: the sunshine, the leafy trees, the little clanging tram from Samois, the singing of the saws and fresh sweet smell of sawdust from the timber yard, the houses, the people, and the sombre château of Prince Orloff.

The fiacre stopped in front of some big gates, and the cocher said 'Prieuré'. I paid him, and from sheer nervousness gave him a tip that caused him to raise his hat. Over the wall I could see the mellow roof of the château, and from the courtyard came the plashing of a fountain, a grateful sound that hot spring day. By the door of the conciergerie was a bell-handle with the words 'Sonnez fort'. I pulled hard and waited. Everything was quiet. I pulled again. After a time two small boys appeared and without a word took my bags and put them in the conciergerie, and the elder, whose name was Valya, motioned to me to sit. They disappeared. A long time passed, and while I was sitting I let impressions sink in; and I soon sensed something very unusual in the atmosphere. Whether it was a result of something left by the ancient monks, or the little court of Madame de Maintenon, or of the work of Gurdjieff and his pupils, I did not know; but it was similar to what one feels in old temples and churches; and I knew that in coming here my deepest wish, though unconscious and unformulated, had been granted.

The thread of my musing was cut by Mme de Hartmann, who came in and shook hands. 'Did Mr Gurdjieff get my letters?' I asked. 'I've been waiting to hear.' 'Your letters?' she said. 'Mr Gurdjieff doesn't answer letters. Why do you wait so long? We have been back three weeks now. But I will show you your room. Perhaps you wish to rest. Yes? Excuse me, I have much to do.' She took me to my room, which was on the first floor, and luxuriously furnished in French antique style. My window opened out on to the spreading lawns and shady paths, flower-beds and little pools, all golden in the sunshine—and beyond, the forest. I leant on the sill absorbing the beauty, and all the tension and apprehension dropped away. Again, the *Pilgrim's Progress* came to my mind:

> Then I saw that he went in trembling for fear of the lions, but taking good heed to the direction of the porter, he heard them roar, but they did him no harm. Then he clapped his hands and went on till he came to the gate where the porter was. Then said Christian to the porter, 'Sir, what house is this, and may I lodge here tonight?' The porter said, 'This house was built by the Lord

43

of the Hill, and he built it for the relief and security of the Pilgrims.' He also asked whence he was and whither he was going.

Christian: 'I am come from the City of Destruction and am now going to Mount Sion—but because the sun is set, I desire, if I may, to lodge here tonight.'

Porter: 'What is your name?'

Christian: 'My name is now Christian, but my name at first was Graceless. I came of the race of Japhet whom God will persuade to dwell in the centre of them.'

Porter: 'But how doth it happen that you came so late? The sun is set.'

Christian: 'I had been here sooner but, wretched man that I am, I slept in the arbour by the hillside; nay, I had notwithstanding that been here much sooner, but that in my sleep I lost my evidence, and came without it to the brow of the hill; and then feeling for it and finding it not, I was forced with sorrow of heart to go back to the place where I slept my sleep, where I found it, and now I am come.'

After I had rested, I went into the forest, where a lot of people were busy cutting brushwood, clearing ground, burning rubbish, or sawing logs. A young woman whom I had known in New York left her work to greet me. Gurdjieff came along, but after a glance in my direction took no further notice of me; neither did anyone else, and, rather dismayed, I wandered off. Feeling the need of company, I attached myself to one of the working groups, and pottered about till the bell rang from the tower and everyone went off to tea.

For the first few days I slept in my room in the 'Ritz', as the pupils called it, the luxuriously furnished bedrooms where guests and newcomers were put. From there I was moved to the 'Monk's Corridor' above; later I was moved again, to the top floor, formerly the servants' quarters, overlooking the stable-yard; this was 'Cow Alley'. I was free to do whatever I liked and apparently no one took any notice of me. But I wanted to work, and when I asked what I could do I was told to help in the forest; so I joined up with one group or another.

I have said that 'apparently no one took any notice of me'. Actually, everything I did, the way I did it, and what I said, was reported to Gurdjieff. I had heard about the hard physical work; and many people of the intellectual type did find it extremely hard. As for myself, accustomed to long hours as a general bush and station hand in Australia and to life in the trenches in France, it was nothing; and in such conditions, very enjoyable. But I had yet to discover how to *work* even semi-consciously.

In doing the movements in the evenings I experienced a satisfaction, physical, emotional, and mental, such as never before had happened to me, even when doing folk-dances with the peasants in Central Europe and Russia. There was something new in these dances, something which was neither folk nor classical, yet partook of both; and ballroom dancing and jazz, which had been a passion with me and at which I had been considered rather good, now seemed inane and meaningless, even sub-human. As time went on and I learnt more of the movements and dances, the more was I able to enjoy good classical dancing, folk dancing, and ballet, and the less I enjoyed 'modern' dancing. It may be that this was one of the smaller things I had been subconsciously afraid of losing. Apropos, when I had been at the Prieuré for about a month, an old friend of mine with whom I had worked in Russia, young Prince M., invited me to a cabaret party in Montparnasse, and although I enjoyed his company and that of his friends, the atmosphere of the place and the dancing made me feel physically sick.

Our daily life followed a routine that frequently changed. The getting-up bell rang from the tower at half-past six. Breakfast consisted of large hunks of toasted bread, with coffee; then came work in the gardens, or the forest, or the house. There was a break from half-past twelve to two for lunch. Tea was at four and supper at half-past six; movements and dances followed until ten or eleven. During the day Mr Gurdjieff gave general talks, and personal talks to individual pupils.

Some days after I arrived one of the pupils showed me round. The château was a gift from Louis XIV to Mme de Maintenon. He had had it built partly from the remains of an old monastery, of which nothing was left but a few blocks of stone; on one of these I could just decipher 'Ad maiorem gloriam Dei'. The château passed to Maître Labori, Dreyfus' lawyer, from whose executor Gurdjieff bought it in 1922, with furnishings and pictures, some by Rosa Bonheur.

Inside and outside the house was beautifully proportioned. It gave one a sense of satisfaction and well-being. A stream from Avon ran through the grounds, thirteen acres in extent, enclosed by a high wall. Hidden from the château by trees was a row of small houses called Paradou, and here lived Gurdjieff's mother and his married sister; his brother Dmitri and his family; Dr and Mrs Stjoernval; and Mr and Mme de Salzmann. Beyond Paradou was an orangery in ruins, and beyond that again, the Study House.

45

The Study House had been built by the pupils about eighteen months before with materials from a disused hangar. It was in the form of a Dervish tekke. Walls and floor were of earth. Inside, over the entrance, was a small gallery with a seat, and hung round the gallery was a collection of stringed instruments and drums from the Near and Far East; while on the walls were several diplomas or certificates in Eastern characters, which had at various times been given to Gurdjieff. The floor of the Study House was covered with carpets from Persia, Afghanistan, and other Eastern countries, and carpets hung on the walls. Inside on the right of the entrance was a box with hangings, Gurdjieff's own seat. Round the walls of the House were raised seats for spectators, separated from the open space by a painted wooden fence. At the far end was a raised platform of earth, covered with linoleum, for movements; and in front a small fountain. The windows were stained and painted in a pleasing harmony of colours; while scattered about on the walls, in a script somewhat like Persian or Turkish, were aphorisms or sayings. The atmosphere was that of a holy place, partly due to the effect of the combination of colours on the senses and feelings (for Gurdjieff understood how to produce definite effects by means of colours, as well as by sound and movements) and partly to the vibrations of the pupils who practised the sacred dances and movements there.

I was taken through the flower garden, now in full bloom, to a swimming pool; by it on a raised bank was a gazebo. There began the kitchen gardens; beyond these again was the forest, with its rides and walks. A place of beauty, dignity and charm, and above all pervaded by an atmosphere like an old church or monastery, yet living and vital.

We passed a group of children playing together—Nikolai Stjoernval, Boussique Salzmann aged five, some of Gurdjieff's nieces and nephews, and Mme de Salzmann with her six months' old son Michel in a pram. We ended our tour at the cowshed. I was curious to see it, since I had known Katherine Mansfield in London when she and John Middleton Murry were producing Signature with Koteliansky, and Orage had printed her first story in the New Age. It was he, she said, who taught her to write. Orage had suggested her going to the Prieuré. She had spent some days there, and it was to be decided if she should stay. She saw Gurdjieff in Paris with Mr Pinder as interpreter. Gurdjieff told her seriously that if she wanted to live longer she must go to a warm, dry climate. 'And how much longer would I live?' she asked. 'I don't know,' he said. She thought a little and then: 'No. If you will let me, I will go back and live the rest of my life at the Prieuré.'

When Katherine Mansfield returned to the Prieuré, Gurdjieff said that she must spend a lot of time in the cowshed, since the emanations of the animals and the fumes would help her. A platform was built above the stalls in the cowshed, and Mr de Salzmann painted the walls and doors in lively colours and patterns. Here Mrs Murry would lie on a chaise-longue and watch the cows being milked, or look at the drawing of an enneagram on the ceiling. Mr de Salzmann had also painted some of the pupils, and as everyone is said to represent in his type an animal or bird, he had given their faces bodies of corresponding forms. Orage had the body of an elephant, another man that of a donkey, another the head of a poodle, another of a vulture. A young engaged couple had turtle-doves' heads, and so on. Never was cowhouse so gay and colourful and interesting.

One of the young women who looked after Katherine Mansfield told me that she had expressed her gratitude to Gurdjieff. 'If I had gone away from the Prieuré and lived the old life,' she said, 'I should have died very soon of boredom. Here, at any rate, I am alive inside, and the people around me are alive. And I am not Katherine Mansfield the writer, but Mrs Murry, a sick woman, looked after without fuss or sentimentality. Another thing—here at last I see what I have always wanted to see; people who are themselves, and not playing a part behind a mask.' She was in a state towards the end where a small shock would be fatal, and the thought of J. M. Murry's coming to the Prieuré excited her, for she said he would never understand what it stood for. She died shortly after he arrived. She had said that Gurdjieff and his people did everything possible for her, and that she achieved more understanding of herself and of others in her short time at the Prieuré than in all her previous life. Yet people still speak and write of the 'charlatan' at Fontainebleau who caused her early death. I was then in Russia, and wrote to Murry, who answered with one sentence, 'K. M. was perfect'. Of course she was not perfect, but her spark of solar energy gave her an understanding, particularly of women. Unfortunately her admirers wished her to be a kind of angel and Murry fostered this wish.

It seems that Gurdjieff and a few pupils had come to Paris from Hellerau, where they had stayed for a time, and with him some of Jacques Dalcroze's best pupils, who, after seeing Gurdjieff's dances, realized that eurhythmics, though providing a foundation for the study of movement, were kindergarten in comparison. Gurdjieff, as soon as he arrived in Paris, began rehearsals for a demonstration. He himself designed the costumes and cut them out; the pupils made them up. The first demonstration in Paris was given in the Théatre des Champs Elysées, but although the theatre was crowded none of the French were interested enough to become pupils; they waited another twenty years. When Diaghileff, who was a friend of Mr de Hartmann's, came to the Prieuré, he was so impressed with the dances and movements that he made several visits. A number of Ouspensky's pupils and others came from London to the demonstration, and Mme Ouspensky herself helped in the preparations. Most of the money for this phase of Gurdjieff's activities came from Ouspensky's English group, of which Dr Maurice Nicoll and his wife were members, as were Clifford Sharp, editor of the *New Statesman*, and his wife; Dr J. A. M. Alcock; and Dr James Young. Later, Dr Mary Bell, Algernon Blackwood, J. D. Beresford, and D. Mitrinovich came to the meetings.

Almost all the first twenty or so people were outstanding in their professions, and were readers of, or contributors to, Orage's paper the *New Age*. Gurdjieff visited the group in London, and a number of pupils were chosen to go to the Prieuré, but only Orage and three or four others stayed there for long. By the time I arrived all the English people except Orage, two or three women, and one or two young men had left to return to their jobs or to work again with Ouspensky. Madame Ouspensky's daughter and her small son still stayed on at the Prieuré.

Having already experienced almost every kind of physical toil and discomfort as soldier, sailor, farmer, labourer; I considered that the Prieuré had nothing to teach me in this respect. But it did not take more than two or three weeks for me to begin to see that I still had much to learn; to realize that I did not know how to do physical work —as a man and not a machine. I had been told to 'chop' stones, and with four girls I spent ten days breaking limestone rock into small pieces the size of a nut. It was a contrast to working in the shady walks of the forest with the men; in the hot sun it became monotonous, dull, and wearisome, and my feelings began to revolt. I worked spasmodically and nervously. Gurdjieff came along one day, with the doctor, Stjoernval. 'Why you work so nervously?' he asked. 'It's a result of the war,' I said. 'No!' he replied, 'I think you always like this. Watch Gertrude, see how she works. All your attention goes in watching the clock, listening for the dinner bell.' The next day Dr Stjoernval said to me, 'You know, Mr Gurdjieff says we should learn to work like men, not like ordinary labourers. Like men, not like machines. Try to save your energy while you are chopping stones. You waste much energy in resenting what you are doing. Make a list of thirty or forty words in a foreign language and memorize them while you are working; at the same time try to sense your body and notice what you are doing.'

I began to be aware that when Gurdjieff said something to you, it registered not only in the mind but in the feelings, in such a way that you could not help but think seriously about it. Soon, by making the effort to do this simple exercise, a change in my attitude to the monotonous labour began to take place. Some of the energy that I had been wasting in resentment was used productively for myself. The work even became satisfying. Some days later Gurdjieff again passed and glanced at me. The next day I was given another job, helping the young men water the far garden. The water had to be carried from the stream outside the south gate a hundred yards away, so that a whole morning was necessary. One day I noticed that the stream ran on the other side of the high wall which bounded the far garden, and it seemed to me that if we could dig a pit by the wall and let the water through the wall, an enormous amount of carrying work would be saved. My companion agreed, but pointed out that the hole might bring the wall down. So I suggested syphoning the water over. We got a length of hosepipe, and by sucking at it the water was persuaded to come through, climb the ten-foot wall, and fall into the pit. Our problem was solved. Some of the pupils came to see it. 'Fancy,' said one, 'all those great minds like Orage, Nicoll, Young, and Pinder, spending weeks carrying water, and not one of them thought of this simple idea.'

Two days later Gurdjieff returned from a trip; we gleefully told him about the water system and asked him to come and see. While we stood by preening ourselves, he looked at it and said, 'Very good, very ingenious. Now, I have another idea. Take away pipe and fill the pit. We look for a spring.' So we continued to carry the water from outside. That same week, I met Dr Stjoernval, who said, 'I will show you something.' He took me in and pointed to a portion of the script, and asked, 'Do you know what it says?' I shook my head. 'It says, "Remember that work here is a means, not an end".'

The spring was not found until five years later, and it fell to me to find it. Its finding became the means for a new understanding of the work and of myself in relation to the work. But I will tell of that in its place.

Gurdjieff sometimes took drastic measures to bring home to us how we were attached to, or identified with, our work and its results. Two Englishwomen, keen gardeners, had worked intensely in the flower garden and produced a fine show of blooms. Young pupils—and especially children—were often shooed away for fear harm might be done. When the garden was at its best, they asked Gurdjieff to come and see it. He did so, and it was arranged that everyone else should come too. He looked round, nodded and smiled and said: 'Very nice, very nice', and went away. That evening the gate 'happened' to be left open and the calves and sheep went browsing in the precious garden.

As a result of these two incidents I read again, and for the first time with profit, George Herbert's 'The Elixir':

> Teach me my God and King
> In all things Thee to see
> And what I do in anything,
> To do it as for Thee.
>
> A servant with this clause
> Makes drudgerie divine.
> Who sweeps a room as for thy laws
> Makes that and the action fine.
>
> This is the famous stone
> That turneth all to gold;
> For that which God doth touch and own
> Cannot for less be told.

From time to time word would be passed round for everyone who could be spared to go to the forest. Gurdjieff would appear and begin what we called a 'scurry' party, from the Russian 'skorey'—quick. Tools were handed out, and individuals and parties given various jobs —clearing, cutting brushwood, making fires, clearing ditches. Everyone worked urgently and purposefully, to his limit, but (and this was one of the aims) with attention. Gurdjieff himself worked, urging us on with 'Skorey!' 'Skorey!' It was exciting, and much could be learnt about oneself if one could self-remember; for these parties were related to what in the Institute's programme was called 'dulio-therapy'— 'slave cure', when a man voluntarily submits himself completely to the command of a teacher. Gurdjieff once quoted the Greek saying: 'Be slave freely, not slave will be'.

After two or three hours of work, he would say 'Davolna!'—

3. Front, from left, Mr. Gurdjieff's wife, mother and sister.

4. Building the Study House.   Left, Mr. Gurdjieff, right, Mr. de Salzmann.

enough! Sometimes he sat on a log, sometimes he went to the Study House. Tea and food were brought, and we sat down to refresh ourselves. Usually someone brought up a question, and he talked to us, speaking partly in Russian, partly in English. We tried to remember what he said and to piece it together afterwards, for he always spoke so that we were compelled to use our minds, compelled to ponder.

Someone once asked a question about 'freedom', and Gurdjieff began: 'Freedom leads to freedom. That is truth, not in quotation marks but in the real sense. Truth is not just theory, not just words; it can be realized. The freedom I speak of is the aim of all schools, of all religions, of all times. It is a very big thing. Everyone, consciously or unconsciously, wishes for freedom. There are two kinds, the Lesser Freedom and the Greater Freedom. You cannot have the Greater Freedom until you have attained to the Lesser Freedom. The Greater Freedom is the liberation of ourselves from outside influences; the Lesser, from influences within us.

'For us beginners, the Lesser Freedom is a very big thing; it is not subject to our dependence on outside influences. Inner slavery comes from many sources; it depends on many independent things, sometimes one, sometimes another. There are so many that if we had to struggle with each one separately in order to free ourselves from them, half a lifetime would not be enough. So we must find a means, a method of working, that will enable us to destroy simultaneously as many as possible of the enemies within us from which these influences flow. Among these enemies two of the chief are Vanity, and Self-Love or Self-Pride. In one teaching these are called emissaries or representatives of the devil; and for some reason or other they are spoken of as Madame Vanity and Mr Self-Love.

'As I have said, there are many of these inner enemies; but I have mentioned only these two, since they are characteristic. It would take us too far to mention them all now.

'These representatives of the devil stand all the time on the threshold and prevent not only good but bad influences from coming in; they have a bad side and a good side.

'They are a kind of sentinel, and to deal with them I personally advise you not to spend your time wiseacreing about them but to deal with them by reasoning simply and actively with yourself. For example, let us take Self-Love or False Pride, which occupies half our time and half our life. When anyone or anything touches this we are hurt, at once and for a long time after; and the wounded feelings, by inertia, shut the door and keep out life. I live. Life is outside. I am in life when I am connected with outside. If I imagine that life exists only inside me, this is not life. I cannot live to myself alone, I am linked with the outside world, and so is everyone.'

Here Gurdjieff went and sat between two of the Russians, Merslukin and Ivanoff. He continued:

'For example, I am sitting between Merslukin and Ivanoff. We live together here. Now we will suppose that Merslukin calls me a fool; at once I begin to consider. I am offended and hurt. Ivanoff looked at me disapprovingly, as though he despised me. Again I am hurt, and for a long time. I consider interiorly and forget myself. And so it is with everyone, all the time. No sooner does an experience of this kind fade away than another takes its place.

'We must not forget that our machine is so constructed that there are not different places for different experiences at one and the same time. In us there is only *one place*—this he said emphatically—'where an experience can occur. If this place is occupied by one kind of experience, and an undesirable one, it cannot be occupied at the same time by an experience of another and desirable kind.

'Well, Merslukin called me a fool. But why should I feel hurt? Actually, for me personally, I am not hurt—not because I have no pride or self-love; perhaps I have more than any of you; but perhaps it is my pride that does not allow me to feel that I have been insulted. I think about it, I reason about it. I say to myself: "If he called me a fool, does it follow that he is wise? Perhaps he is a fool himself. He acts like a child, and you cannot expect children to be wise. Perhaps someone has been talking to him about me and he has got foolish ideas. So much the worse for him. I know that in this case I am not a fool, so I am not offended. If a fool calls me a fool I am not hurt inwardly.

'On the other hand I may have been a fool. In this case I should thank him for letting me see that I have behaved like a fool. In neither case am I hurt.

'About Ivanoff; we will suppose that he gives me a dirty look. But instead of letting this offend me, I pity him because he squints at me. Something or someone has upset him. But can he discover the real cause? I understand myself and can judge myself impartially. Perhaps someone has told him something about me and this has given him a certain impression of me. I am sorry that he is such a slave; that he should look at me through the eyes of another. This only shows that he himself has no existence—he is no more than a slave.

'And so with all of you—everyone is the same; but I give these two examples as a basis for active reasoning. All the trouble lies in the fact that we do not possess ourselves and that we have no real pride. Real pride is a big thing; unfortunately we do not possess it. Pride is a kind of measure of the opinion that one has about oneself. If a man has real pride, it proves that he *is*. Pride is also our chief enemy, the great obstacle to our wishes and achievements, the weapon of the representative of hell.

'Pride is also an attribute of the soul. By pride we can discern the spirit. Pride is the evidence that its possessor is of heaven. Pride is "I", "I" is God. Pride is hell, pride is heaven. These two, having the same name, externally the same, are different and opposite, and no ordinary consideration and observation of them will ever distinguish one from the other.

'There is a saying: "He who has real pride is already half free". Yet, although we are full to the brim with pride, we must admit that we have not obtained the least bit of freedom for ourselves.

'Our aim must be to have real pride; only then shall we be freed from many of our foes within; and we may even free ourselves from those two called Madame Vanity and Mr Self-Love. How can we distinguish real pride from false? It is difficult to observe and discriminate in another; it is a hundred times more difficult to do so in ourselves.'

He paused and looked round and with a sly smile added sarcastically: ' "Thank Heaven," I hear you say, "that we who are sitting here run no risk of confusing one with the other. The fact that we are here and have worked on ourselves shows, of course, that we are empty of false pride; so there is no need for us to look for it." '

Resuming his usual tone, he concluded, 'In any case you must try to learn to reason actively. You must make an exercise of it. Each must recall some occasion, past or present, of hurt pride; and each, with the participation of others, must reason about it. Later I shall call on one or more of you to speak about his case, which must be actual and not imagined.'

One result of work in the Institute was that all kinds of things began to stir in me. My weaknesses became 'stronger', that is to say they showed themselves more clearly. As my old personality began to dissolve, it was as if a pot had begun to boil and the scum to rise. I had imagined that I 'loved' people, in the weak pseudo-Christian way that my religion had taught. It came as a shock to have the beginnings of a realization that I hated certain people. One of the Russian women said, 'I don't like your emanations. You hate me.'

'Hate you! Of course I don't.'

'Oh yes, you do. But don't let yourself be identified with it. In the beginning this work often brings out the worst in us. That is why we are here; to see it. It will pass.'

When I thought about it I saw that I did indeed hate her, and for no reason except that our personalities did not agree; I was surprised at the force of my hatred. Very soon it did pass, and I forgot about it. I then began to be aware that a hatred of one of the young men was growing in me. It was not his personality, but something in our essences, that aroused my dislike. When Gurdjieff put us to work together I could hardly bear to look at him, and everything I said came out in a tone of resentment. Then, one Saturday evening in the Turkish bath, Gurdjieff, as was his wont, began to talk, this time about how personalities can hate each other, or essences hate each other. He said that we must understand this and reason with ourselves and realize what is taking place in us, and not be identified with what we are feeling at the moment; then we shall change. In the same way as they hate, personalities and essences can also love each other.

'You must understand,' he said, 'that both ordinary hate and ordinary love are mechanical. Later you may understand something about real love.'

We dressed and began to leave. As I was going out, Gurdjieff, in front of everyone, pointing to the man I mentioned, said to me, 'You hate him. You think he is the tail of a donkey. But you—not even tail of donkey. You are less; you are what comes out of donkey.'

On another occasion I was talking to the Russian, M., and he answered me in that rather supercilious arrogant manner that Russians sometimes use, which seemed to mean 'You poor ignorant young man'. It was as if I had received a blow in the solar plexus. I was hurt and I went away and brooded. Then I thought to myself, 'This is what Gurdjieff was speaking about. Perhaps I was to blame.' When I thought about it a little more, I saw that really I had been the cause of his speaking to me in the way he did, and the hurt feeling passed.

Gurdjieff constantly manipulated people and situations so as to provoke friction, to create negative emotions between them and give them an opportunity of seeing something in themselves. He asked Orage to put into good English a talk that had been translated from the Russian; he then gave it to Madame de Hartmann to correct, and told someone to let Orage know. Orage, when told about this, for a moment looked annoyed, but then began to smile.

In my childhood, and indeed later on in life, all sorts of persons, from my parents to my superior officers in the army, were constantly telling me what to think, feel, and do. Outwardly I accepted their views, inwardly I doubted them; I doubted whether they were speaking from inner conviction due to direct experience. Now I had met a man who, I was convinced, was speaking from his own experience when he pointed out my faults and weaknesses. By his own efforts he had over-come these things, and he fully understood my needs. The older pupils also, when they answered my questions about the system, spoke only from their own direct experience.

I have said that the physical work as ordinarily understood was far from difficult, except for those who had never done any—such as some of the rich, and the 'intellectuals'. And I had heard that the food was plain, scanty, and Spartan; but for me at the ordinary meals it was plentiful and satisfying and tasty, and at Gurdjieff's guest meals abund-ant and delicious. For breakfast, toasted bread and butter and coffee; for lunch, stew with vegetables and a pudding; at 4.30 tea and bread and butter; and for supper a little meat with vegetables, and pie to follow. When it was wet or cold we ate in the Russian dining room; on fine days, outside at small tables. The 'Russian' dining room was dark and bare of furniture except for a big table and benches. Gurdjieff ate with us except when there were guests, which was often.

Guests were given lunch or dinner in the 'English' dining room with the older pupils; usually some of the new pupils were also invited. This dining room was a spacious apartment with the original furniture. Here Madame de Maintenon had fed her little court and entertained Louis XIV. There was a big table which could seat about twenty-five people, and two side tables seating twenty each; altogether, seventy or more people could eat in comfort. Gurdjieff's place was in the middle of the big table facing the windows. Behind him, on the mantelpiece, a photo of his father showed a benevolent old man with a beard and moustache, wearing an astrakhan cap. On Saturday nights after the Turkish bath everyone ate in the English dining room. The older pupils and men and women guests sat at the big table. At one of the side tables were the young people; at the other the children. These Saturday even-ing dinners and other special occasions were patriarchal feasts. At the beginning of the meal people sat quietly, then conversation began, but it never rose to an unpleasant pitch. Gurdjieff would tell newcomers and guests how he had suffered from the poor food he had had to eat in America and England. He would describe the properties of the food on the table, how it was prepared so as to retain all the active elements which kept the stomach in good condition and enabled it to give the necessary energy. Sometimes he would begin to speak to someone in a tone of voice that caused everyone to stop and listen intently, for what he said might be for the person addressed, or it might be for someone else. In any case, if the cap fitted you, you were glad to wear it.

Quite simple statements that one had heard a hundred times repeated by people mechanically, now became charged with meaning. For example, I once caught the words: 'You live in the past. The past is dead. Act in the present. If you live as you always have lived, the future will be like the past. Work on yourself, change something in yourself, then the future perhaps will be different.'

When he spoke in this way his eyes sparkled with light, and one felt that one was hearing a truth for the first time. It sank in. Another thing, one did not say to oneself, 'This is for so-and-so', but 'This is for me'. When he wished to convey something to a particular person, that person never failed to receive it. What he now said about living in the past applied, of course, to many people; but particularly, I felt, to me. As I thought about it, I saw that one of my faults was to be always recalling the past; repulsion and fear for the unpleasant past like the war and schooldays; and a longing for the 'days that are no more'. It is, for some, a slow job to bring themselves into a state where they can neither fear recurrence of the unpleasant past, nor long for a return of the pleasant. As my grandfather used to say: 'The mill cannot grind with water that is past', and the poet: 'We look before and after, and sigh for what is not'.

In all my travels I think I have never eaten food so delicious as at these dinners—food from every quarter of the world. There was soup, meat with spices, poultry, fish; vegetables of all kinds, most wonderful salads whose juice we drank in glasses; puddings and pies, fruit of all sorts, dishes of oriental tit-bits, fragrant herbs, raw onions, and celery. Calvados and slivovitz for the elders to drink, and wine for the young and the children. A speciality was sheep's head after the meat course, done in Caucasian style, delicious and very rich. Gurdjieff would tell a guest that in the East the sheep's eyes were considered the tastiest part, and would honour him by offering him one—which was refused except by someone who wanted to show off. All the food supplies and the cooking were supervised by Gurdjieff, and there seemed no end to his recipes. He himself was a wonderful cook, and knew how to prepare hundreds of oriental dishes, though he himself never ate a great deal. This, I used to think, is just how dinners should be; to be able to savour the food and enjoy it, without being identified with it on the one hand, or being unconscious of it on the other.

Sometimes he would say to someone, 'Eat, eat! English people pick at their food. They never know what they are eating. Do you know why? They export all their good food and live only on margarine and Australian frozen mutton. Never have fresh food!'

Dinner over, he would get up and lead the way into the salon, where coffee and liqueurs were handed round. He would talk—and there was almost always teaching in his talk. After the coffee, Hartmann would play music.

Gurdjieff's dinners, and those in old Russia or Ireland or France, or even England up to the end of the eighteenth century, had this in common—you were expected to enjoy your food and drink, and to appreciate the fact that people had spent time and labour in preparing it, in contrast to society dinners in London and New York, where incessant talk was the rule and comment on the food bad form.

Among my farming relatives the growing of food naturally occupied most of their lives. In their homes, and in my home, the preparation of food for eating took up a great part of the daily round, while the enjoyment of it provided a never-failing topic of conversation. What an enormous amount of time is spent on the growing of food compared with the preparation of it for eating! And how little time is spent in eating a meal compared with that spent in preparing it; and how very much less in the process of expelling the waste matter from the organism.

In the Prieuré, everyone took turns to be kitchen boy or kitchen-maid, and the experienced ones to be cook. The job of kitchen boy was not sought after, even as a means of self-development. It meant working from 5 a.m. till 11 p.m., missing the movements, the music, and Gurdjieff's talks—a never-ceasing washing of plates and dishes, scouring pots and pans, scrubbing stone floors, snatching a bite at intervals, with all sorts of odd people drifting in to heat up a cup of coffee or get a bit of food.

It was as kitchen boy that I first met Madame Ouspensky. On that occasion she took her place as cook for the day, and carried herself with the air and style of a Grand Duchess—indeed a remarkable woman. Gurdjieff often smilingly teased her; sometimes after a brush with him she would walk indignantly out of the salon saying: 'Niet, niet, George-ivanitch!'

A weekly event always looked forward to was the ritual of the Turkish bath. The bath had been constructed the year before by the pupils. It was sunk in the ground, the roof just showing above. Steps led down to the undressing-room; beyond this was a large boiler for heating the rooms, the water, and the steam. The men's bath was at 7.30 every Saturday evening, the women taking theirs earlier in the afternoon; a dull affair it must have been, since they did not have Gurdjieff to entertain them as he did us. To undress we sat on a long bench of beaten earth, Gurdjieff's place being opposite. While we were undressing and warming up, he would talk or joke. At my first visit, he said: 'You know, it is a rule that everyone who comes to my bath must be able to tell three funny stories. Can you do this?'

When we had undressed and got warmed up, Gurdjieff led the way into the hot room, a large circular room supported by a central pillar. After a period here, we followed him into the small Russian steam-room, and packed ourselves on benches, one above the other, like herrings. For a long time I could never go into the steam-room without an attack of claustrophobia. When the steam was turned on, and while it lasted, I could hardly refrain from rushing out. Always I had to screw up my courage to the sticking place and keep it there until the steam was turned off, when we climbed down from the benches and flicked each other with bundles of twigs among the clouds of dispersing steam. Back in the hot room we shampooed and massaged each other on benches. There was a hot and cold shower, a hose pipe, and a little cold water fountain on the floor to squat over.

After the washing and massaging, we drifted back one by one into the cooling room and smoked or dozed. When Gurdjieff had rested he would talk or perhaps exchange jokes with the Russians. Salzmann had a never-failing supply of funny stories which often sent Gurdjieff into fits of belly-laughter. Orage was very witty and amusing, though usually his jokes had to be translated by Hartmann, the only one of the Russians who spoke English well.

In the Study House one day Gurdjieff said: 'I understand that some of you are not clear about what you call the formatory "centre". This is not a centre, it is an apparatus. It consists of a number of machines connected with the centres.

'Shocks from one centre pass through the formatory apparatus, and if the associated thoughts, feelings, or sensations are strong enough they will set up corresponding associations in another centre. The associations between centres are conveyed through the formatory apparatus connexions. The centres are of spiritized matter, so to say; the formatory apparatus not; it is a machine that we are born with.'

He gave as an illustration a factory with various departments—and partners, the centres. There is a general office in charge of a secretary. In us the general office is the formatory apparatus, and the secretary our upbringing and education—our automatically acquired points of view. All messages from outside, between departments, and between partners, are received in the office and transmitted by the secretary with all references and relative correspondence. But the secretary is lazy and often given to fits of day-dreaming; she presses the wrong button, gets messages mixed up. And so with the formatory apparatus in us.

This talk, in time, cleared up many things for me. We depend on this secretary. Accidental shocks set something going within us, and we talk and talk—or write! There are those who talk incessantly, like a gramophone record which repeats and repeats; not only barkers at fairs and markets, intellectuals and politicians, but many nice well-meaning people pour out an unending stream of words.

At first it was extremely difficult for me to ask Gurdjieff questions. On the one hand was timidity, a fear of saying something foolish, or being thought stupid, an inner inertia, and on the other the feeling that I did not know what to ask. This state of wishing to ask and not being able reached such a pitch that I suffered. One day I saw him coming down the track in the forest, driving the one-horse wagon. He stopped and watched what I was doing, then got down to adjust the harness. At that moment, making a tremendous effort, I said: 'Mr Gurdjieff, what is it that makes it so difficult for me to speak to you, to ask you a question?' He looked at me without saying anything, then took my arm, and it was as if a warm flow of electricity passed through me. Getting up on to the wagon, he signed to me to sit beside him, and drove on. For half an hour we drove about while he gave directions to various people, then he gave the reins to me, told me to take the horse to the stable, and went into the house. We had not exchanged a word. But from that time I had a different feeling towards him, and though it

59

never became easy for me to ask him questions, my attitude became different, and I discovered that if I pondered a question and was able to formulate it clearly, sometimes the question was already answered.

On Sunday there was no work except for those in the kitchen, and no dances or movements in the Study House. After lunch in the English dining room Gurdjieff with two or three pupils usually went to Paris in his little Citroen car, to his apartment on the Boulevard Pereire. In the evening, he would meet and talk with people in the Café de la Paix by the Opéra, or perhaps organize a dinner at l'Écrivisse in Montmartre. The Café de la Paix was his 'office', as he called it. Morning and evening, whenever he was in Paris, he could be found there, ready to talk with anyone who wanted to see him and drink coffee with him.

When staying at the Prieuré, he made a daily trip into Fontainebleau to drink coffee and meet people at the Henri Deux, and every few weeks he made a trip in his car to some part of France or other, taking pupils with him.

Even to sit with him while he was talking in Russian with others was an experience. Like one of the Rishis, he was 'blazing with energy', and one left him revitalized. As a small electric machine can be charged with energy just by being near a more powerful one, so a person could be magnetized by being near Gurdjieff, by his force and 'being'.

After I had been at the Prieuré for a time, I began to think about my grandfather. The association was first called up by the portrait of Gurdjieff's father, about whom he writes in the Second Series of his books, *Tales of Remarkable Men*. My grandfather and Gurdjieff's father were rather alike in looks, and although my grandfather was English of the English he looked, in old age, somewhat like a Russian priest. He was 'uneducated', a farmer who worked with his men. Save for a few old books such as the *Pilgrim's Progress* and the Bible, he read little, though he had a great store of wisdom that came from a long line of yeoman farmers. He was no business man, and never became rich like his brother, also a farmer; and he never took advantage of the weaknesses of others. He remembered a great many sayings that he had picked up here and there. When I heard them as a youth they made little conscious impression on me but the subconscious effect must have been considerable, for little by little I began to recall them, since they were appropriate to my present way of life. I suspect that he got some from George Herbert. Among them were the following:

By doing, we learn.

He who pities another remembers himself.

God, our parents, and our Teacher can never be repaid.

God keep me from four houses—a money-lender's, a gambler's, a hospital, a prison.

Lawyers' houses are built on the heads of fools.

The doctor owes his living to the patient—the patient owes him only money.

You can take out of the sack only what is there.

He thinks not well who thinks not twice.

One half of the world does not know how the other half *lies*.

None knows the weight of another's burden.

What one day gives another takes away.

He that is warm thinks everyone else is so.

Three helping one another bear the burden of six.

Love your neighbour, but do not pull down your hedge.

None is a fool all the time, but everyone is a fool sometimes.

The higher climbs the ape, the more he shows his bum.

Advise none to marry or to go to war.

One hand washes the other—and both the face.

Before marriage keep your eyes wide open; after keep them half shut.

There would be no great ones if there were no small ones.

When the fox begins to preach keep your eye on the geese.

Wednesday is here, and the week half gone.

To have a great deal of money is fear—to have none brings grief.

A well-fed man does not know what the hungry man is thinking.

Before you own a man as a friend, eat a bushel of salt with him.

Show a good man his fault and he will turn it into a virtue; a bad man, and he will double it.

Nothing dries sooner than a tear.

All my life my grandparents, by the mere fact of their being, have had a great influence on me; and studying Gurdjieff's ideas and working according to his method has made me realize what an important influence it has been.

The movements and the dances were extremely interesting. I did not find them difficult in the way some people did, but, as with everything else that I had acquired in ordinary life, I had to begin over again and forget what I had learned. It took me a long time to learn to sense and feel each movement, gesture, posture. Such a simple thing it seemed, to 'sense', but, being English, brought up on physical drill and army training, I had to be reminded over and over again to 'sense' my body.

The first 'obligatory' I began to do as if it were a series of physical jerks. At last Gurdjieff rebuked me severely in front of everyone, which so mortified me that I left the platform and sat down. In a few minutes he came to me and quietly explained something. I returned to my place in the class, and from that time began to understand something of the inner meaning of the dances, and I spent every spare moment of each day practising.

Eventually I was allowed to take part in the 'Initiation of the Priestess' and felt that I was taking part in a religious ceremony—as indeed I was. Our teachers were Mme de Salzmann, Mme Galumian, and Mme Olgivana H.—French, Armenian, and Montenegrin respectively. I began to learn fast, and soon was doing all the obligatories and taking part in the big dances. The music was played by Hartmann on an ancient upright piano, which under his touch produced magic music. When Gurdjieff wanted a new piece he would pick it out on the piano with one finger, supplementing the notes by whistling. Then Hartmann would begin the melody and by degrees fill in the harmony, Gurdjieff standing over him until it was as he wished. He would give Hartmann no respite until he got it as it should be. Only a first-rate musician like Hartmann could have produced such music, and he, on at least one occasion, found the situation so impossible when Gurdjieff was going for him that he got up from the piano and left the Study House.

The movement of the Thirty Gestures was composed at this time. Gurdjieff called the three teachers to him, showed them the movements a few times with explanations, gave Hartmann the melody, and went and sat down. They began to work at once on the gestures; and in a short time, less than an hour, were teaching them to us. But we young pupils had to spend many hours working on them before we were able to do them passably well.

Like all great art, the dances and movements were more modern than the moderns, yet rooted in the past.

It came to me one day with a shock of surprise that for the first time in my life, here at the Prieuré, I had no wish to be elsewhere. The vague unrest that had disturbed my life no longer existed. Here I could find all that I had longed for. Not that I did not suffer at times, but with a different kind of suffering. If most of it was not voluntary suffering, at least it had ceased to be completely automatic; though there were times when I felt as if the whole world's weight of suffering lay on my spirits. Gurdjieff, seeing me in this state one day, told me to come to the café in Fontainebleau for coffee. Casually glancing at me he said to Orage, who was there, 'Orage, when things seem to be at their worst they usually get a little better.' It was as if some of his power was directed to me, and with this my spirits began to rise. Apart from 'Thank you' for the coffee, I did not speak a word until I was back at the Prieuré. But the bad mood, the depression, which would sometimes last for days, had disappeared.

Hartmann told me that when they were in the Caucasus he was taken ill with typhus, and the attack became so severe that he was not expected to recover. 'But, you know,' he said, 'one day I became conscious, and I saw Gurdjieff bending over me with the sweat pouring down his face. All his force seemed to be directed at me. He gave me a piece of bread and went away. I sat up and began to eat it, and I realized that he had saved my life.'

Another time, at the same café at Fontainebleau, the Henri Deux, he was talking with Hartmann, Stjoernval, and Salzmann in Russian, while Orage and I conversed in English. Then he began to speak to Orage about turkeys, and looking at me, said with a smile, 'He not peacock or crow, but turkey.' Seeing that I did not understand, he nodded to Orage, who said, 'The characteristic of a turkey is that it is always puffing itself up, showing off, not only to others, but even to itself when it is alone.'

I must have had an expression of dejection on my face, for Hartmann said, 'I should tell you that although Mr Gurdjieff says many things about turkeys he is very fond of the bird.' Only very much later did I have a realization of this characteristic in myself, and become able to observe it impartially and even with amusement. And surveying my life I saw how, even as a small boy, this turkeyness had constantly manifested itself, trying to appear to myself and others to be 'someone', and not a mere nonentity. Now I was able to face the turkey, and it ceased to gobble.

At dinner one day, Gurdjieff again spoke about paying, about the different ways of paying, about paying the debt incurred by one's arising—the debt to nature. He said, 'You pay me to be allowed to work here. But by working here you will know and feel how nine-tenths of the world lives. By working physically in the right way you can gain very much in understanding. If you help your neighbour, you, in turn, will be helped; perhaps tomorrow, perhaps in a year, perhaps in a hundred years. But you *will* be helped. Nature must pay the debt; it is a law. If we like what we do when working we are at once rewarded by the satisfaction received. If we do not like it, and make effort, the reward must come, but later. It is a mathematical law, and all life is mathematical. The present is a result of the past, and the future will be the result of the present. Everything with life has to struggle; in looking back over the past we usually remember the difficult times, times of struggle; but struggle is life.'

Someone asked why we are born, and why we die.

He said, 'You wish to know? Really to know you must suffer. You must learn to suffer not as you do now, but consciously. At present you cannot suffer one franc, and to understand a little you must suffer a million francs.'

To another, who asked about negative emotions, he replied, 'Every bad thought and feeling reacts on you, on others, and on me, and bad thoughts and feelings keep out life.'

Among the aphorisms in the Study House were these: 'Here there are neither English nor Russian, Jews nor Christians, but only those with a common aim—to be able to do.'

'The energy produced by conscious work is immediately converted for fresh use; that used mechanically is lost for ever.'

'Here, we can only create and direct conditions, but not help.'

'The more difficult the conditions of life, the greater are the possibilities for productive work—if you work consciously.'

Gurdjieff seldom used the words 'system', 'method', 'self-remembering', 'self-observation'. Terms of any kind become petrified; by constant use by the formatory apparatus they become expressions without content. Life in the Prieuré was in itself a process of constantly reminding us to remember ourselves, to observe ourselves, to notice what we did, how we moved, spoke, felt, thought. Conditions were such that opportunities were given us to melt down our old personalities so that essence could grow and our own individuality take the place of a personality that was not our own. One aphorism was: 'You are here having realized the necessity of contending with yourself; then thank everyone who provides an opportunity.'

There were no 'arranged' lectures or talks. Gurdjieff might talk anywhere, at any time. One had to be continually on the watch when he was about so as not to miss something, and we learnt to 'sense' when he would be likely to sit down and talk. The same with the music. At any moment he would call Hartmann to play, morning or afternoon, in the Study House or the salon. Word would go round, and we would leave our work in the forest and go up and sit and listen, and one did not wallow in emotional daydreams as one is apt to when hearing music in general.

Once while we were resting in the forest, the blue smoke curling from the fire, only the far-off sounds from distant Avon breaking the stillness, Gurdjieff said: 'Why everyone so quiet? No one have question?'

After a pause one said, 'I find it difficult to distinguish between essence and personality.'

'Each of us,' replied Gurdjieff, 'is composed of two men—essence and personality. Essence is everything that we are born with: heredity, type, character, nature; essence is the real part of us. Essence does not change. I, for example, have a swarthy skin which belongs to my type; it is part of my essence. Personality is an accidental thing, which we begin to acquire as soon as we are born; it is determined by our surroundings, outside influences, education and so on; it is like a dress you wear, a mask; an accidental thing changing with changing circumstances. It is the false part of man; and can be changed artificially or accidentally—in a few minutes by hypnosis or a drug. A man with a "strong personality" may have the essence of a child, overlaid by personality.

'When we speak of inner development and inner change, we speak of the growth of essence. The question now is not to acquire anything new but to recover and reconstruct what has been lost. This is the purpose of development. When you have learnt to distinguish personality from essence and to separate them you will understand what has to be changed. At present you have only one aim—to study. You are weak and dependent, you are slaves and helpless in the face of everything around you. Time and work are necessary to break the habits of years, and later it will be possible to replace certain habits with others. Man is dependent on externals, but externals are harmless in themselves and you will learn to replace influences that hinder your development with those that can help.'

A question was asked about observing oneself.

Gurdjieff: 'At first conditions for work must be prepared. At present you can only try to notice what you do, and gather material that will be useful for work. You cannot yet observe when your manifestations come from essence, and when they come from personality. You cannot tell while you are gathering material because man has only one attention, directed on what he is doing. His mind does not see his feelings or his feelings his mind.'

He also spoke about being able, later on, to divide our attention into two or even three parts. But when someone asked how this could be done, he said, 'You cannot do this yet. Later we will speak about it. People in general have no real attention. What they think is attention is only self-tensing. First you must strive to acquire attention. Correct self-observation is possible only after you have acquired a measure of attention. Begin with small things.'

One of us asked: 'What sort of small things do you mean? What can I do?'

Gurdjieff: 'There are two kinds of doing—mechanical, automatic doing, and doing according to your real wish. Take some small thing which you are not able to do, but which you wish to do. Make this your God. Let nothing interfere. Only strive to fulfil your wish. If you succeed in this small thing, I shall give you a bigger task. At present many of you have an abnormal appetite for doing things which are too big for you. This appetite keeps you from doing the small things which you could do. Destroy this appetite. Forget these big things. Make your aim the breaking of some small habit.

'If you *wish*, you *can*. Without *wishing* you never *can*. Wish is the most powerful thing in the world. Higher than God. Of course I speak of conscious wish; and with conscious wish, everything comes.'

One of us asked: 'Would it be a good task to bear the manifestations of others?'

'To bear the displeasing manifestations of others is a big thing,' he replied. 'It is the last thing for a man. Only a man who has perfected himself can do this. Make it your aim to acquire the ability to bear one manifestation of one person that you now cannot endure without nervousness. Setting yourself a voluntary aim and compelling yourself to achieve it creates magnetism and ability to *do*.'

Another said: 'I think my worst fault is talking too much. Would it be a good thing to try not to talk too much?'

Gurdjieff: 'For you this is a very good aim. You spoil everything with your talking. It even hinders your business. When you talk so much your words have no weight. Try to make an exercise not to talk so much. If you succeed many blessings will come to you. It is a big thing, not small. If you succeed I will tell you what to do next.'

To another he said: 'For you a good task would be to try to ask questions. You wish to know, but you don't speak. For you this effort would be very good.'

In answer to another question about observing oneself, he said:

66

'Many things are necessary for observing. The first is sincerity with oneself. This is very difficult. It is much easier to be sincere with a friend. We find it difficult to look at ourselves, for we are afraid that we may see something bad, and if by accident we do look deep down, we see our own nothingness. We try not to see ourselves because we fear we shall suffer remorse of conscience. There are many dirty dogs in us, and we do not want to see them. Sincerity may be the key to the door through which one part may see another part. Sincerity is difficult because of the thick crust that has grown over essence. Each year a man puts on a new dress, a new mask, one over the other. All this has gradually to be removed. It is like peeling off the skins of an onion. Until these masks are removed we cannot see ourselves.

'A useful exercise is to try to put oneself in another's place. For example, I know that A. is in a trying situation. He is dejected and morose. Half of him is trying to listen to me, the other half is occupied with his problem. I say something to him that at another time would make him laugh, but now it makes him angry. But knowing him I shall try to put myself in his place and ask myself how I would respond.

'If I do this often enough I shall begin to see that if someone is bad-tempered there may be a reason for it which has nothing to do with me personally. We must try to remember that often it is not the person himself but his state that behaves irritably towards us. As I change, so does another.

'If you can do this and remember yourself and observe yourself you will see many things, not only in the other person, but in yourself, things you never even thought of.'

'Only he can be just who can enter into the position of another.
'Judge others by yourself and you will rarely be mistaken.'

Speaking of art, he said, 'Love not art with your feelings. Real art is based on mathematics. It is a kind of script with an inner and outer meaning. In early times, conscious men—who understood the principles of mathematics—composed music, designed statues and images, painted pictures and constructed buildings—all of which were such that they had a definite effect on the people who came in contact with them: on their feelings and senses.

'There is a room in a monastery in Persia, for example, the proportions and volumes of which are such that everyone who goes into the room begins to weep.'

I recalled what I had heard about the early Gothic cathedrals which were designed by men who understood the principles of mathematics, and how these principles could be applied. The proportions, the volume of the interior, the air pressure, acoustics; the effect of light filtering through the stained glass, the music—the effects of these on people were mathematically calculated so that, unconsciously, people were raised to a higher plane. In such a state some could receive high ideas. And no one knows who the men were who designed the first cathedrals.

Of all the works of art I saw in the East, the Taj Mahal and the Sphinx made the greatest impression on me. The one is no more than three hundred and fifty years old, the other five thousand or more, and even so, according to Gurdjieff, it is a copy of one in Babylon eight thousand years ago. Both are in the esoteric tradition, that hidden, everlasting current that vivifies the life of man and saves him from falling into a permanent state of savage barbarism.

Objective works of art are products of esoteric schools. The cathedrals of Notre Dame de Paris and Notre Dame de Chartres are products of a Christian esoteric school, the Taj Mahal of a Sufi esoteric school. Sir Arthur Bryant relates that dukes and counts and even kings, as well as tradespeople and peasants, considered it a privilege to be allowed to help in the building of the early cathedrals, hauling the stone and mixing the mortar. In England too—Ely, St Albans, York Cathedrals are also, perhaps, objective works of art. It can be said that all great works of art proceed from esoteric schools. In China, too, there are examples. The Temple of Heaven has three circular tiers or platforms; that nearest the ground is the largest, the middle one is smaller; the top one is the smallest, and on this the Emperor worshipped alone.

There is a great temple in Northern China which I visited one sunny day in winter. The way to it was flanked by a single long coloured-tiled wall. From the road, where the wall began, the temple in the distance looked remote and minute, with an outline of roofs and arches; some of yellow tiles, some green, some blue, some purple. As I approached, the various roofs of differently coloured tiles changed places, formed designs, melted into one another. The effect of the perspective, the changing shapes, made an extraordinary impression on me—it was as if they, not I, were moving; they conveyed an impression of light and colour, of emotional and mental freedom, a harmonious wholeness, a sense of perfection that something in me longed for.

At the Prieuré, the impressions of these temples—Chinese, Moslem, Christian—constantly came to my mind; they were one with the old fairy tales and myths, and with some of Gurdjieff's music and dances; they had spoken to me in the same language, and what they said was heard with the feelings. Men in the past built for the glory of God, as well as for living and business. The wonderful cloth-hall of Ypres, destroyed in the first World War, was an example. In the nineteenth century they began to build only for business, for money, and from pride and vanity, and a blight fell on architecture. Architecture, like everything else, has its place on a scale; it involves as well as evolves, until it reaches the negative absolute, bottom 'doh', in the commercial building of recent times.

Gurdjieff never let slip an occasion for reproving a pupil—sometimes angrily, sometimes gently. We were working in the Study House. He was sitting in his special seat, observing us. For a moment or so I forgot myself and did something rather silly. At once he shouted at me, 'Idiot, Doorak, why you do that? You wish to spoil my work?' I was so mortified and hurt that I was on the point of walking out. But he began to tell me how necessary it was to keep a pinch of red pepper handy, that it was his job to stick the fork in 'you know where'. In other words, I must be constantly on the watch to remember myself.

One day, while working in a part of the forest that had been partly cleared, I tripped and fell on a pointed stick which ran into my leg. The stick broke, and I had to pull it out. I called to the men to get a barrow. They lifted me into it and wheeled me up to the house. The wound looked serious, and Gurdjieff at once sent Dr Stjoernval to my room and told one of the young Russian women to look after me. Everything possible was done for me. I ran a high temperature, and for a day or so was very feverish. The Russian woman slept in my room and nursed me, and in a week I was out and about again, although a long time passed before the wound was finally healed. I was touched by the kindness everyone showed me. Although Gurdjieff might humiliate you before others, wound your vanity and self-pride, provoke your jealousy and envy; although pupils might seem to slight you or treat you with indifference—if you fell ill everything possible was done for your comfort and welfare.

In general, there were no fixed rules in the Prieuré; but there were many which were changed every few days or every few weeks. But there was one, fundamental, great, unspoken rule, of which everyone was aware. 'A pupil must not do that which would harm the work.'

As to the changing rules, one was that for a period of a week every letter written in the Prieuré must be censored; another, that no one should go outside the walls except on Gurdjieff's business; another, that no one must go to Fontainebleau without permission, and so on. Often they were exercises—not to be taken literally; but if you were caught breaking the rule, so much the worse for you.

Three of us had been in the habit of climbing the wall and going down to the Seine for a bathe—a very agreeable relaxation after hard toil during the scorching summer days. We evaded the rule by eluding the 'guards', and seldom missed our bathe. It was a kind of game. Gurdjieff frequently spoke of the need to exercise one's ingenuity, to be able to be 'cunning', not in the modern, but in the Biblical meaning. He frequently spoke of someone in a tone of contempt as being 'naïve'. Of course we were considerate externally so far as the organization and the running of the place were concerned, and in our attitude to Gurdjieff and the older pupils.

No one was allowed in the Prieuré grounds without Gurdjieff's personal permission. But it so happened that two friends of S., one of those very near to Gurdjieff, rang the bell of the conciergerie one day and asked to see S. Gurdjieff was away for the day. P., the boy on duty, told S., who went to the gate and asked his friends in, gave them coffee, and walked round the grounds with them. They left within an hour. The same evening in the salon after dinner, Gurdjieff called the boy and said to him, 'Did I tell you not to admit anyone without my permission?'

'Yes, Mr Gurdjieff.'

'Did you let some people in today?'

'Yes, Mr Gurdjieff.'

'Why?'

P. stood silent, and G. began to berate him; but, in the middle of the tirade, Z. got up, and said, almost shouting, 'Georgeivanitch, why do you go for P.? You know it wasn't his fault. S. told him to let the people in, and P. didn't know what to do. He is to blame, not P.'

Gurdjieff said a few more words to P., and then sat down next to S. and began to talk of something else. All this time S. said nothing. The rest of us sat round drinking coffee, intensely interested, trying as usual to understand what it was all about, for Gurdjieff never made a scene like this without a purpose.

One day, in the Henri Deux, he was talking about how men had degenerated; and that, from nature's point of view, certain animals were far better than man. 'Even rats,' he said, turning to me, 'are better than man.' I began to wonder why he should so pointedly mention rats. Then I remembered that a few days before I had been in the stables when a rat had run along a beam, and when I saw it I had jumped and begun to tremble. This was reported to him. Before the war I had no fear of rats, but experiences in the trenches with rats had associated them with all the filth, the cruelty, the fear, misery, and suffering of front-line trench warfare. I had been into a temple in the East full of poisonous snakes, without the least fear, but I could not see a rat without shuddering and feeling sick. I know that it is so and why, but even now, only by firmly remembering myself can I overcome this shuddering revulsion. But Ganesha, the elephant-headed god of knowledge and learning, has as his symbol a rat, one of the most sagacious and cunning of creatures.

Speaking again of personality and essence, Gurdjieff said that only a conscious man can distinguish between them. 'All the ordinary roles we play are personality; but if, by accident, we find ourselves in unusual conditions, we may behave according to essence. Some grown-up men, for example, when they have had a good deal to drink, or are under the influence of some young woman, will behave like little boys—which essentially they are. On the other hand, in times of danger they may behave either intelligently and rationally or like frightened children. Under the shock of grief, the stern business man or the statesman may become human and tender. Our task is to die to this personality, which is a false thing, not our own; it may be necessary to melt it down in the fires of great suffering, but when this is done correctly, in its place will grow *individuality;* a man will become an individual, possessing real will and an "I". He will be himself.'

He said that a good deal of our lying, greed, envy, jealousy, and hate is often caused by an accumulation of corresponding energies. Unused energy causes frustration, which is deflected into the expression of negative emotion. Man has real individuality inherent in him; it is his own, his birthright, which he has sold for the mess of pottage of false personality.

Identification occurs when our energy and attention is fixed on one aspect of a thing; it is one-centred work, a form of hypnosis, and must be distinguished from concentration and attention, which are useful and necessary.

71

In the Institute our weaknesses were observed and noted, and we were given opportunities of seeing them; and we had to see them for ourselves. Attention was necessary so as not to miss anything that was said or done. Apparently casual remarks or actions might reveal a great deal to a person. The teaching was given in fragments and often in unexpected ways, and we had to learn to put the pieces together and connect the fragments up with our own observations and experiences.

Gurdjieff spoke of the need to think differently about certain expressions in common use: sin, prayer, fasting, confession, repentance, supplication, submission, atonement, death, resurrection, life. Under the ordinarily accepted definition of these terms there lies another meaning, a real meaning, which is connected with a state of change in man's psychology. Fasting, for example, the abstention from ordinary food, can be very useful if it is carried out under the guidance of a teacher. In orthodox religion it has become just a custom, but properly carried out it can purify the system and change the metabolism of the body. And there is another kind of fasting, which is not connected merely with our food; the abstention from useless unwilled manifestations, the constant giving way to negative emotion.

In answer to a question about so-called supernatural faculties, such as second-sight and telepathy, he said that these arose from the moving-instinctive centre through muscular contraction or through molecular fluctuation of the emotional centre. A movement in one centre is at once communicated in waves to the other centres, and to all parts of the organism.

In early times, before they became spoilt, people could communicate with each other and even see what was going on a great distance away. Now this faculty is preserved only by those who are called 'uncivilized' people, among some of the Lapps, for example, or Red Indian tribes, or even Australian aborigines. Or it happens to some people by accident, and then it is regarded as something 'queer'.

I was very much interested in this, as I had had experiences of the kind. During the war, I and another officer were told to take our companies to work on Salisbury Plain. We were driven in trucks for ten miles, then had to march four miles across the deserted, treeless plain to our work. Expecting to return in daylight, we took no bearings; but it was getting dark before we finished. I left first with my men, and in fifteen minutes it was a pitch-dark, frosty, cloudy February night; and I realized that I did not know the way. But at that moment, a lost sense came into play: I knew that I knew, and went straight on. One of my subalterns began to speak of our losing ourselves on the plain, and I told him to keep quiet. For over an hour we walked, without a word, over the rolling plain, so dark that we could not see ten yards ahead. I tried not to think, but to be quiet inside and to let my innate sense of direction, or 'instinct', take charge. At last I sensed that we were getting near to the trucks, and in five minutes we suddenly came upon them; in half an hour we were eating hot food in camp. The other party was discovered next morning just after daybreak, wandering over the plain—cold, tired, hungry, and lost.

Some months later, that same year, we were on the Somme. I was told to take a party at night to investigate a wood about half a mile beyond our front line. Having placed my men inside the wood, I went forward with the sergeant to look, or rather 'feel', round. Suddenly I stopped. I could not go on. Something said 'danger'. The sergeant apparently felt nothing, for he was going on unconcernedly, when I stopped him. I tried one or two other points, but each time that I tried to go on, the feeling against it was so strong that it was as if I were up against a kind of steel net. After a time I withdrew the men and went back to the front line, reporting that I considered the wood to be occupied by the enemy. The next night, men from another company went out to the same place, and walked straight on into an ambush. Several were killed, including the officer in charge; the rest came running back. More than once I saved my own life and the lives of my men by listening to the inner voice of the 'sixth' sense. In the New Zealand and Australian bush I frequently got out of difficult situations by letting the unknown sense have its way, and more than once by letting the horse I was riding have its way.

I have had many experiences of sensing things at a distance, and of foreknowledge of things which actually did happen; so have people of my acquaintance. Unfortunately, spoiled as we are by education and upbringing, these experiences of the sixth sense commonly come in a very general way and we are usually unable to profit by them. It is often difficult, moreover, to distinguish between what is set going by the imagination and what is really sensed and felt. In any case, the real experiences have little or nothing to do with the mind; they come from the moving-instinctive and feeling centres.

When Gurdjieff said, 'We do not aim to construct something new, but to recover what is lost', it applies, from one aspect, to the vanishing sixth sense. So far as I have been able to discover in the investigation of all kinds of phenomena, none of the so-called 'modern techniques' are of any use. The only really useful method is that ancient one given out in a modern form by Gurdjieff, though that is only one of the many aspects of his teaching.

Before I met him I regarded these experiences as accidents. A great many 'simple' people possess this extra sense—fishermen and farmers for instance. Officials, 'intellectuals', and 'experts' are almost devoid of it, which is probably why they are almost always wrong. Human beings, besides being machines for transforming substances, are also instruments for receiving and transmitting vibrations. It is also possible for them to make use of the apparatus for their own benefit.

This summer of 1924, my first at the Institute, was one of those very hot blazing summers that sometimes visit northern France; and all meals, except for the special ones in the English dining room, were taken out of doors. Plates of food were handed to us from the kitchen window which looked on to the gravel court; I had taken my plate, and on my way back to the end table, I passed Gurdjieff, who was sitting with some others. As I came nearer, he gave me a quick glance, and a cigarette fell from the box he had taken from his pocket. I hesitated; one part of me, or one 'I', said 'Pick it up', another said, 'No, don't'. While 'Yes' and 'No', which lasted a few seconds, went on in me, someone else picked it up. I went to my table and sat down, and after thinking about it, told my neighbour.

'He was testing you,' he said. 'Five different types would have reacted in five different ways.'

'Not in the army,' I said.

'No. But I am speaking of non-machines. In the army, if five machines, or five hundred, are connected to the same switch, they all act as one. Here we are beginning the process of being metamorphosed from machines into men. Gurdjieff experiments with people according to their types. Some people who hear about this object; they regard it as humiliating to be used like dogs and monkeys for experiments. But if you take it in the right way you will have opportunities for learning a very great deal about yourself. It is a privilege.'

Each day one was able to have a new experience—but only in the degree that one worked and made effort to overcome the laziness and inertia of the body, and the likes and dislikes of the feelings. The aphorisms took on a real meaning:

He who has rid himself of the disease of tomorrow has a chance of achieving what he is here for.

Man's greatest achievement is to be able to *do*.

I love him who loves work.

Help only him who strives not to be an idler.

One of the strongest motives for work on yourself is the realization that you may die at any moment.

When Gurdjieff spoke about the uselessness of most of our suffering, which comes from our own corns or treading on other people's or others treading on ours, one was reminded of the aphorism: 'One of the chief aids to felicity is to be able to consider exteriorly always; interiorly, never.' And, 'Consider only what others think of you, not what they say.'

Gurdjieff was always giving people shocks in order to make them use their critical faculty. To one young pupil he said, 'Never believe anything you hear me say. Learn to discriminate between what must be taken literally and what metaphorically.'

Some of us were having supper with him in his apartment on the Boulevard Pereire. A young man, an American, asked him why he always shut the windows at mealtimes. Gurdjieff went into a long explanation of how necessary it was to keep vibrations from being lost through open windows, and so on and so forth, while the young man listened wide-eyed. He left before the rest of us. When he had gone, Gurdjieff said, 'You see, he takes everything literally, without pondering. He will go back to Prieuré and shut all the windows all the time, and I shan't be able to get a breath of fresh air.' The windows were closed, of course, to keep out the noise of the street.

To another pupil he said, 'You never believe anything I tell you. You always doubt. Even when you know you must believe you begin to doubt.'

There was an aphorism: 'If you have not a critical mind by nature your staying here is useless.'

Some pupils saw, or affected to see, something 'mystical' or 'esoteric' in Gurdjieff's lightest word or gesture. Since he was so far above us in knowledge and understanding and 'being', this was not surprising. One had all the time to be on the alert; and when one was in a state of self-remembering one seldom made a mistake. It was comparatively easy to remember oneself when Gurdjieff was there, for his state of consciousness kept one awake; all the time we had to learn to discriminate between what ought to be taken seriously and what jokingly, and he often made exaggerated statements in order to shock us.

Some of us younger pupils tried to formulate for ourselves vanity and self-pride.

When we said, 'My pride was hurt', or 'She or he is as vain as a peacock', what did we understand by it? The consensus was that, in its bad aspect, self-pride, or self-esteem or self-love, was an over-weening opinion one had about the qualities or attainments that one had been born with or had acquired; an ignorant presumption that the qualities of the organism are due to merit, and that consideration should be given to us by others on this account. When someone failed to give us our due, something in our feelings was hurt and we suffered accordingly. From a certain aspect, Self-Pride or Mr Self-Love was the active part; Madame Vanity belonged to the passive feminine part in us. But vanity was even more difficult to define. Orage said, 'It is that something for which we will sacrifice almost anything rather than that it should suffer.' Perhaps it is not possible to define vanity except by examples; we can see its manifestations in others, but to see them in ourselves—at the time, and not afterwards—is almost impossible. In times of mass psychosis these two enemies, vanity and self-love, are intensified. On one occasion in the war the commanding officer of my battalion sacrificed, from vanity, the lives of twenty men rather than admit that he was wrong. In another sense vanity is the expenditure of time, energy, and money on what is essentially worthless and use-less; the expectation of lasting benefit from the things of this world. 'Vanity, vanity, all is vanity, saith the Preacher.' Joseph Conrad said: 'Vanity plays lurid tricks with our memory.' Rochefoucauld: 'Vanity causes us to do more things against our inclination than does reason.' Tolstoy: 'Life without vanity is almost impossible.' Shakespeare: 'Vanity keeps persons in favour of themselves who are out of favour with all others.' 'Vanity,' Somerset Maugham has written, 'is the most devastating, the most universal and the most ineradicable of the passions that afflict the soul of man, and it is only vanity that makes him deny its power. It is more consuming than love. With advancing years, mercifully, you can snap your fingers at the terror or the servi-tude of love, but age cannot free you from the thraldom of vanity. Time can assuage the pangs of love, but only death can still the anguish of wounded vanity. Love is simple and seeks no subterfuge, but vanity cozens you with a hundred disguises. It is part and parcel of

76

every virtue; it is the mainspring of courage and the strength of ambition; it gives constancy to the lover and endurance to the stoic; it adds fuel to the fire of the artist's desire for fame, and it is at once the support and the compensation of the honest man's integrity; it even leers cynically in the humility of the saint. You cannot escape it, and should you take pains to guard against it, it will make use of those very pains to trip you up. You are defenceless against its onslaught because you know not on what unprotected side it will attack you. Cynicism cannot protect you from its snares nor humour from its mockery. It is vanity finally that makes man support his abominable lot.'

In the *Conference of the Birds*, Attar relates, 'Then came the sparrow of feeble body and tender heart, trembling like a flame. She said, "I am frail as a hair. I have no one to help me, and I have not the strength of an ant. I have neither down nor feathers—nothing. How can a weakling like me make her way to the Simurgh? A sparrow could never do it. So, since I am not at all fitted for this enterprise, I shall be content to seek my Joseph here."

'The hoopoe replied: "O you who are sometimes sad, sometimes gay, I am not deceived by these artful pleas. You are a little hypocrite. Even in your humility you show a hundred signs of vanity and pride." '

We talk all the time of vanity and self-pride, but until we can see examples in ourselves they remain only words and expressions. We do not want to see them, for we should suffer. We cannot see them, for our buffers prevent us. Yet, if we wish to grow from essence, we must see them, but gradually.

Gurdjieff once asked me: 'Do you know who has the most vanity?' I said, 'Actors, film stars, high officials?' He said, 'No, angels and devils.'

On several occasions Gurdjieff spoke about symbols and their use, among them the Enneagram, which contains among other things the working of the Law of Three, the Law of Seven, and the Law of Ninefoldness, the keys to which may be found in *Beelzebub's Tales*. A great deal of material was put together in the form of 'A Lecture on Symbolism'. Briefly the idea is that every man has in him a desire for knowledge, differing only in intensity, but the mind of the seeking man often comes up against a blank wall when he asks 'Why?'—though usually the question is 'How?' not 'Why?' Man does not realize that under the surface of things is hidden the oneness of all that exists. Man has always sought this oneness in religions and philosophies, and has tried to define it in words—which become dead and empty. Words and ideas change according to time and place, but unity, oneness, is eternal and unchanging. Certain men of real understanding, realizing the inadequacy of words, have, through the ages, constructed symbols for the passing down of real knowledge. One who studies a symbol and arrives at an understanding of it, realizes that he has the symbol in himself. 'Everything in the world is one and is governed by uniform laws.' As in the Emerald Table of Hermes Trismegistus: 'As above, so below.' The laws of the cosmos may be found in the atom; but the nearest object for man to study is himself. In this respect the formula used by Socrates (though originating in Egypt), 'Know thyself', is full of meaning. By studying the laws of the universe man may see the working of the law in himself, and when he seriously struggles with his denying part, his negative part, he will be engaging in the struggle that goes on in the whole of the universe—'the divine warfare'—and he will be constructing in himself the great symbol which issues from remote times and which we know as Solomon's Seal. Solomon's seal is every man who looks into himself'.

From *The History of Magic.* Abbé Constant.

78

Gurdjieff in his teaching always tried to make us understand that we must use it in our life-work. The struggle between 'Yes' and 'No' goes on endlessly. We are full of idle wishes—'it wishes'—and to these we must oppose our 'I' wish. If this is done in the right way, a good result follows.

He gave as an example the following: 'Suppose I very much need some information, or something, from someone. But this someone has offended me. "It" does not wish humbly to ask, and I shall have to struggle with my self-love and self-pride, which would suffer in the case of refusal. If I persist in my struggle against the denying part and overcome the inertia set up, and go to the person, something in me will be strengthened and my understanding will have deepened. On the other hand, if I do not go, though I shall have saved nervous energy and possible unpleasantness, my understanding will not have increased.'

Later he spoke about initiation. 'Initiation is usually regarded as an act by which a man who knows transfers to another man knowledge and power, which become the latter's inalienable possession with no effort on his part. This, of course, can never be. There is only self-initiation, which is acquired by constant effort. It is impossible to give to a man anything that could become his own without effort on his part. One can only show and direct, but not initiate. One can only give to a man just as much as he is ready to receive.'

As I have said, Gurdjieff always followed up a talk on theory with practical work; and I, with others, found myself being manoeuvred into situations in which I became conscious of 'Yes, here is something I ought to do'; 'No' from the body, a resistance accompanied by all kinds of reasonable excuses to myself for not going on with the struggle. When the effort was made, the neutralizing force came into play, and a feeling of growing strength was experienced. Sometimes the effort was not made, with a consequent feeling of weakness in the solar plexus.

While taking part in a certain dance based on what is called the 'Enneagram' something began to work in me, in my feelings; it was occasioned partly by the music, partly by the postures and the movements. The music was a simple recurring melody and harmony, but arranged in such a way, and so beautifully, that it pierced the depths of one's being. It was as if I were understanding something, becoming conscious, partaking in a ritual. I sensed something of the meaning of the enneagram of the law of eternal recurrence, eternal repetition, and of the possibilities of a way out; and in time the enneagram became for me a living moving symbol that gave me a feeling of joy whenever I looked at it; I could learn something every time I pondered it. The chronogram of Mary Stuart read: 'In my end is my beginning'.

★   ★   ★

It was a hot morning in July; the forest, at least the part where I was working, might have been in the tropics. By mid-morning I was very thirsty and left my work to go up to the house to get some tea. On the way, by the great lawn, I came upon three of the Russians who were talking with anxious expressions on their faces. With my small knowledge of Russian I could not catch much, but the name 'Georgeivanitch, Georgeivanitch' was constantly repeated. I stopped, and they told me that Gurdjieff had had a bad accident; the ambulance was bringing him to the Prieuré and might arrive at any moment. We walked up to the house and into the courtyard, and reached the gate just as the ambulance arrived. Gurdjieff was brought out on a stretcher, his head covered with bandages; he was unconscious, but he murmured, 'Many people, many people.' He was carried upstairs to his room.

A hush descended on us; everyone went about his work quietly and seriously. A few were weeping, though there was a complete absence of conventional expressions of sorrow. Gurdjieff's condition was very serious; the doctors were not very hopeful for his recovery; the wonder was that he had not been killed instantly.

Later in the day I went up to the garage in Fontainebleau to get something from his car, a small Citroen, which had been towed there. The radiator was crushed, the engine was off its seating, the steering column was broken, screen and doors and windows smashed, the front axle and wings crumpled. Gurdjieff had been found lying on the grass verge on the road that runs from Paris to Fontainebleau, his head on a cushion of the car. How he had got out of the car, whether he got himself out or was carried, was not clear. The car had run into a tree.

It seems that the day before he left Paris on his weekly return trip to the Prieuré he had done something unusual. He had told Mme de Hartmann to go to the garage and tell the mechanic to examine the car carefully—bolts, nuts, steering and lights especially; she had never known him so insistent. Also, giving no reason, he had made over his papers to her and given her power to act in his name. Another unusual thing, he told her to go back to Fontainebleau by train; and he dismissed her look of surprise with a gesture.

What happened, no one knows, since Gurdjieff himself remembered only 'a charge and a crash' until he woke some days later in his room —'a piece of live meat in a clean bed', as he said. He may have been dazzled by the lights of an oncoming car, or he may, for a moment, have nodded.

That such an accident could happen to Gurdjieff was a shock to us; some thought that he should be invulnerable, free from the law of accident. One fanciful lady, a theosophist, spoke mysteriously of 'the dark brethren' who were trying to destroy Gurdjieff's work. But Gurdjieff himself pointed out that if you are on this planet you are subject to the laws of physical accident, whose causes may lie far away in the past. The great teachers knew this. Jesus rebuked the disciples when they attributed to sin the deaths of the men on whom the tower of Siloam fell. We only see, or think we see, the immediate causes of accidents.

There is another aspect. All teachers—Buddha, Hermes Trismegistus, Muhammad, the Christian Gnostics—have taught that something undesirable has become mixed in us, which can only be purged by conscious labour and voluntary suffering. This 'something', the result of the organ Kundabuffer, is the cause of our forgetting, of our sleeping, and so brings about hundreds of unnecessary difficulties. In the *Mahabharata*, Vyasa tells stories of gods, heroes, and devils having to work out on this planet the results of former unconscious (and therefore evil) actions: as the Russian liturgy expresses it, the 'results of voluntary and involuntary sin'.

The whole of life is a series of unexpected happenings, of which simple people, farmers and gardeners for example, are very much aware; and so in our own lives rarely do things turn out as they are expected to do (as sometimes even they logically should) except by accident. At the best things turn out perhaps fifty-fifty.

There was silence in the Prieuré; we spoke with lowered voices; the bell in the belfry no longer rang; there were no dances or music in the Study House, and everyone wished with his whole being for Gurdjieff's recovery. Madame de Hartmann took over the running of the place, and Dr Stjoernval and Gurdjieff's wife did the nursing. Madame Ouspensky came from London and stayed for a few days.

But it was as if the mainspring of a great machine had broken and the machine was running on its momentum. The force that moved our lives was gone.

When Dr Stjoernval told us, about a week later, that Gurdjieff was out of danger, it was as if the prince had entered the castle of the sleeping princess: everything began to come to life. The children again played their noisy games in the grounds; our voices resumed their normal tones; Mme Galumian started classes of movements in the Study House; and Hartmann played music to us in the evenings. Beginning with the obligatories we worked through all the movements and dances, everything that anyone could remember. None of the movements and steps had been noted down, since Gurdjieff carried everything in his head; and when we tried to reproduce the Initiation of the Priestess, a Fragment of a Mystery, we found, to our dismay, that we could not do it. We could remember our own parts, but no one could recall the sequence. The same with the Big Seven. It was these two pieces which had produced such a great impression on me in New York—two fragments of objective art. Fortunately, we had the music composed by Hartmann under Gurdjieff's direction.

Routine work was much more difficult without the stimulus of Gurdjieff's presence; we young pupils had to make much more effort to work with attention when there was no one about 'to stick the pitchfork in you know where'. A pupil confessed to me that unless Gurdjieff was with him he could not work at all—but it must be said that this one was known as 'the Prieuré donkey'.

About a month later Gurdjieff appeared in the garden, supported by his wife and Mme de Hartmann. He was wearing his thick black coat and astrakhan cap. His head was bandaged and his eyes concealed behind dark glasses. His sight was so impaired that he did not recognize us. Against the doctors' instructions and warnings he had made a tremendous effort to get up. At first he would take a few steps, then stop. After fifteen minutes he was taken back to bed. But each day he stayed a little longer and walked a little further. When in October the torrid heat gave place to the bright warm days of autumn, he had his chair brought, and from this directed us to make huge wood fires in the open. Sitting, he would gaze into the flames for an hour or more; the idea was that he drew strength from the blaze. We all helped, and the blazing fires and our activity seemed to help him. This continued until it looked as if we should have to cut down half the forest to keep the fires going. Then one day he stopped us, and began to

5. Preparing for the demonstration at the Theâtre des Champs Elysées, Paris, 1922. Standing left, Dr. Stjoernval, sitting right, Dr. Maurice Nicoll.

6. Fitting costumes.

7. Sewing costumes. Back left, Mme de Hartmann,
Mme de Salzmann. Back right, Mme Galumian,
Mrs. F. Lloyd Wright.

8.   Initiation of a priestess.

watch us working, though without saying a word or seeming to recognize any of us. It was difficult to realize that this was the powerful, active, vital man of a few weeks before who had shocked us into life. Yet one could still sense and feel that undiminished force of his being. Soon he began to direct from his chair, and we began to work as before, striving to sense and remember ourselves, to work with attention, and to realize that if we worked consciously, then we should be helping him as well as ourselves. Everyone who was not on kitchen duty worked outside—Stjoernval, Salzmann, Hartmann— men, women, and children. Gurdjieff seldom spoke, and not since his accident had he smiled. One day we were hauling a fallen tree out of a ditch. Hartmann and I were working up to our knees in water, the other pupils on the bank. Suddenly the tree slipped and fell against my injured leg. I shouted 'Damnation!' Everyone stopped and stared and looked. 'It's all right,' I said, 'no harm done, just uncomfortable.' A slow smile spread over Gurdjieff's face; everyone began to laugh, and a new feeling, almost of joy, emanated from the group. This coincided with a phase of his recovery, and from then he began to talk to us a little.

We began to get into our stride again, and to look forward to the new future when work would be organized in the old way. But one morning word went round that Gurdjieff wanted everyone without exception to assemble in the Study House. He was in his armchair in the centre of the floor. We grouped ourselves round him, sitting on the floor and waited. In a quiet voice he began to speak, sometimes in English, sometimes in Russian. He said that now all work in the Prieuré had come to an end. He was going to liquidate the Prieuré. 'In two days,' he went on, 'everyone must be gone from here, only my own people stay. For a long time I live for others, now I begin to live for myself. Everything now stop—dances, music, work. You all must go in two days.'

As he was speaking our faces grew so long that one would have thought they would touch our chests. After some further talk in Russian he made a gesture with his hand, and we slowly got up and went outside, standing in groups on the lawn and asking each other what it meant.

It was a shock, as it was intended to be. We did no more work that day, but talked among ourselves, trying to discover if anyone understood what it was all about. 'Is this,' we asked, 'the end of all the hopes that have been raised in us? Has everything really come to an end? Is his work really finished?' Everyone was mystified—old pupils as well as young. 'Why is this?' asked some of the Russians of me. 'What is to do? We give up everything, come here, and all is finished. What is to do?' They seemed like characters in a Chekhov play. I knew as much, and as little, as they did.

The next day most of the Russians, some of the Americans, and others, packed up and left, never to come back to the Prieuré. They took him literally. Some of the Englishwomen went but they came back later. The rest of us also left. We went to Paris and stayed at the shabby little Unic Hotel on Montparnasse. But before we left we had a talk with Mme de Hartmann, with the result that Gurdjieff said that the Americans could return after a few days and stay on, also those 'near' to him could return. Actually everyone, except his family and those who were looking after him, did leave for a few days.

When we returned to Fontainebleau the Prieuré seemed empty. Only a third of us were left, including the old pupils—those closest to Gurdjieff. Work was resumed in the gardens and the forest, and every evening Hartmann played music to us in the Study House, both Gurdjieff's music and Russian pieces. At the end of October Gurdjieff was walking by himself again, though slowly, and again he began to set us tasks.

I was told to work with Olgivanna; we pulled one at each end of a cross-cut saw, cutting up logs for the winter and piling them up in the woodsheds. She told me about their life in the Caucasus with Gurdjieff. In Tiflis he had asked her if she had a wish, a real wish. She said, 'I wish for immortality'. He said, 'What you do now?' 'I look after my house and servants,' she replied. 'You work yourself? Cook, look after baby?' 'No, my servants do that for me.' 'You do nothing, and you wish for immortality!' he said. 'But this does not come by wishing but by special kind of work. You must work, make effort, for immortality. Now, I will show you how to work. First, tell servants to go and begin by doing everything yourself.'

'He did show me,' she added. 'He showed me how to do ordinary housework, not as a servant would do it, but to work and at the same time use his method.'

For two weeks we pulled at the long saw, and every day Gurdjieff came round and watched us. He would have a few minutes' conversation with Olgivanna, and then walk to another group. From what I could follow of the conversation it seemed to be about her plans for the future; and eventually she left, with her little daughter Svetlana, for America, where in course of time she became Mrs Frank Lloyd Wright. For fourteen years thereafter I never saw her but once, and then only for a few moments. Like all the women who really worked with Gurdjieff, she was remarkable and unusual; she possessed an inner something, she had individuality, and she could turn her hand to anything.

This episode of sawing made a great and lasting impression on me because of what happened at the end; which, again, came as a result of the months of work. I began to notice that I was experiencing something different while doing this physical work, something that I had never experienced in my long years of the labouring life. Then, one day, Gurdjieff came along on his daily visit and, while he was watching me carrying in the wood and piling it, something in me said, 'I am sensing myself, I am remembering myself'. This awareness of increased consciousness was accompanied by a feeling of real joy. Then he said, 'Enough, I think. You now know very well how to work with wood. I give you new task'.

This apparently meaningless sentence, the way it was said, clinched something in me. I had had, as they used to say, 'a conviction of sin' —a realization that my life hitherto had been completely mechanical and automatic; now it was as if a magician had said: 'Leave the form of a machine and assume your rightful form of a man'. This was my first initiation; and Gurdjieff's words the ritual that accompanied it. A mystery had taken place. At lunch that day, looking round at my companions, I saw them and myself differently, and I was reminded of a passage in the story of the Golden Fleece: 'When the Argonauts returned to the ship after taking part in the mysteries at Samothrace they seemed to Atalanta and Meleager like gods, not men; a faint nimbus of light shone about their brows. But when they were in the ship and had put on their usual clothes the radiance faded—they were once more men, but changed.'

One day, Mme de Hartmann told us that Gurdjieff was going away for a cure, and that if any of us wished to speak to him before he went we could do so that afternoon. There were now eight of the younger pupils left, all from America. I was very nervous, not knowing what to ask, yet not wanting to lose the opportunity. We sat on the grass in the bright autumn sunshine and waited. At length he came out and slowly walked to his chair. First one and then another got up and went to him. I put off my turn as long as possible, for my mind was a blank, but as I got up, the questions came to me, and, sitting at his feet I said, 'Mr Gurdjieff, I would like to have stayed at the Prieuré, but I've made arrangements to start a book business in America; also, I want to get married, though I have no one in mind at the moment. And I want to help others.' 'All these can be of use,' he said. 'Very necessary to get money for life. You go and start your business, then later perhaps we go into business together. About marrying; first you must distinguish between woman and wife. Wife is always, woman temporary. If you marry now perhaps not last. Later perhaps. Also, before you can help others, be of real use to others, you must know yourself and be able to help yourself. Now you are egoist, mind always on yourself. You must learn how to be egoist for good aim, then you will be able to be real altruist and help others.'

That was all; but the force behind the words, like a fresh breeze, cleared my cloudy mind of sentimentality, the 'slight emotion exaggerated by muddled thinking' that had accumulated over the years about sex and 'doing good'. When he went indoors to rest, I walked through the forest pondering his words.

Gurdjieff went away next day, and I did not see him until the following summer. November came, it was cold. The Study House was shut, and we cleared the English dining room and practised movements there, and even learnt some new obligatories.

I returned to London at the end of the month to complete my business arrangements. My old friend Walter Fuller, who was then literary editor of the *Weekly Westminster*, invited some people to hear me talk about life at the Prieuré. It fell flat, for I could give them no intelligible picture of the life, the system, or the method of teaching. They sensed that I was no longer interested in the causes we had worked for together—socialism, social reform, education. 'And your experiences don't seem to have made you any happier', they added. They continued to work for causes, to tell others what ought to be done; but I cannot see that the life of man has improved since then, either his inner or his outer life. A great obstacle to the good life is the hubristic attitude of the so-called 'intellectuals' on the one hand and the bureaucrats on the other, whatever their race or creed; those who are convinced that they know, and wish to put others on the path. And they are always wrong. In a way we are all like this, and must be until we begin to be able to look into ourselves and face the truth about ourselves. As the Sufis say: 'However much knowledge a man has, unless he has examined himself and confessed to himself that really he understands nothing, all that he has acquired will be as "the wind in his hands" '.

Seeds had been sown in me and had begun to germinate, but, as every gardener knows, there is often a long period between germination and sprouting, between sprouting and becoming a plant, and longer still before the tree appears with blossoms and fruit. Becoming a new and developed man is a still longer process.

II

NEW YORK AND
FONTAINEBLEAU 1925-6

TOWARDS THE END of November 1924 I returned to New York, rented an apartment in Washington Square, and proceeded to gratify my whim of having a bookshop. This I established in 47th Street, in one of the old brown stone houses. Twice a week I went to Orage's group, which was meeting in the apartment of a psycho-analyst who was interested in the ideas. More people joined the group, and we were transferred to Jane Heap's 'Little Gallery' on Fifth Avenue at 11th Street. Finally, Muriel Draper, one of America's brilliant society women, offered her apartment in East 40th Street, and there the big group continued to meet. Orage had other groups, which met elsewhere. Among the members of one of these were Herbert Croly, editor of the *New Republic*, and John O'Hara Cosgrave, literary editor of the *New York World*, a daily. Our own group consisted of what in England might be called the 'intelligent middle-class'—mostly young middle-aged people who were doing well in their ordinary life-work, profession or business. There were also one or two quite rich people. For each meeting we paid two dollars. There were also classes for movements and dances, twice a week, in the O'Neil Studio, organized by Mrs Howarth and Miss Lillard, who had been at the Prieuré in its first two years. For these we also paid two dollars a lesson, the better-off pupils paying more. It was clearly understood that each should pay according to his means. Also, most pupils found ways of getting money for the Prieuré from some activity outside their daily job. In our group there were between fifty and sixty people.

The nominal time of Orage's meetings was eight o'clock. Usually he would walk in about nine; but the interval gave us an opportunity of sitting quietly and relaxing, or of speaking to those whom we had no opportunity of meeting during the week.

'Well,' Orage would say, 'any questions?' After a pause, someone would ask a question, and he would answer. Once started, questions flowed. Each asked according to his type and in accordance with his level of understanding—or lack of understanding—and each received an answer accordingly. An emotional-instinctive type like myself took everything uncritically, through the feelings, and continually asked for more. A mental type like S. had to have an intellectual explanation for every point; he would go on and on in spite of the protests of 'For goodness' sake, S!' from some; while Orage, with infinite patience, would try to get him to feel and sense something. To me, he would point out that it was necessary to think more, necessary to use my mind; and he would tell S. to try to feel more, to feel with his feelings and not with his head. Orage, sitting before us in his chair, was the active force opposed to the passive force of us as a group; from the questions and answers there emerged a third force; the result was a degree of understanding, according to the effort each was able to make.

We would go to the meeting tired after a long day's work, but by the end of the evening so much energy had been generated that, instead of going home, we would adjourn to a Child's restaurant and 'chew keva' until, very often, two in the morning. Orage's knowledge of things and people was astonishing. He knew a great deal of what went on behind the scenes in public and literary affairs. He could also divine what was going on behind our own façade. He seemed to know the answer to every question; his replies were so right that many of us got into the habit of talking everything over with him—mundane problems as well as psychological ones. In the beginning this helped very much, but some of the weaker ones came to rely on him entirely, and consulted him on everything. With all his knowledge he was a warm human being, with human weaknesses and defects, striving to perfect himself. As he said, he himself was learning by working with us; he needed us as we needed him. He taught from Gurdjieff as he understood the teaching; and stood in relation to Gurdjieff as we did to him. We were impatient to 'know' more and more, and were sometimes annoyed that the teaching was not handed out on a plate complete with explanations.

Between Orage and some of us there was established a very close emotional and mental relationship, and he would appear to be 'all

89

light' in whom was no darkness (our heroes must be all white). It was not possible, at first, to be impartial about Orage, since we were unable to be impartial about anyone, least of all ourselves. As he would say, 'Before you can be impartial about other people, you must learn to be impartial about your own organism—this is one of the aims of Gurdjieff's teaching.' There were, of course, differences and struggles between pupils in the group, which provoked friction, but this only served to make the roots strike deeper, and to weld us into a kind of brotherhood. But one easily becomes attached to people emotionally and wants to give everything at once; and when the other person inevitably does something which seems not 'right' one reacts strongly and negatively, and thereby produces a train of suffer-ing—and so becomes a source of evil. 'Love emotional, whether for man, woman, or a cause, evokes the opposite', said Orage.

A pupil, who at times became immersed in self-pity, was saying how difficult life was, and how everyone and everything seemed to be against her; if only things and people were different life would be livable. She knew she was a worm, but did not see how she could do anything about it. Orage merely repeated a verse of a song:

> I wish I were an Elephantiaphus,
> And could pick off the coconuts with my nose,
> But oh, I am not, alas I cannot be, an Elephantiaphus,
> But I'm a cockroach, and I'm a waterbug;
> I can crawl around and hide behind the sink.

The pupil began to laugh, and we also. Orage, like Gurdjieff, was able to arouse our sense of humour and make us laugh at ourselves.

From time to time Orage gave us simple exercises to do, 'kinder-garten' he called them. He told us to write down in a column what we considered were our positive or 'good' characteristics, and in the opposite column our negative or 'bad' ones, and to put the paper away and to look at it again only after a year or two. I made such a list and forgot about it. It may have been two or three years later that I came across it among some papers and read it. With a shock I saw that none of what I had looked on as my 'good' characteristics—and it was a fairly long list—really existed; my true characteristics were almost exactly opposite to these 'good' ones. I had been seeing reality—reality about myself—upside down. I *was* upside down and inverted.

He gave us two other exercises at this time. One was 'reviewing the events of the day', an exercise in memory, will, and concentration. The idea was that before going to sleep one should begin slowly to count 2.4.6.8.10—10.8.6.4.2, and so on, up to a hundred. Having got this rhythm started, to try to picture oneself impartially—getting out of bed, dressing, having breakfast, going to the office in the bus, meeting people and so on, and so to bed—as if we were watching a not very interesting film, otherwise we might get identified with it. 'Don't think about it,' he said, 'thinking will falsify the picture. During the review, you will have periods of forgetting and you will stop counting. You must mend the film and start counting again. Also, you may want to go to sleep and a great effort will be needed to keep going. And often, when you get into bed, you will forget to do it. As with all real exercises, the organism is in a conspiracy to make you forget.'

The other was an exercise in attention.

'Take your watch and fasten your eye on the second hand; watch it as it makes a revolution of a minute and do not let your eye wander. When you are quite sure that you can focus your attention for one revolution you will have begun to develop your power of thinking. Having accomplished this, while keeping the focus of attention on the small hand, count to yourself from 1 to 10 and then backwards. This requires a double attention; one part is on the movement of the hand, the other on the counting. You may find it easy at first, but keep on until it becomes difficult. Having got so far, continue to keep your eye on the moving hand and continue to count mentally, then, at the same time, repeat to yourself a verse of a rhyme. Do it for two or three minutes.'

Much later, more difficult exercises were given; but the most difficult were those given by Gurdjieff, and done only under his direction. Some included the conscious use of air and impressions.

During the winter, Orage heard from Mme de Hartmann regularly. Gurdjieff was recovering. He had bought an old and large car and was again taking parties about, himself driving. Sometimes he made his companions get up at six o'clock on a cold winter morning and leave the warm hotel. He would drive, without a word, until hours later they stopped for coffee. He was making tremendous efforts to overcome the unwillingness of his sick planetary body, which wanted to take things easy, to lie about and do nothing. Some said, 'But ordinary people have done this—made tremendous efforts. Look what men did in the war!' The difference was that in war men make effort under compulsion.

'Then,' said one of the group, 'you consider that this effort of Gurdjieff's is an example of real will?'

'Yes,' replied Orage, 'as I have said, real will can be defined as only that which is self-initiated, not obliged, not wanted by the organism. An effort to accomplish an "I" wish, not "It" wish. Gurdjieff's efforts are those of an elephant—ours are ant-like.'

'How can I begin to acquire real will?', someone asked.

'Well,' said Orage, 'take a whim that you have, a harmless whim, and make an effort to gratify it. Something that you have wanted, for a long time, to do, and compel yourself to see it through. This will give you a taste of real will. It often takes more effort to do what you want to do than what you do not want to do. The perverted puritanism in us whispers that when we are "denying" ourselves, we are pleasing God. When the average English or American Puritan does something he really likes, he often has a feeling of guilt and has to make an excuse to himself that it is "good" for him, especially if it has to do with wine or women. Gratifying harmless whims is a means for acquiring real will, but don't cultivate them.'

In March, Orage told us that he had received a manuscript from the Prieuré. Gurdjieff had written it in Armenian; it had then been translated into Russian by Mme Galumian, an Armenian pupil, and then into English by English-speaking Russians, together with emendations by some not very literate English pupils.

'I've sent it back,' he said, 'and have told them that it is completely unintelligible. I've no idea what it is about. But Mme de Hartmann says that Gurdjieff has planned to write a book in which he will put the whole body of his ideas. If this chapter is an example, I can only wish he would not. I don't see the point of it.'

However, it was not long before a revised version arrived, which he read to us. 'This is entirely different,' he said, 'Now I begin to smell something very interesting.'

He read it to us many times, but we could not make much of it. Soon, however, something began to work in us; and as more chapters came over, the impact on our feelings became stronger. The book was to be called *Beelzebub's Tales to his Grandson* or *An Impartial Objective Criticism of the Life of Man.* Beelzebub while travelling in a space-ship with his companion Ahoun, and his grandson Hassein, relates to the latter his observations of the life of man on the planet earth that he had made during his descents to earth from the planet Mars. Some of the group said that a stumbling-block was the extraordinary style. Orage said that it was far more intelligible than Joyce's *Ulysses*, or Gertrude Stein's book, both of which had recently appeared in America in the *Little Review*. One of the group, a writer, spoke our thoughts.

'Orage,' he said, 'you've got a big job on your hands if you're going to put that into readable English. People will be put off by the style, for one thing, and the average person won't understand it at all. Much of the grammar and punctuation is not even literate.'

'I don't propose to rewrite it,' he said. 'In fact, apart from general editing, I shall leave it as it is until, probably the final revision, whenever that may be. The book will take shape. It is full of ideas. As I see it, it is really an objective work of art, of literature of the highest kind; it is in the category of scripture. It seems that Gurdjieff planned it while he was lying in bed after the accident. It is consciously designed to have a definite effect on everyone who feels drawn to reading it. Anyone who tried to rewrite it would distort it.'

I cannot say that I had understood much, if any, of the theory of the Gurdjieff system; the work for me at the beginning, fortunately perhaps, was entirely practical; but the effort even to try to understand the system was beginning to have the effect of making my lazy mind work. I was beginning to see the difference between thinking with my feelings and thinking with my mind, and I was beginning to notice the difference between feeling and sensing. Also I noticed a slight, though perceptible growing strength in the solar plexus—a diminution of that acute sinking feeling that, in the face of a rebuff, almost doubled one up at times—an inherited weakness intensified by the war. (Orage said that in some Eastern teachings the solar plexus is said to be the seat of power, or real will.) I began to be able to deal with situations and people more competently.

Orage's mind stimulated one's own; it was alive, very different from the minds of the rigid 'intellectuals' I had mixed with at the 1917 Club in London, whose talk was no more than the flow of associations streaming from their formatory apparatus. Orage felt as well as thought. And though none of us, and no intellectual, not even my old friend C. K. Ogden, was ever a match for him, Orage could, like Gurdjieff, put a simple person at his ease.

It was during this year 1925 that I first became aware of 'negative emotion'. When, one day, a pupil in the group in New York said to me apropos of my attitude to him, 'You have an awful lot of negative emotion', I was indignant and spoke to Orage about it. He said, 'One of the things I have to thank Gurdjieff for (and Ouspensky for passing on the idea), is his teaching about negative or lower emotions. You yourself give way to negative emotion very readily. You are touchy, easily hurt, you harbour resentment, you cannot bear the least criticism; and almost everyone is the same. Negative emotion is unconscious, and therefore evil.' This was a shock. I had never thought of my suffering as being 'negative emotion', but as a result of the 'pressure on the spirit', a result of the war, of ill-health brought on by life in the trenches. It was a surprise to realize that all this could be summed up in the expression 'negative emotion'. The preparatory work I had done during my visit to the Prieuré enabled me now, months afterwards, to begin to face the fact of my negativity. But it is one thing to know with the mind, quite another to understand.

Orage said: 'If we pass on our suffering to others it becomes "evil", which, as Professor Saurat says in *The Three Conventions*, is "suffering apart from creation". The saints are eaters of suffering; they consume it, transform it, and use it for the creation of *being*. When we wallow in self-pity, resentment, or unreasoning hatred of others, we become channels of suffering, we pass it on. Pity is divine, self-pity diabolical. We do not want to face the fact that we are often cluttered up with the sentimentality of self-pity. Self-pity is a disease of the emotions; it is being sorry for oneself and blaming parents, conditions, and people for one's own wretched personal state; self-pity is one of the manifestations of negative emotion that makes others dislike us, in which a hubris, an overweening conceit, often conceals itself in abject humility, a feeling of worm-likeness.'

'But isn't any suffering of use?' I asked. 'Yes, it can be. Only you must ask "What kind of suffering?" If we accept our suffering without resentment or complaint, we are, according to Gurdjieff, either paying off an old debt or laying up future merit.'

The expression 'negative emotion' is useful, since it defines so much of the feeling that motivates human activity. Almost all newspaper reports and 'news' has to do with negative emotion. I must say that I never heard the expression at the Prieuré nor did I hear Gurdjieff use it.

There are so many of these negative feelings that the English language has to use scores of words and expressions to denote the various kinds and shades of them. To take some beginning with the letter 'D' for example: despondency, dejection, depression, despair, doleful, downcast, drooping, dismayed, disheartened, dispirited, dreary, dread, dumps, disconsolate, desolate, disgust, discontented, dissatisfied, disappointment—one could go on for pages; and others, like touchiness, irritability, pique, backbiting, resentment; and all that goes with the expression 'accidie' or 'acedia'. Then there are the basic ones such as hatred, envy, jealousy, anger, which have a positive aspect as well as a negative. 'Envied to be imitated', says Gurdjieff. 'Never fear to hate the odious', says Orage. Beelzebub speaks about the beings of this planet, who know only the denying force, from which negative emotions spring. Then there are the various forms of sentimentality— the English attitude to animals, in which sentimentality masquerades as humanitarianism. Introspection, useless self-reproach, certain kinds of 'love', are negative. Ordinary life, social and business, is largely a polite mask which hides a seething mass of negative emotions.

Depression is a common form of negative emotion. With some it is a kind of disease which comes on periodically, even regularly at certain times of the year. Some take to drugs or drink to escape it. The causes are various: food, climate, unsatisfied sex or over-expenditure of sex energy, lack of money, planetary influences; with some it is inherited. Gardening and some kind of handicraft, are among the best cures, also washing-up, clearing out a lumber room—physical work of various kinds. An almost infallible cure is to do these while remembering oneself, and to do the task more slowly or faster, than usual. The difficulty is to make the initial effort. But, as Gurdjieff's father said, 'Once you have shouldered it, it is the lightest thing in the world'.

What is 'negative?' It is that which is devoid of positive attributes. It is a minus, the negation of something, that which denies—the opposer, the devil, the adversary. To be negative is to be passive when one should be active. Negativeness is that part of the Holy Denying, the Holy Firm, which has been distorted and corrupted in us, that in us which has become corrupt. But the garbage and filth put in the compost heap can be transformed to sweet-smelling soil from which grow flowers and fruit. So with us.

95

Paul, who understood this system as interpreted according to his time, said, 'Behold, I show you a mystery; we shall not all sleep, but we shall all be changed, in a moment, in the twinkling of an eye, at the last trump; for the trumpet shall sound, and the dead shall be raised incorruptible. For this corruptible must put on incorruption, and this mortal put on immortality; then shall be brought to pass the saying that is written: "Death is swallowed up in victory".' This is not a state in a fancied future, but a psychological process that can take place now.

At the Prieuré there was a great deal of expression of negative emotion. Gurdjieff seldom reproved young pupils who were getting into a state of anger and resentment; but he would say a few words, and they would suddenly stop, as if they had woken up. At suitable times he would provoke a display of negative emotions, because until you realized that you had them you could do nothing about them. Repressed, they turn sour and become poisonous; given way to, destructive; so life is what it is. Only the alchemy of the method can transform them. Negative emotions are the raw material which we can use to work on ourselves. They are the steam that drives the piston, as it were. Energy controlled according to the Method is beneficent; uncontrolled it is maleficent.

To refrain from the expression of negative emotions can be productive of good only when it is accomplished by the effort to remember oneself. Only when one is in a state of self-remembering can negative emotion be transformed into positive emotion.

In speaking of the denying force, Gurdjieff sometimes used the word 'dabbel'. 'You wish to be an angel,' he said, 'but dabbel also necessary. Angel can do one thing, dabbel can do everything.'

The following is from conversations I had with F. S. Pinder:

'Negativity is a "nothing"; though it has a kind of activity in spreading to other things that have a possibility of being "something" or "nothing". It is a minus, a lessener in respect of any potential activity. It is a something that draws energy into itself. In the objective sense, exclusively, it is a receiver, a Passive on all cosmic scales—for the sole purpose of conceiving and affording the cosmic processes a means of transforming the conception into an Active.

' "The cause of all misunderstandings is to be sought for only in woman"—this is the language of symbols, not literary grammar. Therefore it can be seen after meditation and pondering that a male who is a Passive-Active, instead of an Active-Passive, is a monstrosity, an "ape". A female who is an Active-Passive instead of a Passive-Active, as she should be, is also a monstrosity, an "ape"—suffragettes, the big woman who wears the trousers, many intellectuals and women in public life; they are a kind of minus quality. The Devil in Goethe's *Faust* says: "Ich bin der Geist der stets verneint"—"I am the spirit who always denies", also, "Das ewige Weibliche zieht uns hinan"—"The eternal feminine draws us on".

' "Yes", the affirmation, or active response; "No", the negation or yielding. Always one "bars" the other, or outdoes the other, gets it down. Objectively, any lessening of the strength of "yes" in relation to "no", or vice versa, results in psychopathy—they must be equalized, and from this equalization feeling is obtained.

'Take the thinking centre: the thinking part says "Yes", the moving part "No"—reconciling says 50-50, and fuses into a simple noumenon or concept; and potentially an objective thought—but not whole and complete, for we have three centres, all of which must be functioning in the same way; and a big "Yes" against a big "No" produces a big feeling—when all three centres are working at their fullest vibrations and in harmony.

'We have not reached that state.

'We still have to fight against negative emotions that affect the feeling parts of the thinking and instinctive-moving centres.

'Let us take the sensations of the instinctive-moving centre. They may be plus or minus, affirming or denying, pleasant or unpleasant, necessary for enabling us to get through life, as when tasting a piece of meat we find that it is "off", and the organism rejects it. The same with fresh and foul air, cold and heat; we can use these positive and negative instincts to get through life with the minimum of discomfort; and in moving about—when we are tired of walking, we sit down or go back.

'The state of being bored is negative; boredom begins where the mind leaves off, and it will affect the formatory apparatus through the thinking centre and the feeling centre.

'An emotion is really being "moved up one" or "moved down one", so to speak. "Love of feeling evokes the opposite"; and we can see that unrestrained joy, over-confidence, a superfluity of gladness, fellow-feeling, sympathy, and so on (which are generally regarded as positive) may easily be turned into their opposites; for we ordinarily have no permanent or fixed emotions as we should have; and this is not possible in the ordinary waking state of consciousness, where we all are. Examples are all around us of how love turns into hate and jealousy, and how from that we may lose him whom or that which we love.

'Permanent negative emotions may be seen all around us and in us —in manifestations of petulance, irritability, vanity, egoism, selfishness, conceit, boasting, and so on and so forth; these are permanent until we wake up and struggle against them "up the steep slope", when they may be gradually transformed.'

Gurdjieff constantly reminded us, in all sorts of ways, that 'dabbel is also necessary', but that we must not remain passive and allow ourselves to be the slave of our denying part, our negative emotions. He said that we must not become the slave of our passive part as represented by a woman. A man should not be dominated by a wife or a mistress.

Varro relates that Socrates said: 'The faults of a wife should be either destroyed or borne with. By helping her get rid of the fault a husband makes her more agreeable, and by putting up with the fault, he becomes a better man.'

When Alcibiades, who represented ordinary life, asked Socrates why he put up with such a nagging and bitter-tongued woman as Xantippe, he replied: 'By putting up with her at home I become used to it, and I make an exercise of it which enables me, when I go about, to tolerate the ill-will and insults that I meet from people.'

Part of Gurdjieff's training consisted of bringing out and developing the active part in his men pupils, and the passive in the women; it brought out the masculine in men and the feminine in women. The men had to learn to be active towards themselves, towards their own inertia and weaknesses, and to be active in their relationships with other men and women; as the true active part of the man developed, so did the passive, the creative part; and of course, the reconciling.

It is possible consciously to use an attribute, such as vanity, in special ways and derive benefit from it. Anything that is against the work is negative. Negativity is mechanicalness, unconscious, and therefore evil.

A writer, well known in London, a follower of Adler, once said to me, 'One of the striking things about the effect of Gurdjieff's teaching on his pupils is that the men—at least those I have known—become more masculine and the women more feminine.'

★   ★   ★

98

In the spring of 1925 I returned to England to buy books. From there to Paris, Vienna, Berlin, also to buy old books and prints. After arranging my business affairs I went to Antibes for a holiday, and from there to Fontainebleau. Gurdjieff greeted me:

'Ah, Mr America, first you must have Turkish bath and get rid of the American smell, then we can talk.'

'But I'm not American, I'm English!'

'You Mr America. American smell, English smell, all the same, one worse than the other.'

And so for two years he continued to address me as Mr America, until I discovered that he wanted me to see on the one hand that I was unconsciously adopting an American personality, and on the other that having previously bottled up my feelings like an Englishman, I was now beginning, like an American, to emote on any occasion. It was part of the process of showing me things about myself, so that I might be able to achieve a measure of real individuality which would take the place of my ever-changing personality; individuality based on an awareness of my own significance.

At this time, May 1925, Gurdjieff had almost recovered, though his eyes troubled him, and he had to rest much more. He was also putting on weight physically; indeed he was weightier and bigger in every way in the sense of Being, yet, paradoxically, he was lighter—he radiated more 'light'. Life at the Prieuré followed its usual course, though familiar faces were missing. There were Turkish baths on Saturdays, and meals in the English dining room. Dancing in the Study House had begun again; and Hartmann played both the music for the dances and Gurdjieff's hymns and other pieces. Gurdjieff again gave us tasks in the forest and gardens, but did not take much active part himself. He had resumed his trips to his flat in the Boulevard Pereire and his sessions in the Café de la Paix. And he was driving another little Citroen.

His main task was now writing, and everything and everyone was made use of to further his aim of completing *Beelzebub's Tales*. He always carried a supply of cheap exercise books and pencils with him, and he wrote anywhere and at any time—in his room, in the garden, in the café at Fontainebleau and the Café de la Paix in Paris, and during halts in his drives in the country. But it was often an effort for him to write, and he resorted to tricks to compel his organism to work. He would, for example, get two or three of us with him at the café to talk. The flow of ideas would start and he would take out his pencil

99

and paper and begin to write, while the others conversed or sat silent. Once he asked me to meet him at the Café de la Paix at eleven o'clock the following morning. He was there, apparently watching the flow of traffic and the people. He asked me what I wanted to drink. I said 'armagnac'. He ordered it, we drank, and he began to write. For two hours he wrote without saying a word, except at intervals to order coffee or drinks. At one o'clock he stopped.

'You see,' he said, 'what a lot I have done. Very good work this morning. Now take this back to the Prieuré and ask Mme de Hartmann to have it typed.' That was all. All the time I was sitting there it was as if I were being charged with electricity, magnetized with energy from Gurdjieff; as if a force were passing between us. Although I had felt listless and tired when I arrived, and had sat for two hours apparently doing nothing, I was now charged to the brim with bubbling energy, like a battery. Actually, I had made an effort to be active inside—not passive and fidgety. Also I had learnt something: I was reminded of what a Rishi in India had told me—that it was possible for a teacher to teach a pupil without a word being said. 'There are times when it is necessary to do nothing—but not to be idle', as a Chinese saying has it.

There were no new people at the Prieuré this summer. Orage arrived soon after I did, and one or two turned up from America later. And it rained and rained; it was one of those wet summers of Northern France when everything is always damp; clouds and warm rain, week after week, with occasional hours of hot sun, like a wet summer in England or on Long Island in America.

Orage and I were sitting in the Russian dining room one wet morning talking over a cup of tea. Gurdjieff came in, looking very handsome in a light grey suit, and carrying a walking-stick. He stopped, sat on the table, and lit a cigarette. Then he began to talk about the accident. He said that it was a habit of his when driving along that part of the road from Paris to Fontainebleau to put his hand out of the window and pick an apple off a row of trees that grew there. On this occasion as he did so the wheel of the car must have bumped into something, for he remembered nothing further. He said he must have unconsciously taken a cushion from the car and put his head on it to prevent the blood running into it. Of the rest of his story I could make nothing. He was speaking in parables, conveying something to Orage. After a pause, in which he lit another cigarette, he continued:

'You know, Orage, when you give something to a man, or do something for him, the first time he will kneel and kiss your hand; second
time, he takes his hat off; third time, he bows; fourth time, he fawns;
fifth time, he nods; sixth time he insults you, and the seventh he sues
you for not giving him enough.' Then, glancing at me, he said: 'You
know, Orage, we must pay for everything.'

When he had gone, I asked Orage what he meant.

'He was probably getting at us for not knowing how to give,' he
said. 'Neither of us, it seems, has yet learnt. Perhaps Gurdjieff himself
has had to learn how to give.'

Orage, always pouring out love on people; I, from fear, always
holding back. To one of his older men pupils, not Orage, Gurdjieff
once said: 'You love me too much. When you leave me you will
suffer, because you love me too much.'

Pondering what Gurdjieff had said, I began to see that everything,
even salvation, has to be paid for. Jesus said: 'You shall not come forth
until you have paid the uttermost farthing.' For literally everything
we have, someone has had to pay, in toil, sweat, or suffering or struggling of some kind. And we must learn how to pay our debts, learn
even to pay with money for our salvation. There is an old English
adage:

> What I kept I lost,
> What I had I spent,
> What I gave I kept.

Being asked what Communism had done for him, a Russian said:
'Before the revolution, a loaf of bread was just a loaf of bread from
a shop. Now when I see a loaf of bread I also see the peasants toiling
in the cold and rain and the hot sun to grow and harvest the grain; I
see the mills grinding it and the bakers baking the dough; I realize all
that goes to making a loaf of bread.' Though a revolution is not
necessary to enable us to see and sense reality.

Early this year Gurdjieff introduced 'The Science of Idiotism' and
the ritual of toasting the idiots. At first it seemed to be a way of
enlivening meals and making them more interesting. But one soon
realized that it represented something very serious and profound in
the study of oneself and others. Gurdjieff used the term 'idiotism' partly
in the old Greek and partly in the mediaeval English sense. Up to the
time of Donne, idiotism meant the speech or language peculiar to a

country; the peculiar character or genius of a language, or a deviation from its strict syntactical rules. Donne in 1631 wrote: 'It is the language and idiotism of the Church of God that it is to be believed as an Article of Faith . . .' In 1440 Capgrave wrote: 'Right be as twelve idiots, St Austin saith. He meaneth the twelve apostles, for they not learned were'. Jeremy Taylor speaks of 'The holy innocent idiot or plain easy people of the laity'. In Greek 'idiot' had the meaning of a private person, and one who possessed something of his own. But Gurdjieff attributed other and deeper meanings to the term. His understanding of the human psyche was such that when he gave a person his special 'idiot' it seemed almost miraculous, for to others it gave a clue to the pattern of the person's behaviour; though it took the person some-times a very long time to see it for himself. Gurdjieff said that the science of idiotism was a mirror in which a man could see himself. Not everyone had the right to be included in a category, of which there were twenty-one. Apart from the toasts, during the day's work he might call a person idiot, *doorak*, in the opposite sense, meaning that he was senseless.

Although, at the Prieuré, there were men and women who were 'representatives of contemporary art' as Gurdjieff called them, and of art at its highest as we know it, of music, painting, and design, singing, writing, yet I do not remember a single discussion. Not that it was forbidden but that it became unimportant compared with our purpose there. In the west wing was a fine oak-panelled library, one of the most remarkable libraries I have ever been in: it did not contain a single book.

The only book I read at Fontainebleau was the *Bhagavadgita*. In India I had met Annie Besant, who had spoken to me about the Gita and the vast store of Indian literature, of which I had never heard. Later, Orage spoke of the wonders of the *Mahabharata*, the *Bhaga-vadgita* being one of the many discourses in that great work. Yet until I went to the Prieuré and was lent a copy, I had never seen it. It was a revelation. I read it again and again; and ever since it has been a source of comfort and enlightenment. It also served as an introduction to the *Mahabharata*, which, eventually, I read from beginning to end at least twice.

The *Bhagavadgita* came at a time when my mind and feelings, thanks to the system, were beginning to expand. Disillusionment with organized religion and its sterile morality had made it impossible for me any longer to read the Bible. When, much later, free of old associations, I was able to read it, its teaching came back with all its simplicity and depth and with renewed force. I began to understand things that hitherto had been incomprehensible. Sayings which I had heard hundreds of times mechanically, began to have real meaning. So it was with the sayings of the Chinese teachers, Lao Tzu for example; with Sufi poetry, with the Gnostic teachings, Socrates and Plato, and the Egyptians. In *Some Sayings of the Buddha*[1] is to be found an almost exact description of the state of 'Self-Remembering' as we understand it. The measure of understanding I have been able to get from the ancient wisdom has been one of the results of the Gurdjieff system.

I see now that I owe a great deal to the simple faith of my father. As a young man he left the Church of England and joined the Wesleyan Methodists—the religion of man number one; and it filled his life with a kind of inner happiness. He had no doubt that the Wesleyan form of religion was the best that could be, and that by following it he one day would arrive at the heavenly mansions. My father was a good simple man. Yeloff the bookseller, in *Tales of Remarkable Men*, speaks of the need for people to have some faith or other, and that one should not try to convert them to another faith, since it is something built up within them from an early age. To destroy a man's faith, he says, is a great sin. If a man finds something that gives him more understanding and inner freedom and accepts it voluntarily, that is another thing.

Gurdjieff was a religious man, as was Orage—not orthodox, but in *essence*. He was speaking one day at lunch about how the teachings and the picture of Jesus have been distorted. Two of the visitors that day were Englishwomen, who began to talk in a rather sentimental manner about 'Jesus and his love'. Gurdjieff said: 'I hate your Jesus, poor Jewish boy'—the emphasis being on 'your'.

At dinner one day, he said: 'An important thing. Man cannot stay long in one subjective state. Very many things can arise from a sub-jective state. Never can you know the subjective state of another; the subjective state of two people is never the same, for subjective states are like finger-prints, different for each person. And no one can explain his own subjective state to another. A man does not really know why he is angry with you. You can say, "*He* is not angry with

[1] Translated by F. L. Woodward, Oxford, 1925 and 1939.

me—his *state* is angry with me". Remember this, and never reply with your interior, which is inner considering, and don't harbour associations of revenge and resentment. Good wishing can be effective over great distances—bad wishing also.'

He had been writing in the garden, and came to where some of us were sitting at the tables outside the dining room. He began to speak about Triamazikamno, the Law of Three, of the three forces, three principles. The only thing I remembered of this talk was his reference to the ancient Toulousites. Later, discussing this, one of the pupils drew a diagram of a symbol in the cathedral at Toulouse. It may be seen in some English churches.

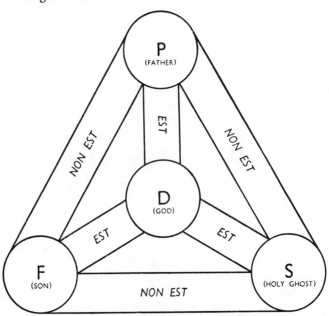

Diagram to illustrate the Law of Three, found in Toulouse Cathedral and in certain English churches.

As we studied it, we saw the connexion between the diagram and the Athanasian Creed. The Creed is a discourse on the Law of Three —at least the first part is; and the diagram is a symbol of that which is far older than Christianity. And now the Creed took on quite a different meaning from the literal one I had heard as a boy—that all those who did not believe in it, in the Church's sense, were actually condemned to suffer in hell. The Creed says:

Whosoever will be saved: before all things it is necessary that he hold the Catholick Faith.

Which Faith except every one do keep whole and undefiled: without doubt he shall perish everlastingly.

And the Catholick Faith is this: That we worship one God in Trinity, and Trinity in Unity:

Neither confounding the Persons: nor dividing the Substance.

For there is one Person of the Father, another of the Son: and another of the Holy Ghost.

But the Godhead of the Father, of the Son, and of the Holy Ghost is all one: The Glory equal, the Majesty co-eternal.

Such as the Father is, such is the Son: and such is the Holy Ghost.

The Father uncreate, the Son uncreate: and the Holy Ghost uncreate.

The Father incomprehensible, the Son incomprehensible: and the Holy Ghost incomprehensible.

The Father eternal, the Son eternal: and the Holy Ghost eternal.

And yet they are not three eternals, but one eternal.

As also there are not three incomprehensibles, nor three uncreated: but one uncreated, and one incomprehensible.

So likewise the Father is Almighty, the Son Almighty: and the Holy Ghost Almighty.

And yet there are not three Almighties: but one Almighty.

So the Father is God, the Son is God: and the Holy Ghost is God.

And yet they are not three Gods: but one God.

So likewise the Father is Lord, the Son Lord: and the Holy Ghost Lord.

And yet not three Lords: but one Lord.

For like as we are compelled by the Christian verity: to acknowledge every Person by himself to be God and Lord:

So are we forbidden by the Catholick Religion: to say, There be three Gods, or three Lords.

The Father is made of none: neither created, nor begotten.

The Son is of the Father alone: not made, not created, but begotten.

The Holy Ghost is of the Father and of the Son: neither made, nor created, nor begotten, but proceeding.

So there is one Father, not three Fathers: one Son, not three Sons: one Holy Ghost, not three Holy Ghosts.

And in this Trinity none is afore, or after other: none is greater, or less than another:

But the whole three Persons are co-eternal together: and co-equal.

So that in all things, as is aforesaid: the Unity in Trinity, and the Trinity in Unity is to be worshipped.

Here is a clear statement, in the language of the Church, of 'The Holy Affirming, The Holy Denying, The Holy Reconciling', which, in *Beelzebub's Tales*, is described in the language of objective science.

Whoever the author of the Creed was, he understood the Law of Three, though he had to interpret it in the religious language of the time. Even the name Athanasius is derived from 'against' or 'not' death; 'thanatos', death: 'a', not. The Law of Three has to do with the struggle that goes on between the active and passive forces, in the universe and in ourselves, the struggle and the reconciling, the result of which can crystallize something in us, transubstantiate something, over which mechanical death has no power. Death will lose its sting, and the grave will not triumph. Again, this is not only poetry, but something practical, a psychological process.

One of us said: 'I was brought up in the Christian religion, and always I was struck by the difference between those who talked about the teachings of Jesus and called themselves Christians, and their behaviour.' Gurdjieff replied: 'This question of Christianity is a big one. Generally speaking there are three kinds of Christians—he who wishes to be a Christian, he who wishes to be able to be, and he who is. Only the third can live according to the teachings of Jesus Christ with his essence as well as his mind. A pre-Christian is one who follows Christian precepts with his mind only; a non-Christian, a pagan, cannot follow them with mind or essence.'

One of the kitchen helpers had stolen into the dining room to listen to the talk instead of doing his task. Reproving him, Gurdjieff said: 'Your task is now in kitchen. If you neglect life tasks you will neglect this work. You must try to do everything well, in all circumstances. Help is given to those who help themselves in the right direction. By striving to do everything well we shall help the work, the teacher, and the group.' I could not catch all that followed but I heard: 'Remember what I write in *Beelzebub*, "If take then take. Whenever I do anything I do a lot of it".'

★   ★   ★

I returned to New York in November and worked with the groups through the winter and early spring. The summer following, 1926, I was again at the Prieuré. A small pipe-organ had been put in the salon, and every day Hartmann played Gurdjieff's music. Hearing it on the organ gave one a fresh understanding of it. Gurdjieff composed many new pieces this summer and autumn, which were arranged by Hartmann, among them music for Easter and Christmas: 'the Holy Affirming, Holy Denying, Holy Reconciling', and 'Hymns from a Truly Great Temple'. Almost every afternoon and evening the music was played. All who could would leave their work, go to the salon and sit quietly. At week-ends, when there was usually a number of people, Hartmann played many pieces. Some of them were so moving as to be almost unbearable, and the tears would stream involuntarily down our cheeks; one had to remember oneself with all one's might in order not to have to go out. Hartmann said that he himself found some of the pieces almost too difficult to play. One of the pieces consisted of slow and solemn chords of the most divine harmony, and in the overtones one could hear a sort of joyful singing as of the voice of a seraph. I have never heard anything like these hymns of Gurdjieff, except perhaps some of the very early church music such as can be heard in Notre Dame, and some of that of Bach, who at times touches the higher emotional centre.

Listening to the music, one could observe in oneself three different processes proceeding simultaneously: one in the mental centre, another in the emotional, and still another in the instinctive centre.

One was reminded of Madame Vivitskaya in the story of Prince Lubovedsky in *Tales of Remarkable Men*. She was travelling with Gurdjieff's party in Central Asia. They had stayed at a monastery and had heard some music which had aroused great interest, and moved them deeply. The next day when they started out they asked her why her finger was bound up. 'It was that damned music,' she said. The effect on her had been so powerful that she had not been able to sleep. She had gnawed her finger, puzzling over the effect it had had on her.

There had been a reading from *Beelzebub's Tales*, in the chapter on Purgatory, in the salon after lunch in the English dining room. In answer to a remark from someone Gurdjieff began to speak about 'silly angels' and said that if a man works on himself and purges himself of undesirable elements he will be better than an angel, a being with more understanding and experience. One of us, who perhaps had had a glass of armagnac too much, asked a question and began to wiseacre a bit. Gurdjieff, turning on him, reproved him for not trying to understand, which, by association, brought to my mind a passage in the *Pistis Sophia*. Andrew says to Jesus: 'Don't be angry with me, but have patience and reveal to me the mystery; it is hard for me and I do not understand'. Jesus said: 'Well, ask, and I will explain clearly.' 'It is a matter of wonder to me,' Andrew said, 'how men in the world and in the body of this matter, if they come out of the world, will pass through these firmaments and rulers, lords, gods, great invisibles, and enter into the Light Kingdom.' Jesus said angrily: 'How long must I put up with you? Are you so ignorant that you still do not understand? Don't you know that you and angels and archangels, the gods and lords and rulers, and the great ones of the emanation of the Light, and their whole glory, are all made out of the same paste, matter and substance—you are all of the same mixture . . . but the great ones, in purifying themselves, have not suffered nor been in affliction . . . But you, you are the refuse of all these, and you suffer and are in affliction through being poured into different kinds of bodies in the world. Now, Andrew, and all of you, when by your sufferings you have purified yourselves, you will go on high to the Light Kingdom, and if you reach the region of the great Lord of the Light, you will be revered among them because you are the refuse of their matter and have become more purified than them all.'

This also helps to explain Gurdjieff's constantly telling us that we were 'merde de la merde'.

Attar, in the *Conference of the Birds*, says, 'When the soul was joined to the body it was part of the all; never has there been so marvellous a talisman. The soul had a share of that which is high and the body a share of that which is low; it was formed of a mixture of heavy clay and pure spirit. By this mixing man became the most astonishing of mysteries.'

The Sufi poet, Jalali, says: 'If thou art good enough to be a man thou art too good for an angel. Adam's race of whitened dust are shrines that angels worship at.'

Dante, before he ascends the mountain of Purgatory, is told that his face must be cleansed of the tears he shed in Hell; and Virgil washes his face with dew. The penitent's first duty in going to Purgatory is cheerfulness; having seen his sin and acknowledged it, he must put it out of his mind and not wallow in self-pity and self-reproach, which are forms of egotism.

A pupil, speaking of the difficulty of arousing people's interest in Gurdjieff's ideas, referred to Lucian's 'Charon'. Charon says: 'And although their lives are short as leaves, Hermes, you see how they struggle with one another to get power and honour and possessions, in spite of their having to leave it all behind and be doomed to take our ferry with only an obol for the fare. Now that we are on these heights don't you think it would be good if I were to shout out a loud warning and tell them to cease their useless toil and to strive to keep the fact of death ever before them? I would cry: "O you foolish men, why do you strive after these vain things? Stop this toiling and moiling. Are you going to live for ever? These honours and riches are not lasting, nor can you take them with you. You will go out naked, leaving your houses and lands to others!" Don't you think that if I were to shout this to them it would help them to exist more wisely?'

Hermes: 'Don't you see what their abnormal way of living has brought them to? Even if you used an auger you could not unstop their ears. They have plugged them with the wax Ulysses and his friends used against the Sirens' songs, and would not hear if you shouted until you burst. What the river Lethe does in your underworld is done on earth by ignorance. Very few there refrain from stopping their ears, and so are able to understand the reality of things.'

A Persian proverb says: 'The wise man understands the fool, for he himself was once a fool; but the fool does not understand the wise man, since he never was wise.'

And there is another Persian saying: 'Up! Up! Only a little life is left, the road before you is long, and you are immersed in illusion.'

Gurdjieff often spoke about the need to repair the past—not to dwell on it and indulge in useless self-reproach, but to feel remorse of conscience. Remorse, in the Middle English language, is 'Ayenbite of inwit'—the 'Again-bite of in-knowing, of understanding.' Compare the French 'remordre'—'bite again'—the opposite of self-calming.

He said to a pupil: 'Past joys are useless to a man in the present; they are as last year's snows, which leave no trace by which they can be remembered. Only the imprints of conscious labour and voluntary suffering are real, and can be used in the future for obtaining good.'

On another occasion he said: 'What a man sows, he reaps. The future is determined by the actions of the present. The present, be it good or bad, is the result of the past. It is the duty of man to prepare for the future at every moment of the present, and to right what has been done wrong. This is the law of destiny. Blessed be the prime source of all laws!'

To someone who complained that nothing was ever as it logically should be, he said: 'Every satisfaction is accompanied by a non-satisfaction.'

In speaking of the need to help one another, he said: 'We usually know others better than they know themselves, therefore mutual help is necessary and profitable. But often self-love and self-pride prevent our profiting when we are told of our faults and weaknesses, for we often deny or try to justify ourselves.

'In all our actions we should strive to attain that which is useful for others and agreeable to ourselves.'

He often spoke about 'the unlucky sometimes becoming the lucky'. Apropos, Lao-tse relates: 'An old man lived with his son in an ancient disused fort on a hill. One day his horse, on which he depended, strayed and was lost. His neighbours came and sympathized with him on his bad luck. "How do you know this is bad luck?" he asked. Some days later his horse appeared, together with some wild horses, which the man and his son trained. His neighbours this time congratulated him on his good luck. "How do you know this is good luck?" asked the man. And as it happened, his son, while riding one of the horses, was thrown and became permanently lame. His neighbours condoled with him, and again spoke about his ill-luck. "How do you know this is ill-luck?" he asked. Not long after, war broke out; and the son, because of his lameness, could not go.'

We had been speaking among ourselves about electricity and magnetism, or animal magnetism, and how some people have more animal magnetism than others. When one of us asked Gurdjieff about this, he said: 'Man has two substances in him, the substance of active elements of the physical body and the substance made of the active elements of astral matter. These two by mixing form a third substance. This third substance is a mixed substance; it gathers in certain parts of a man and forms an atmosphere round him as an atmosphere forms round a planet. The atmospheres round planets are continually gaining or losing substance because of other surrounding planets. Man is surrounded by other men as planets are surrounded by other planets. When, within certain limits, two atmospheres meet—and if the atmospheres are sympathetic—a contact is made between them and lawful results occur—something flows; the quantity of atmosphere remains the same, but the quality changes.

'A man who has worked on himself and understands, can control his atmosphere. It is like electricity, and has positive and negative parts; and one part can be made to flow like a current. Everything has positive and negative electricity. In man, wishes and non-wishes are positive and negative. Astral material is always opposed by physical material or matter.

'In ancient times priests, real priests, understood the use of magnetism, and were able to cure disease by blessing with the hands. Some priests laid their hands on a sick person, others could cure at a short distance, others at long distances. A priest was a man who possessed the third, the mixed, substance, and could use it to cure others.

'A priest was a magnetizer. Jesus Christ was a magnetizer. Sick people are those who are deficient in this mixed substance, magnetism, or "life". This mixed substance can be seen if concentrated. An aura, halo, or nimbus is real. It can still be seen by some in certain holy places and certain churches: and sometimes around certain people. Mesmer rediscovered the use of this substance.'

Someone asked: 'How can *we* use this substance?'

Gurdjieff: 'To be able to use it you must first have it in yourselves. To gain it, it is the same as with gaining attention—by conscious labour and voluntary suffering: that is, by doing small things voluntarily, consciously. Begin by doing some small thing you wish to do and are now not able to do. By making this effort and *doing*, you will acquire magnetism.'

Gurdjieff spoke about learning to play roles, but one should begin with something quite small and simple. He himself was a master of the technique. With officials, for example, he could play the role of a simple man, almost devoid of intelligence, and so disarm them. Once, two psychologists from England came to the Prieuré on their way to a conference in Geneva; presumably to get Gurdjieff's views on the various schools. They were acquainted with Ouspensky. Gurdjieff gave them a wonderful lunch, but every time they asked him a question he turned it aside with a joke. After lunch he took them for a walk round the grounds and back to the Study House, cracking jokes and behaving like an eccentric. I was standing by the door, and he asked me: 'What a day is today?' I said: 'Tuesday.' He turned to them with a smile: 'Fancy! He say Tuesday, and all the time, I think it Wednesday.' And he led them into the Study House. The men were bewildered. When they left his attitude changed. 'Now,' he said, 'they will leave me in peace to pursue my aim.'

Another aspect of Gurdjieff was his ability on the one hand to make himself almost invisible and on the other to make himself appear like one of the Rishis, blazing with energy and radiance. When visitors were being shown round the grounds they would sometimes pass him with only a glance, like an American who was talking to me about what a wonderful man Mr Gurdjieff must be, and that he would like to meet him. Just then Gurdjieff passed by and went into the house. 'That is Mr Gurdjieff,' I said. 'Wal,' he replied, 'isn't that queer! I spoke to him in the grounds and thought he was the gardener.'

In ordinary life people play roles unconsciously. Gurdjieff played them consciously, and those who worked closely with him usually knew when he was playing a role.

In 'A Letter to a Dervish', he wrote: 'The sign of a perfected man and his particularity in ordinary life must be that in regard to everything happening outside of him, he is able to, and can as a worthy action, perform to perfection externally the part corresponding to the given situation; but at the same time never blend or agree with it. In my youth, I too, as you more or less know, being convinced of the truth of this, worked on myself very much for the purpose of attaining such a blessing as I thought predetermined by Heaven; and after enormous efforts and continuous rejection of nearly everything deserved in ordinary life, I finally reached a state when nothing from the outside could really touch me internally; and, so far as acting was concerned, I brought myself to such perfection as was never dreamed of by the learned people of ancient Babylon for the actors on the stage.'

Gurdjieff never let pass anything that we did or said in moments of forgetfulness. If he was present when it happened he took it up at once; and if he were told about the incident he would wait for an opportunity to 'make us eat dog' in the presence of others. I had made a silly flippant remark to someone apropos of Gurdjieff. Three days later I found myself in the Study House, sitting on the rich carpets with himself, Stjoernval, Hartmann, and some others. We were drinking coffee. He said to me: 'Repeat what you said to so and so the other day.' At once I realized how silly I had been in a moment of forgetfulness. A tremendous resistance came over me against acknowledging that I had acted as one without responsibility. He again asked me, smiling. But I kept silent and suffered. Then he said: 'If you do this

Foma, (Hartmann) shall play you any piece you wish.' After a struggle I repeated it, overcome with humiliation. Gurdjieff smiled and said: 'What you wish?' I said: ' "A Fragment of an Essene Hymn".' He nodded to Hartmann, who went to the piano and played it. This incident hit me so hard in the solar plexus that I never forgot it.

Once, in a harassed state, when I was trying to cope with a situation which involved myself, Gurdjieff, and three women, I asked him: 'Why do you let them stay here when they say such things about you, when they oppose you in every way?'

He said: 'You not understand; they do not say what they really feel. Men are logical, women not logical. You make mistake because you expect a woman to react as a man would react. Men are men. Women are women. Another thing, sometimes necessary to have people round you that you dislike. If people always pleasant, you like them—no incentive for work. These women give you very good opportunity for work, and I, also, must make effort!'

As usual, Gurdjieff was right. It was lack of understanding on my part. His patience and his work made very useful pupils of them.

In the *Pilgrim's Progress*, Christian and Faithful meet Talkative, who proceeds to discuss with them the mysteries of religion. At last Faithful says to Talkative: 'If a man have all knowledge, he may yet be nothing, and so be no child of God. When Christ said to the disciples "Do you know all these things?" and they answered "Yes", He added "Blessed are you if you do them." For there is a knowledge that is not attained by doing. A man may know like an angel yet be no Christian . . . There is knowledge that rests on the bare speculation of things, and there is knowledge that is accompanied with the grace of faith and love which puts a man upon doing even the Will of God from the heart. "Give me understanding, and I shall keep thy law; yea I shall observe it with my whole heart." (Psalm 119, 34.)'

Talkative, angry, leaves them, and goes back.

During this summer Gurdjieff was making notes on the chapters about Ashiata Shiemash, and one evening he began to talk to us, especially to Orage, about conscious Faith, Hope, and Love, particularly the last. Gurdjieff then went to his room, as he often did, early, to rest, sometimes inviting people to talk. On this occasion he told Orage to come. The next day Orage said to me: 'Read this. I talked with Gurdjieff last night for a long time, and afterwards I went to my room and wrote till four this morning. This is the result.' It was the draft of an essay 'On Love'—the three kinds of love affecting the relations between men and women. It was the most interesting thing I had ever read on this universal subject, and I read it and re-read it. It was published later in the *Atlantic Monthly*. When Orage returned to England he wanted it published there, and as no publisher would take it, I paid for its publication in book form in London. Since then it has run into several editions. It is a gem; though, for most, an almost unattainable ideal. This short essay, apart from what is written in *Beelzebub's Tales*, which is in a different category, is the only modern published exposition of the possibility of attaining a state of *conscious* love between men and women. Even those who are happily married can learn something from it.

In reply to a question about the second food, air, Gurdjieff said: 'There are two parts to air, evolving and involving. Only the involving part can vivify the "I". At present this involving part serves only for general cosmic purposes. Only when you shall have in yourselves a conscious wish will you be able to assimilate this, for you, good part of air, which comes from the prime source.

'In order to be able to assimilate the involving part of air, you should try to realize your own significance and the significance of those around you. You are mortal, and some day will die. He on whom your attention rests is your neighbour; he also will die. Both of you are nonentities. At present, most of your suffering is "suffering in vain"; it comes from feelings of anger, jealousy, and resentment towards others. If you acquire data always to realize the inevitability of their death and your own death, you will have a feeling of pity for others, and be just towards them, since their manifestations which displease you are only because you or someone has stepped on their corns, or because your own corns are sensitive. At present you cannot see this. Try to put yourself in the position of others—they have the same significance as you; they suffer as you do, and, like you, they will die. Only if you always try to sense this significance until it becomes a habit whenever your attention rests on anyone, only then will you be able to assimilate the good part of air and have a real "I". Every man has wants and desires which are dear to him, and which he will lose at death.

'From realizing the significance of your neighbour when your attention rests on him, that he will die, pity for him and compassion towards

9. Dervish prayer.

10. Dance of the Whirling Dervishes.

11. A. R. Orage, 1930.

him will arise in you, and finally you will love him; also, by doing this constantly, real faith, conscious faith, will arise in some part of you and spread to other parts, and you will have the possibility of knowing real happiness, because from this faith objective hope will arise—hope of a basis for continuation.'

Gurdjieff worked as usual every day on *Beelzebub's Tales*, re-writing and revising, working, as usual, in cafés and at the Prieuré—sometimes indoors, sometimes in the garden; sometimes with people round him, sometimes alone. When chapters were read out in the salon after dinner he would watch the expressions on our faces. He had begun to draft the chapter on America; and if an American visitor turned up he would have parts of the chapter read, and always he would begin to laugh during certain passages. We also would join in the laughter, although most of us were never sure what he was laughing at. I suspect that it was at ourselves.

In the bookless library one day he said: 'Orage, why do English and especially Americans, say "All right" even when it isn't all right?' Orage replied: 'Yes, when everything goes wrong we say: "All right, what do we do now".'

Salzmann thought this very funny, and began to joke about the expression 'All right'. And Gurdjieff said: 'I will use this in my chapter on America. "When nothing's right," then "All right!" ' '

When a chapter was being read, he would often tell the reader to pause, and the reader would put a comma at the place. Hence the sometimes strange punctuation in the English translation.

Often he would ask about a passage or a chapter, 'What does it make you *feel*?' The emphasis being on 'feel', never 'What do you "think" of it?'

There were frequent disputes about the use of the right word. Gurdjieff would have it 'the city Samlios'. The reader would say 'That is not English, we say "the city of Samlios".' 'Do you say "the man of Smith"?' asked Gurdjieff. 'No, "the man Smith".' 'Then why not "the city Samlios"?'

'Because it isn't English.'

'Then English is idiot language,' rejoined Gurdjieff.

He wanted to make the expression 'the next day' definite. The reader said: 'You must say "the very next day".'

'But "next day" is next day. Why "very"?'

'That's how we say it.'

With a quick movement he stroked his moustache, then made a gesture with his hand, which was meant to express, 'Even for me the English language defies all rules of logical expression.'

On another occasion the expression occurred: 'To see if it would not be possible'. He said 'I mean, "to see if it *would* be possible".' The reader said: 'That is what it does mean.'

Gurdjieff said, '*not* possible means impossible. I mean "possible". Is it not possible sometimes to think straight in your language?'

The strange names in *Beelzebub* are combinations of words or roots, or parts of words, in various languages; symbols, to make the reader ponder and reflect.

A constant balance was maintained between objective ideas and the needs of everyday life. The need of money, for example; and a great deal was needed to carry on the work. It was difficult for some to understand that money, for Gurdjieff, was money for the work. People revealed a great deal about themselves in their attitude to money, and in the way they gave it. Gurdjieff's attitude made it difficult, for with money as with other things he never did as others did. When people had made an effort to get money for him they were sometimes surprised to find that he would spend it on a large party or a trip; though he never, except for occasional clothes, spent it on himself.

His disposal of money, as I have said, was often determined by the attitude of the giver. A pupil from New York, a rather mean but well-to-do woman, gave him a cheque for about fifty dollars, but written in francs to make it appear larger. The same evening after dinner in the salon he, with Mrs X sitting by him, had all the children brought in. Beginning with the youngest he distributed the francs among them, to the amount of exactly five hundred. To other pupils who gave him money, Gurdjieff would give it back and say: 'You keep. You need it now. Perhaps later you will have money to give.' He was always helping people who really needed money.

'You are naïve about money,' he said to me. 'Most people are. But you are also a miser, not only in money, but in everything. While you remain naïve everyone will take advantage of you. If a person is "nice" to you, you will give money, from feeling, and regret it afterwards. Same in your business. If you are easy with people from weakness they will not respect you but take advantage of you—in dollar business and in other things. You must learn to be, how you say in English, can-

116

ning?' 'Cunning,' I suggested. 'Yes, cunning. But for a good aim and in the right way.'

He constantly reminded us that we must do everything well, that we must always be ready to adapt ourselves to changing circumstances, to be resourceful, and to learn to be able always to turn a set-back or a disadvantage to our own use—to regard life as a gymnasium in which one could use conditions for the development of will, consciousness, and individuality, to learn to be not ordinary but extraordinary.

'The extraordinary man,' he said, 'is just and indulgent to the weaknesses of others; and he depends on the resources of his own mind, which he has acquired by his own efforts.'

As I say, when he was speaking to me I felt that I could *do*. But always there was the inertia of the organism to contend with, its wish to take things easily, to talk instead of to do; the tendency to become caught up in outside life, to go with the stream of things. It is so easy to drift. In life, once effort ceases, the movement is downwards. This has been known from remote times.

When Aeneas has prayed, before his descent into the underworld, the prophetess answers: 'Seed of the Blood Divine, man of Troy, Anchises' son, the descent to Avernus is not hard. Every night and every day black Pluto's door stands open wide. But to retrace your steps and return to the upper air—that is the task, that is work.'

The Golden Bough, the Method, is necessary.

★   ★   ★

In the late autumn of 1926 I was again in New York. In December an offer was made for my book business; and in a few weeks it was sold and passed out of my hands. With some surprise I recalled that less than four years previously I had been afraid that if I became interested in the Gurdjieff system I might not be able to carry out the project that then seemed so dear to me; and now it had slipped away with not only no regret but even with relief. I saw how that from my childhood I had been so identified with books that I had almost worshipped them. I had been a bibliolatrist, a bibliomane, a bibliophile, a bibliopolist, and even a bibliotaphist. Now, a feeling of thankfulness pervaded me for having been cured of the book disease. I called to mind what Gurdjieff had said to me during the previous summer in the train from Paris to Fontainebleau. I and another man were talking animatedly about first editions and rare books. Gurdjieff listened, and then said to me: 'I tell you, time will come when not one single book will be sold in England. If you still wish to sell books better for you to sell pornographic books than what you sell now.'

A naïve young man who was with us took this quite literally, and later spread the story that Gurdjieff had said that the time was not far off when no books would be published in England, and he had advised one of his pupils to sell pornographic books to make money. Of course, what Gurdjieff said was meant for me alone. It was one of his characteristic cartoons, a caricature even, of speech, to shock me into becoming aware of my identification with books as things in themselves. Though I had begun to discover, in the course of my business and my connexion with the First Edition Club in London, that there is an association between the identification with books— book-collecting, book-hoarding, and book-stealing—and sexual mal- adjustments. Identification with books, even stealing books, is only one of the many manifestations of the diversion of sex energy from its real purpose, that of normal sex relations and its use in inner develop- ment. Yet a man can still have ordinary sex relations with women and at the same time be too passive, especially if the feminine creative part of himself is strong. As I have said, Gurdjieff and his teaching developed the masculine in men and the feminine in women. His methods of treating psychological diseases were unorthodox and some- times ruthless, but the cures were remarkable; those with homosexual tendencies became masculine, and lesbians became, as he expressed it, 'women mothers'.

With the profits from the sale I bought a barn and some acres of land in Connecticut and there built a house, a more congenial occupa- tion for me than bookselling. Not long afterwards I was married. My wife had been at the Prieuré during its first two years, so we went abroad and spent most of the summer there. Gurdjieff was surprised, I think, and obviously pleased to see us. He began telling those around that we had performed a miracle, had squared the circle; as he ex- pressed it, round idiot had married square idiot. Behind his joking there was a world of meaning and much material for reflection.

This summer was most interesting. Orage and some of the group of New York were there, and Gurdjieff gave all his spare time from writing to working on us individually and collectively. In these few months were crowded years of activity and impressions. I remember little of his actual words, but I remember the strong impression he made—the way he manipulated us, mixed us up, his asides at meal-times. His method brought about an eventual change in all of us, including Orage. Each day we would meet and discuss what Gurdjieff had said, what he had meant. The results manifested themselves, for me, the following year, and I will relate them in due course.

The ritual of the Turkish bath was observed every Saturday, and the lunches and dinners in the English dining room. Revised chapters of *Beelzebub* were read out in the salon, and every day there was music. Instead of the rain of the summer before there were weeks of bright hot weather.

Several young couples were at the Prieuré. One day, as we were waiting for coffee in the salon, one of the newly married young women beckoned to her spouse and pointed to the empty seat beside her in no uncertain manner, and he, being the perfect American hus-band, obediently got up and sat beside her. Gurdjieff gave, not her, but him, a dirty look, and after a pause began to say that a man must not be a slave to woman; he also spoke about the low status of Ameri-can women compared with that in older countries, because the men had relinquished their responsibility. He added, 'If you are first your wife is second. But if your wife is first you must be zero, only then will your hens be safe.' He then asked for some papers to be brought in and told someone to read the following: 'The Greek sage, Socrates, was a follower of this method (the method that Gurdjieff taught) and, in order to obtain shocks for evoking an intense manifestation of his inner struggle, he even looked for a corresponding wife, and, having married her, he compelled himself to endure externally, patiently, for the rest of his life, the constant scolding and nagging of his Xan-tippe.'

Some said that Gurdjieff often tried to provoke bad feeling between husbands and wives. It was not so. He tried to make them understand what a real relationship between husband and wife should be. I do not know of a single instance of married couples separating through Gurdjieff, but I do know of many who were brought closer together through him. His ways of dealing with people were always difficult and baffling, because unusual; but when it came to an understanding of the human psyche Gurdjieff was always right. When immediate circumstances seemed to make him appear wrong, later developments proved him right.

Physical work was organized on a fairly large scale this summer. A tramline was laid by the side of the track through the forest in the grounds leading from a stone quarry near the south gate. We wheeled tons and tons of large rocks and dumped them along the track, where we broke them up to make a road. One day, as I was working, a very strong feeling came over me that I must return to London at once. It was so compelling that I made no effort to resist it, and went up to the house and gave the excuse that urgent business had called me to England. I left at once and reached London that night. It was too late to call on my dearly loved friend Walter Fuller, as I usually did when I arrived in London, so I went on to Harpenden to spend the night with my parents. When I opened *The Times* the next morning there was an account of Fuller's sudden death, and a long obituary, for he was well-known in literary and journalistic circles and was then editor of the *Radio Times*. For several days I was numb with grief. When I returned to Fontainebleau after the funeral, Gurdjieff was very kind. He took me about with him, and one day spoke about the importance of not giving way to grief. To do so is bad for oneself and perhaps bad for the one that is gone. One cannot help feeling real grief, which is very different from the pseudo-grief which people often indulge in. But one must try not to be identified with the suffering, but to use it; in doing so one will help oneself and others.

Gurdjieff often asked me to sit with him at the café while he was writing *Beelzebub*. At this time I was trying to set down the story of my travels round the world. One day I pulled out my paper and pencil and began to write. He stopped, looked at me, and said: 'Ah, you also write!' and asked me what I was writing. I told him. He put down his pencil, flicked his moustache and said: 'If you write now people will say you are ill man. Better you wait, then perhaps can write.' I put the paper away. But the writing itch was strong and by degrees I finished the manuscript. It was no good and was properly turned down by the publishers. Years passed before I was able to get something accepted.

Gurdjieff often staged scenes in order to give us shocks. It appears that Orage had told Gurdjieff that he would stay at the Prieuré for two months, since, for reasons of his own, he had promised certain people in New York to return at the end of this period. As the time drew near Gurdjieff tried to persuade him to stay, for he needed him to go over the English version of the chapter on America on which he was then working. Also, he liked to have Orage near him, for few knew better how to joke and have fun with him without exceeding the bounds between master and pupil. Orage's mind was more nimble than Gurdjieff's; and to be with these two was better than a play. Orage was always stimulating, and as Gurdjieff saw him usually for only two months of the year, he made use of every possible moment to have him near him, and to teach him—often when they were joking. It seems that Gurdjieff thought, or pretended to think, that he had persuaded Orage to stay. On the Sunday before he was due to sail Gurdjieff organized a big party to go to Paris. After lunch seven cars were ready in the courtyard, with everyone waiting to start. As Gurdjieff was leaving his room one of the women told him that Orage was sailing the following day. He came down to the courtyard and began to storm at Orage for leaving his work at the Prieuré and going back to nonentities in New York. The air became charged with electricity. Orage said nothing, then, rather white, took his suitcase out of Gurdjieff's car and went to his room. In a few minutes Gurdjieff followed him, and a little later they both emerged, calm and composed, and got into the car. The cavalcade drove off, and after a stop at a café, arrived in Paris and went to Gurdjieff's favourite restaurant in Montmartre, l'Ecrevisse, or 'Madame Crayfish' as we called it, for dinner. Twenty of us sat down. We all stayed at the small hotel next to Gurdjieff's apartment, and talked in Orage's room until early morning. He said that having given his essence promise to return to New York he was bound to keep it. A personality promise could be changed if necessary; an essence promise never.

One day in Paris I met an acquaintance from New York who spoke about the possibilities of publishing modern literature. As I showed some interest, he offered to introduce me to a friend of his who was thinking of going into publishing, and we arranged to meet the following day at the *Select* in Montparnasse. His friend arrived; it was Aleister Crowley. Drinks were ordered, for which of course I paid, and we began to talk. Crowley had magnetism, and the kind of charm which many charlatans have; he also had a kind of dead weight that was somewhat impressive. His attitude was fatherly and benign, and a few years earlier I might have fallen for it. Now I saw and sensed that I could have nothing to do with him. He talked in general terms about publishing, and then drifted into his black-magic jargon. 'To make a success of anything,' he said, 'including publishing, you must have a certain combination. Here you must have the Master, here the Bear, there the Dragon—a triangle which will bring results . . .' and so on and so on. When he fell silent I said 'Yes, but one must have money. Am I right in supposing that you have the necessary capital?' 'I?' he asked, 'No, not a franc.' 'Neither have I,' I said.

Knowing that I was at the Prieuré he asked me if I would get him an invitation there. But I did not wish to be responsible for introducing such a man. However, to my surprise, he appeared there a few days later and was given tea in the salon. The children were there, and he said to one of the boys something about his son whom he was teaching to be a devil. Gurdjieff got up and spoke to the boy, who thereupon took no further notice of Crowley. There was some talk between Crowley and Gurdjieff, who kept a sharp watch on him all the time. I got a strong impression of two magicians, the white and the black— the one strong, powerful, full of light; the other also powerful but heavy, dull, and ignorant. Though 'black' is too strong a word for Crowley; he never understood the meaning of real black magic, yet hundreds of people came under his 'spell'. He was clever. But, as Gurdjieff says: 'He is stupid who is clever'.

Orage said about this: 'Alas, poor Crowley, I knew him well. We used to meet at the Society for Psychical Research when I was acting secretary. Once, when we were talking, he asked: "By the way, what number are you?" Not knowing in the least what he meant, I said on the spur of the moment, "Twelve". "Good God, are you really?" he replied, "I'm only seven".'

During the summer the idea had been arising in me that if my teacher, Gurdjieff, would tell me a certain something, a little secret, I would understand everything. Like the man in the fairy tales who is given three wishes and feels that everything is within his grasp; but he does not know what to ask for, and so wishes for the wrong things. It seemed to me that Orage, and especially Gurdjieff, were able to tell me something which would make everything clear, instead of as now 'through a glass darkly', and I found that this idea was shared by others. A young couple from the group in New York had been staying at the Prieuré. Twice they had said 'Goodbye' and twice they returned. When they came back for the third time I asked in surprise, 'Why have you come back again?' They said, 'Gurdjieff asked us, and we have been feeling that each time he will tell us what we want to know, and that he may tell us this time.' 'And what do you want to know?'

I asked. 'That, unfortunately, we don't know; we only know we want to know.'

I spoke to Hartmann about it, and he must have told Gurdjieff, for a day or so later the draft of a chapter in the Second Series was read —'Professor Skridloff'. In the story, Father Giovanni speaks about the difference between knowledge and understanding. 'Understanding', he says is the essence of that which one obtains from information intentionally acquired and from experiences that one has oneself lived through, whereas knowledge is only the automatic remembrance of words in a certain sequence. Knowledge can be imparted by one person to another, but it is a hundred times easier for a camel to pass through the eye of a needle than for anyone to give to another the understanding formed in him by anyone whatsoever. He said that even if he wished to impart some of his own understanding to his beloved brother he would not be able to do so. We wanted the understanding to which we were not entitled; we had yet to realize that understanding can be gained only by one's own efforts under the direction of a teacher.

Autumn came early to Fontainebleau-Avon this year, and fires had to be lighted in our rooms in late September. In the evenings a log fire burnt brightly in the salon while Gurdjieff talked or Hartmann played. We still practised the dances in the Study House, though there were no demonstrations.

Life at the Prieuré was a paradigm of the patriarchal life. Gurdjieff —with his wife, mother, brother and sister with their families, children, nephews and nieces, pupils and friends—was the great patriarch. Name-days and birthdays were remembered. It was a real man's life, an ideal for us men; as Orage said: 'We would all like to live as Gurdjieff does, but we have neither the guts nor the knowledge.' Gurdjieff stressed the importance of having good relations with those of one's own blood, especially father and mother. A wife is different—not a blood relation; a man can have several wives, but only one mother or father, his health even can be affected by a bad relationship. He said to me 'Your father, to you, is like God, and you, through father, can become like God.' An aphorism in the Study House said, 'It is a sign of a good man that he loves his Father and Mother'.

In the chapter 'My Father', in the Second Series, he tells that his Father spoke of rules by which, if kept up to the age of eighteen, young people can attain an inner freedom and prepare themselves for a happy old age. One, to love one's parents. Two, to be chaste. Three, to be outwardly courteous to all without distinction, whether they be rich or poor, friends or enemies, power-possessors or slaves, and to whatever religion they may belong—but inwardly to be free, and never to trust anyone or anything. Four, to love work for its own sake and not for gain.

III

ORAGE'S COMMENTARY ON
BEELZEBUB

WE RETURNED to New York towards the end of 1927, and resumed our work with the Group. During the winter Orage reviewed our study of *Beelzebub's Tales* of the past three years. I made copious notes of his talks and collected and collated notes and fragments from others. Later, when Orage came to London to live, I discussed the material with him over a period of three or four years and revised it. The following commentary, compiled from hundreds of pages of notes, is but a small portion of them. Although I have tried to put the notes in sequential form they are not strictly chronological. At various times he referred to the same passages, often from different viewpoints, hence there will be some repetition; and, although some of the notes may appear fragmentary, everything is connected.

Orage said: 'Some of you still criticize the faulty grammar and punctuation and ask why I do not do something about it. Well, although from the first writing the sense is in each chapter, Gurdjieff is constantly re-writing and revising. As you may know, he writes in pencil in Armenian; this is translated into Russian, and then into literal English by Russians; it is then gone over by one or two English and American pupils at the Prieuré who have only a rough knowledge of the use of words. All I can do at present is to revise the English when it obscures the sense. Although I've talked over the chapters with Gurdjieff and discussed the *sense* of them, he will never explain the meaning of anything. His task is to write the book, ours to make the effort to understand. The style and sense are Gurdjieff's. The surprising thing is that, in spite of the difficulties of translation the sense and style come through so well. It can be said that in English, this being a more flexible language than French, it is possible to play with words, so that the English translation will have a quality of its own.'

Orage cautioned us about attempting to explain to new pupils the meaning, as we understood it, of things in *Beelzebub*; one could only throw out hints. With those on the same level of understanding as oneself, discussion was useful. In the weeks that followed he reviewed the chapters; we, on our side, striving to contribute. And since we were all more or less on the same level of understanding the talks were very helpful indeed. What follows of his commentary is only an outline, so to say, of Beelzebub's Tales to Hassein—hints of the richness and depths of the wisdom. Each reader will understand according to his own inner development; at first it is like a bud; then it opens out, like a flower.

'The preface to the book,' Orage said, 'is what an overture is to an opera; the ideas to be developed are indicated lightly, they are expressed, not by direct statement, but by parable. The preface is called "The Arousing of Thought". The book opens with an invocation to all three centres, to wholeness, but especially to the Holy Ghost. The book is to be read from the real heart, that is, with emotional understanding. Normal people would begin any serious venture in an attitude of wholeness, but, on this remote lunatic planet we never do, but only partially. Gurdjieff places his hand on his heart, that is, his solar plexus, which to us is heart, since we have no Holy Ghost, no neutralizing force, since we are third force blind. He has no wish to write; he compels himself to write by will, which is indifferent to personal inclination; and this is the attitude in which each one of us ought to approach the Method. The book is an objective work of art. Objective art consists of conscious variations from the original according to the plan of the artist or writer who strives to create a definite impression on his audience. The art we know is as natural as the song or the nest of a bird. The nest of the oriole seems more perfect to us than the nest of the snipe—but we attribute no conscious value to the bird. So with John Milton and Michelangelo, "Milton sang but as the linnet sings". Gurdjieff will not use the language of the intelligentsia—ideas in the book will not be presented in our habitual thought patterns. Our intellectual life is based on chance associations which have become more or less fixed. Only when these are broken up can we begin to think freely. Our associations are mechanical; a whole mood can be destroyed by the use of one word which has a different group of associations. In a serious discussion, for example, an unthinking person, by letting drop a vulgar word, can destroy the mood of that group.

'Gurdjieff asks: "What language shall I write in?" He has begun in Russian, but cannot go far in that, for Russian is a mixture of essence and personality; Russians will philosophize for a short time, then drop into gossip, into yarns. English is useful for practical matters but inadequate for meditation and pondering on "the Whole". The psychology of the Russians and the English is like solianka, a stew in which there is everything except the essential "you" and the real "I". They cannot tell the truth about themselves.

'Armenian is essence—the Armenian of our childhood, when we spoke from essence. As we grew up we learnt "Russian and English". But one cannot express modern ideas in the language of essence. There remains Greek: but again, Greek of today is not like the Greek of one's childhood; as one grows up, one's behaviour is different. To a conscious person behaviour is a language.

'Many of the books that are written, even literary works, are manifestations of a pathological state; there is, for example, the cancerous style; the tubercular style; the syphilitic style.

'Can you, as literary critics, tell the difference between a style which is only words, and a style which is words plus content? The Song of Deborah in the Old Testament is an example of the latter. But this, though written out of the fulness of a heart, is still not objective art, because its content depends on accidental associations.

'*Beelzebub's Tales* is a book that destroys existing values; it compels the serious reader to re-value all values, and, to a sincere person, it is devastating. As Gurdjieff says, it may destroy your relish for your favourite dish—your pet theories, for example, or that form of art you happen to follow. It will be like red pepper—disturbing to your mental and emotional associations, your inertia.

'For myself, I realize now that for two years I tried to use these ideas, tried to assimilate them into my own set of values, hoping to enrich the values without giving them up. I thought that the new ideas would widen the scope and extend the perspective of the old and give variety to the content. But now I feel that the actual framework is becoming valueless. There comes a time to almost everyone in this work when he asks himself, "Shall I lose the old values that gave incentive, and shall I then be able to go on to new ones, ones of a different order?"

'Further on in the book there are implications that the universe is reasonably and intelligently conducted, and that there are many details to be taken care of, that life is not normal on our planet, but that man, by certain efforts, can become normal. Beelzebub has been exiled. What is it in us that has been exiled? We are identified with the solar plexus, with feelings. The solar plexus is a disorganized and disconnected centre. One result of continued work would be the concentration of emotion into a definite aim in place of the ups and downs of feeling, of the wasteful struggle of conflicting feelings.

'Beelzebub constructed an observatory; but only after many attempts, and when improvements had been made. We have to work a very long time on ourselves before we can begin to observe ourselves properly.

'One of the first objections often made to the Method and the system is that it is selfish and without love. Jesus said, "Take no thought for yourself". Beelzebub says, "Take thought only for yourself" (in the right way, of course), "for only then will you be able to take thought for others". There is a saying of Jesus from the Gnostics: "Follow me and you shall lose me. Follow yourselves and you shall find both me and yourselves". The Gnostics introduced this method that we are studying into Christianity; but when the "Christian" leaders of the young Church became powerful they expelled and persecuted the Gnostics.

'Karnak is an Armenian word, and is connected with the Greek idea of the body being the tomb of the soul.

'*Beelzebub's Tales* are addressed to the dead, asleep in the tomb of the body. The book is of words uttered by "I". What is understood in it will be acted upon. There is nothing in the book that I have not known; but, as yet, I have not woken up and realized it.

'You know the mantram, "More radiant than the sun, purer than the snow, subtler than the ether, is the Self within my heart. I am that Self, that Self am I". We can say that young Hassein represents that self within us. Hassein, the young "I".'

'Concerning the systems of space-ships we can say that Gurdjieff's system is a psychological system which requires active work on the part of the pupil. It replaces the older passive system of faith, love, and hope. What is the cylinder? The barrel was hermetically sealed—sealed with the seal of Hermes, who taught this method, which is the sly man's way. The denser the substances—the fog and gas of negative emotions—provided you know how to use them, the better the ship goes. In the old religions one stayed within the church, and was carried mechanically to a mechanical heaven. In this system one has to initiate things for oneself. It is a pilgrim's progress, full of difficulties and struggle, but, paradoxically, a quicker and surer way than the easy systems imported into Europe from Asia.

'Chapter Six, while being a parable, is also a cartoon. In fact, many of the chapters are cartoons in the religious sense. A cartoon here is a picture of an aspect of a man's life on this planet, exaggerated in a certain way in order to draw attention to it, to make one ponder and so arrive at the truth. This is a satire on the various religious cults, sects, rituals, mysteries, systems of breathing, fasting, and so on: all of which profess to give immortality. Rationalism came and cracked them on their noddles. But rationalism is equally negative.

' "Becoming aware of genuine Being-Duty". This is not duty to society, or "doing one's duty". From one aspect it is concerned with directing and using our body as a machine, actualizing its potentialities. Our body is a machine with many uses; at present the psyche uses the body for only a fraction of these. This is immoral. If we habitually work with only one or two centres we live as one- or two-brained beings; this is objectively immoral for a potential three-brained being. When we begin to ask ourselves, with remorse, like Hassein, "How can I pay for my existence and for all that others have done for me?", then we begin to become aware of genuine being-duty. Every three-brained being, at a certain stage—not necessarily only in this work—asks himself, "What is the meaning and aim of existence? What am I here for? Why was I born? How did I come to be born in this particular family, in these conditions? What must I do?"

'Beelzebub tells Hassein not to think about it too much yet. He is still young and must study. Later he will know what to do. We are young in the work and, like Hassein, must study—prepare ourselves—read the book. For the keys to the answers are all there, though, as Gurdjieff says, they are not near the doors.

' "He who is too lazy now to learn all he can will not be able, later, to put his knowledge into practice". To suffer in purgatory is to know and understand what we ought to do, and not yet be able to do it. But remember: "Zest with ease"; and beware of premature exercises. We are the prodigal son—or something in us is. This story, by the way, came from the Gnostics. In "The Hymn of the Robe of Glory" the son went to search for a robe which had been stolen, but he fell into mechanical life and forgot his aim. He fell on sleep; while tending the swine he woke and remembered his aim and returned to his father.

'Gurdjieff says that a perfected man is superior to the angels, the idea

129

being that men, perfected to a certain degree of reason, are cells in the mind of God. Angels are his emotions. One of the tragedies of the cosmos is that men, instead of being under solar influences, are under lunar influences—therefore lunatics. Legend has it that this is the Ridiculous or Lunatic planet. George Bernard Shaw, who says that this planet is the lunatic asylum of the universe, uses it in this sense. He got it from Lucian, who got it from the Greeks, the Greeks from the Egyptians, and the Egyptians from the ancient Babylonians and the Sumerians.

'Yet life on the maleficent planet has its compensations. While suffering from the advantage of the terrible disadvantage of being human we have the possibility of perfecting ourselves and becoming higher than the angels. There is more joy in heaven over one man perfected by his own efforts than in ninety-nine naturally evolved angels.

'Gurdjieff writes in Beelzebub: "Never will he understand the sufferings of another who has not experienced them himself, though he have divine Reason and the nature of a genuine Devil".

'This has to do with real, not ordinary mechanical suffering.'

'There exist legends in many countries and religions about an accident, a happening unforeseen by the higher powers, which caused a large fragment of the earth to split off and become the moon. Gurdjieff says that there were two fragments: and the smaller one became Kimespai, "Never allowing one to sleep in peace". In ourselves there are repeated the accidents that happened to the planet. At certain ages psychological changes occur in us—two centres are split off. We must discover in ourselves what these fragments are. We are like the dismembered Osiris. With the help of the Method we can re-member ourselves; re-collect ourselves, become whole. What is the comet that bumps into us at a certain age?

'The archangels Algamatant and Sakaki, like all the other angels and characters mentioned, are personified intelligences comparable to the principalities and powers mentioned in the Bible. There are higher, cosmic individuals, the helpers of His Endlessness in the governing of the Universe, in charge of the various solar systems, but, apparently, they are not all-intelligent or all-knowing, otherwise they would have foreseen the possibilities of a cosmic catastrophe. Only His Endlessness is all-wise, all-knowing, all-loving; and his true name, in spite of the thousand names of the Hindus and the hundreds of names of the Muslims, can never be known or uttered by ordinary man.

'We are aware of the moon, whose esoteric name is still "Loonder-perza", of whom Powys writes, "That pale traitress, the moon, the cause of all our woes", but Anulios is unknown to us. If the rationalist psychologist, artist, writer, or reformer feels in himself an ache for perfection, he pays no attention to it, or else dreams that it would be cured by better art, better writing, better living conditions. They have been dreaming of this for thousands of years, and real remorse of conscience that follows a realization of unfulfilled being-duty has no meaning for them.

'The Greek myths alone are full of analogies of a method for self-development, for perfecting oneself—the constant need for conscious labour and voluntary suffering: the Labours of Hercules, the Quest of the Golden Fleece, Ulysses, Perseus and the Gorgon, Ariadne (and the thread by which one finds the way out of the Labyrinth of Life), the war of the Greeks and Trojans for Helen—what does Helen represent in this system? And in the *Mahabharata*, too, from whose inspiration the Greeks drew their myths, the ideas are set out far more elaborately.

'The reading of the book is an exercise in sustained attention, together with imaginative understanding. To understand, an effort must be made with all three centres. Fragmentary effort fails to make a whole. How long can I hold my attention? It varies; and one has to take advantage of those periods when one finds one's attention being held by the narrative.

'Consider the epic quality of the setting of the story. It is a kind of dialogue between Beelzebub, an actualized, ideal, objectively conscious man, whose function has ceased, and who has now a critique, who is stating his conclusions impartially, constructively, and without prejudice—and a young undeveloped being who has a longing to understand.

'Beelzebub, detached and impartial, surveys and observes the body of the cosmos (as we ought to observe our organism). He implies that the universe has a purpose, and that he understands it. Solar systems, planets, beings, the life of man, all organic life, has a practical, not a theoretical or mystical function; and the various parts of the megalo-cosmos, including us men, either fulfil, or do not fulfil, their function.'

A question was asked here about Jesus, and Orage said that Jesus studied with schools which included the Essenes. At first he was hailed as a healer, but this was only a minor part of his work. He came to give people, in place of the complicated machinery constructed by the

Hebrew priests, a simple method; a system—a ship whose engines had few moving parts, so to speak.

Orage continued: 'The singular life of this planet is the result of an accident. Our moon is a result; it was not developed naturally as are the scores of other planets, but prematurely delivered. In consequence, a special kind of life had to be organized so that special radiations and vibrations could be developed in order to maintain the moon and Anulios. Beings on this planet had to be used for this purpose; but, if they realized it, they might refuse to continue their existence. In men an organ was put, Kundabuffer, which had the effect of making them see and sense reality upside down. It was as if something had been radiated into the atmosphere of the planet. As soon as the possibility of danger to cosmic harmony had passed, the organ was removed, but the consequences remained; and men, with few exceptions, have lived in a state of illusion, of dream, ever since.

'How do we explain that if we—who consider ourselves intelligent—impartially and sincerely review our behaviour at the end of each day, find that we have behaved like idiots, cowards, poltroons—that we foul our nests wherever we go? Were we to consider another's behaviour thus impartially, we would condemn him, as we usually do. Yet, for ourselves, we remain unmoved and even complacent. We are so complacent, uncritical, that we take it for granted that we are fulfilling our functions, never realizing that we, and life generally, are becoming more mechanical. The problem of why we are as we are, what life is for, what the body is for, what values we live by, never presents itself to us as something to be sensed and pondered over, as it did, for example, to the writer of Genesis, who said, mythologically but intelligently, that the fall—degradation and mechanicality—came because of our succumbing to the instinctive centre, the passive denying part. As Beelzebub says: "Your favourites, unfortunately, know only the denying part".

'We men were put into the Garden of Eden, and we were expected to take care of the Garden. We fell on sleep, ceased to make effort, and were put outside. But since in the beginning we were not entirely to blame, His Endlessness, from the time of Adam, sent his messengers one after another—patriarchs, prophets, and teachers, to present a method by which we could wake up and free ourselves from the effects of our mechanicality induced by Kundabuffer.

'Why is it that we fail to make use of, or to preserve the treasures of each succeeding civilization—the science and the art of Egypt, the philosophy and religion of India, the wisdom of Chaldea, the system of personal relations of ancient China? Why is it that we are *not* "the heirs of all the ages"? Why this urge to destroy the old? Why, instead of standing on the shoulders of the past, do we have to begin and begin, and arrive at a state in many of the arts and sciences inferior to the ancients? Why do we believe and hope in "progress", when all around us there are proofs that we are deteriorating and are working day and night to produce forces that will destroy even such as *we* have built up?

'The answer is Kundabuffer—our lack of will, our inability to make any effort to work on ourselves. But this is too small a thing for our "reformers".'

'The psyche is constantly under the influence of mass suggestions; it is the same in every man, be he white, brown, black, red, or yellow. Take the conception of the word "hero". Beelzebub tells Hassein that a hero is one who voluntarily undertakes some labour for the benefit of Creation. In this sense Gurdjieff himself is a hero. He spent thirty years tramping through Central Asia, the near and far East, enduring incredible hardships in order to satisfy his longing for knowledge and understanding and to discover and teach a method by which men could perfect themselves.

'On the planet earth, until quite recently, a "hero" was one who most easily fell under the mass psychosis of war and destroyed the lives of many men. The ancients attributed the madness of men in war to gods and devils (in the *Mahabharata* and the *Aeneid*, for example). In former times war may have been necessary for nature's purpose, but now, according to Beelzebub, war has become "a horror of horrors" in the great Universe, and a hindrance to the divine plan. Now, only man and his suggestibility are responsible for the illusion of "the pomp and circumstance of glorious war".'

'The First Descent occurs in the time of Atlantis. Whether Atlantis ever existed is of no interest to us here; but that Atlantis exists in us is of great psychological interest. Atlantis was buried in the depths of the planet. One of our tasks is to disinter the submerged Atlantis, the buried Objective Conscience.

'We ought to continue, while in an intellectual-emotional state, to make an attempt to establish a point of view about the human race. An intellectual attitude is easy, but this alone will not take us very far; it is here today and gone tomorrow. But if we will study something in an intellectual-emotional state, and discuss it practically, we shall establish a threefold state in which it will be possible to realize a truth, and this can be lasting.

'The book is the history of the origin of man, and an objective description of him. The facts are not new; they are in us, in a state of chaos and disorganization; they are not in our *consciousness*. As Gurdjieff says, "We do not try to discover something new, but to recover that which is lost". Some of the parables in the New Testament refer to this.

'As an exercise, try to imagine in one generalization the five main races of man that inhabit the earth. Each has had a history. In what succession did they appear? What are their racial characteristics, their state of evolution and degeneration? What are the objective characteristics common to all as manifested according to the results of the organ Kundabuffer? For example, every man and woman of the five great races is possessed of vanity, self-love, self-pride, egoism, etc. Yet there remains in us a certain objective standard, though often buried deep, that regards these characteristics as deplorable. What do we mean by egoism, for example? From one aspect it is believing that the organism to which I am attached is superior to others, so that I measure others by my likes and dislikes, not by their needs, but by my preferences; and I impudently criticize another for having made a slip while I am guilty of colossal blunders. Egoism is I, I, I. You may remember the anecdote in the *Conference of the Birds*. "God one day said to Moses, 'Go and get a word of advice from Satan'. So Moses went to Iblis, and asked for a word of advice. Iblis said 'Always remember this simple axiom, never say "I", so that you may never become like me' ".

'And vanity, that something for which we will sacrifice almost anything rather than it should be hurt. And self-pity, which is diabolical, though real pity is divine. These are some of the characteristics which we ourselves share with all men. Why? According to Beelzebub it is because we are biological products of an abnormal planet—we are normally abnormal. These faults of character are abnormal to real essence.

'The great religious teachers have not been reformers in the Shavian sense (Shaw never understood Jesus); they have not tried to change or re-form any given culture, but to change the chemistry of the human psyche so that men should think and feel and act normally. At the same time, all great changes which have renewed and vivified the spirit of man—all great art, music, literature, architecture—have come about through small groups of conscious men working according to the inner teachings of the great teachers. All external organized religion, of whatever kind, has come about through the distortion of the sayings of the great teachers; it is part of the process of down-flowing of the Law of the Octave, which, though conscious in its origin, is mechanical when it reaches us—involution. Evolution in us is the result of conscious labour and voluntary suffering, of the struggle against this down-flowing current.'

'Beelzebub's first descent is on account of a young and inexperienced kinsman of his who got into difficulties with King Appolis. (One calls to mind the parallel of Krishna in the *Mahabharata*.) The narrative of the first descent, from one aspect, is a warning against the reformer swayed by feelings, who maintains that "If you trust the people everything's going to be all right"—the reformer who sees the people labouring and suffering for purposes which have nothing to do with their own needs. He sees certain things clearly, but he thinks he knows what ought to be done, and this is where he goes wrong. Hence, if he succeeds in bringing about a reform in his generation, that reform becomes the abuse of the next. Beelzebub warns Hassein about entertaining certain sentimental notions about the human race. He tells him that those "slugs" have double natures. In certain moods they talk as if butter would not melt in their mouths; in other moods they act like monsters and do such things to each other as even wild beasts would shrink from. None of the other religions has been responsible for mutual destruction on such an enormous scale as the Christian, and this has done much to discredit the principle of love in the minds of many serious-minded people. Yet the principle of love in pursuit of real knowledge is indispensable. All the time people are writing and talking about love, yet they have not a glimmering of real that is, conscious love. An aphorism in the Study House says, "Practise conscious love on animals first, they are more sensitive and responsive".

'Beelzebub's descent was from the planet Mars. How do we understand this? Ares, the Greek Mars, was originally the god of games and sports; not of sport as we know it, but of the struggle to train and maintain the body to be of service. In time, as always happens, this idea of Ares degenerated into the symbol of Mars as a god of war and bloodshed. From one aspect, then, we can speak of those on the planet Mars as the Hoopoe spoke of his kind—as being engaged in "divine warfare", "divine struggle".

'We must always keep in mind what Gurdjieff says about *Beelzebub's Tales*: there are three "versions" of the book—an outer, an inner, and an inmost: also, every complete statement in the book has seven aspects. From one aspect then we must ponder what is said about the observatory on Mars, from which Beelzebub was able to observe impartially and critically the life of man on the earth. We have to learn to adopt this impartial attitude towards our own organism.'

Orage constantly spoke about not trying to change something in ourselves without instruction from Gurdjieff or one of the older pupils. If we tried to change something without working according to the Method a worse manifestation might appear. He quoted Belloc:

> Be sure to keep tight hold of nurse
> For fear of meeting something worse.

Orage said, 'If the organism becomes swept and garnished by certain pseudo-occult or revivalist methods—if it becomes purged of negative emotions, instead of the emotions being transformed by the use of the Method—seven devils worse than the first may enter. One of the extraordinary things about the Method is that, by its use, a change to normality is brought about indirectly. Through self-sensing, self-remembering, self-observation, a change is brought about in the organism as a change is made in certain chemicals if a catalyst is present. From another aspect it is as if three children, brothers, were in a room quarrelling and interfering with one another. The door slowly opens and the father looks in. He doesn't do or say anything—just observes. The quarrelling dies down and each child goes on with what he was doing.'

One of the questions asked in new groups was about increased efficiency.
Question: 'Will work in the Method improve my writing?'
Orage: 'Yes.'
Question: 'Right away?'
Orage: 'It is impossible to tell. Certainly, it will eventually.'
Question: 'But it might prevent my writing for a time. Suppose I cannot afford to wait?'
Orage: 'Then do not start working in the Method.'

This brought the discussion to what Gurdjieff often said about striving to do everything well. 'If you will begin by doing small things well, you will be able to do big things well—you will, later, be able to work on yourself well. Small things like cooking, washing up, cleaning a floor—but they must be done with attention.'

Gurdjieff and Orage, when they were teaching, when we were studying high ideas like the laws of the cosmos, were able to bring us down to small everyday things and relate these to high ideas. They never ceased to stress the importance of doing small things consciously, for only then would we be able to *understand* the smallest thing about great laws. For it is possible to *know* everything with the formatory apparatus, yet to *understand* nothing. As the proverb says: 'With all thy getting, get understanding'.

Understanding is one of the most difficult things to understand. As Gurdjieff often said, 'You don't understand what understanding means.'

In the *Conference of the Birds*, the Hoopoe, telling the birds about the Third Valley, says, 'After the valley of which I have spoken there comes another—the Valley of Understanding, which has neither beginning nor end. No way is equal to this way. Understanding, for each traveller, is enduring; but knowledge is temporary. The soul, like the body, is in a state of progress or decline; and the spiritual way reveals itself only to the degree to which the traveller has overcome his faults and weaknesses, his sleep and his inertia, and each will approach nearer to his aim according to his effort . . . There are different ways of crossing this valley, and all birds do not fly alike. Understanding can be arrived at variously—some have found the Mihrab, others the idol. When the Sun of Understanding brightens this road each receives light according to his merit, and he finds the degree assigned to him in the understanding of truth. When the mystery of the essence of beings reveals itself clearly to him, the furnace of this world becomes a garden of flowers . . . But it is necessary to have a deep and lasting wish to become as we ought to be in order to cross this difficult valley . . . As for you who are asleep! How long will you stay as you are, like a donkey without a halter?'

Attar adds: 'There is a man in China who gathers stones, without ceasing. He sheds abundant tears, and as the tears fall to the ground they change into stones, which again he gathers. If the clouds were to weep tears like these it would be a matter for sorrow and sighing. Real knowledge becomes the possession of the true seeker . . . But ordinary knowledge becomes distorted by the formalist mind; it becomes petri-fied, like stones.'

Someone asked Orage what was the difference between self-improve-ment and self-perfecting. He said 'Self-improvement is an "arrange-ment" of something that already exists. Self-perfection is an actualiza-tion of potentialities not yet developed.

'As I have said, one of our great disadvantages is that, as men, we learn nothing from the past. Not only do we learn nothing, but educa-tion and most of what is called informative writing is in a conspiracy to make us believe that the wisdom of the past, compared to what we know, is only the result, as Gurdjieff says, of "the wiseacrings of ancient barbarians". Our civilization is *not* built on preceding civilizations; and science is really a repetition, although it thinks it is discovering things for the first time. Beelzebub refers to at least two civilizations preceding historical times in which electrical inventions were carried to as high a point as in our own time. Gurdjieff says that once he took part in an expedition to the Gobi Desert. In one place, twenty yards below the surface, they found the remains of a city—below that another and still another. Other archaeologists have found similar conditions on the sites of Troy and Jericho. The people living there today have no tradition or even legends of these lost cities. It makes Egypt seem of yesterday. When I was a boy we were taught that the great earth-works in England were the remains of Roman camps. It is now being discovered that they are the remains of a civilization ancient when Rome was young, and that the great stone rings of Avebury are older by thousands of years than Stonehenge. The commonly accepted views of history are the life of man seen through a distorting mirror. Gibbon, in the beginning of his *Decline and Fall of the Roman Empire*, says that "history" is chiefly a record of crime.

'Today, the scientific attitude has taken the place of the religious attitude. One set of superstitions has replaced another. Scientists are engaged in anatomizing the corpse of the universe; they are concerned with "how", not "why". Science sees everything mechanically, through part of the moving-instinctive centre; it has no answer to human needs in a crisis. I am speaking of the ordinary scientist, who possesses an assortment of information, of partial knowledge, not veri-fied by personal experience, and which is often disproved by another "scientist".

138

'Objective science has, as its aim, the investigation of the meaning and aim of existence—not to discover more and more things, but the truth of, the real relation of, things.'

Someone asked: 'How would you define superstition?'

'Superstition,' he replied, 'is an emotional attitude towards a lie.'

Speaking of the chapter on Time, Orage said that Gurdjieff's statement, 'Time is the Unique Subjective', was the key to all that had ever been written and said on the subject.

Beelzebub says: 'Time itself no being can either understand by reason or sense by any outer or inner being function . . . It is necessary to notice that in the Great Universe all phenomena without exception, wherever they arise and are manifested, are simply successively law-conformable "fractions" of some whole phenomenon which has its prime arising on the "Most Holy Sun Absolute", and, in consequence, all cosmic phenomena, wherever they proceed, have a sense of "objectivity", and these law-conforming "fractions" are actualized in every respect, and even in the sense of their involution and evolution, according to the chief cosmic law, the sacred Heptaparaparshinokh. Only Time has no sense of objectivity because it is not the result of the fractioning of any definite cosmic phenomena. And it does not issue from anything, but blends always with everything and becomes self-sufficiently independent; and therefore, in the whole of the Universe, it alone can be called and extolled as the "Ideally-Unique-Subjective-Phenomenon" . . . Time alone (or, as it is sometimes called, the "Hero-pass") has no source from which its arising should depend; but, like Divine Love, flows always independently by itself, and blends proportionately with all the phenomena in the given place, and in the given arisings of our Great Universe.

'We are like a clock with three springs,' continued Orage, 'which vary according to heredity and early environment—all three are wound up to run for three or four hundred years. Gurdjieff says that in the beginning our organs were made to last 1500 years—the age of the patriarchs is not just a myth. What prevents our springs from lasting? The answer is, the abnormal life of man—his physical life, his emotional life, his intellectual life. The regulator of our clock does not work properly; it begins to go wrong at the age of responsibility. Why does the time of childhood and youth seem so long and the rest of life seem to go so quickly, to be so short? Time is the potentiality of experience, the number of experiences contained in a given centre; and these experiences can be successive, sequential, or simultaneous. The "time" of our lives will depend on the rate at which these potential experiences are exhausted. You know the aphorism in the Study House: "Man has a limited number of experiences—economizing them, he prolongs his life".

'Beelzebub speaks of the short duration of life of the beings in a drop of water compared with ours. Similarly, if this room we are in, and we with it, were to shrink to the size of a tennis ball, we would not be aware of it. Perhaps this is what happened to the ants and the bees millions of years ago; enormous creatures then, they degenerated and became a danger to the cosmic scheme, so Nature shrank them. Time and life today may seem the same to them now as then. It may be that if the degeneration of man continues, if his energy continues to be diverted to trivialities, if scientists continue to invent more fantastic means of destruction, if men continue to pollute and poison the rivers and the earth with chemicals and sprays—then Nature may do to them what she did to the ants and bees.

'As we are, experiences happen to us—we do not, and we cannot, use them consciously until we learn to control the physical and emotional energy that pours out when we are confronted by sudden, unexpected occurrences. For example, a person reads something in the paper, or hears of something, and at once he becomes identified; he feels intensely; and valuable emotional and mental energy is wasted; he has shortened his time. The same with difficult experiences with people, which may cause us to unwind, in a few minutes or hours, years of potential normal unwinding.

'Time is the infinite, absolute, potential of all experience.'

To a question asked about space being curved, Orage said, 'We can understand something of this by studying the working of the law of the octave in ourselves. Since space also obeys the law of the deflection of the lines of force, a line taken from a point in space will eventually come back to itself. Space also must be conceived in octaves and is therefore curved.

'There are three dimensions of space and time: Succession—line; simultaneity—plane; seeing three or more successions—eternity. Eternity is observing all potentialities of a series simultaneously. Professor Eddington, speaking of himself as a four-dimensional worm, is on the verge of a concept of three-dimensional time. Really, he is only two-dimensional in his concept; the third dimension enters if you see all your past, present, and future simultaneously. Gurdjieff calls us "sheep"— we move on a sort of one-dimensional line.

'Recurrence is a sphere. Lines of latitude make circles—an octave of them from the equator; and beings have a longevity corresponding to their latitude of time; those nearest the pole being the shortest. Lines of longitude are spatial; longitude is reincarnation in space, latitude is recurrence in time. Without going into a great deal of theory this cannot now be clear to you; the minds you have now are incapable of grasping these ideas. We aim to develop minds to which these ideas will be as easy relatively as ideas of two dimensions are now.'

Someone asked: 'Do you exclude people who apparently can foretell the future or read the past?'

Orage: 'I never met one who could. When I was an investigator for the Society for Psychical Research I never saw or heard of an authentic case. Potentialities may be seen, but longitude and latitude cannot be determined for the actualization. Incidentally, I never came across any so-called supernatural phenomena that could not be explained by natural means.

'One of the aims of Gurdjieff's book is to induce despair in the best trained minds concerning their type of reason.'

'Beelzebub represents the ideal normal man. His function on this planet has ceased. He has the whole of human experience behind him. He has a critique of human nature. He is objective, impartial, unprejudiced. He is indignant, but capable of pity and benevolence. He has made use of his exile to lead a conscious existence, and has spared no effort to actualize his potentialities. He is what we might be. He is what we ought to be. In his talks he presents us with a method by which we may become what we ought to be.

'Beelzebub sees human beings existing in conditions for which they themselves are responsible; conditions not "becoming" to three-centred beings. "Becoming" here means both "fitting" and that which will enable them to "become", to "be". Because of the system of education, cognizance of the cosmos in which they live has disappeared from their psyche. As we are aware of the flora and fauna of nature and of the civilization in which we exist, so three-centred beings should be aware of the functions of the cosmos—the sun in relation to the planets, the earth to the moon. This would be "being-knowledge", that is, direct personal knowledge, not hearsay. A normal three-centred being would understand cosmic phenomena, and how he is affected by radiations, emanations, tensions. Being abnormal, we are unaware of this, or we see it distorted. Why? Gurdjieff himself is a mirror to each one of us, which reflects reality. The book is this kind of mirror. Kundabuffer is also a mirror—but a distorting mirror in which we see reality upside-down. Education is the result of the consequences of the organ Kunda-buffer. Plato said that his republic could be set up only if he could begin with new-born children; but since they have to be educated by adults they would be spoiled. Plato, of course, was the philosopher, while Socrates was the teacher of a method, as well as a philosopher. Many people today have intelligence superior to their conduct; they are free from superstition about religion, science, morals, and politics, but continue to be irrational about their children. They see the stupidities of the educational system, yet continue to bring their children up in it.'

'According to Beelzebub our sun neither lights nor heats. Apart from its psychological implications, what do we know by personal knowledge about the cause of heat and light coming to our planet? Only yesterday, relatively, the whole authority of the Church taught that the sun was a small ball of fire revolving round the earth, created to give us light and heat, and almost everyone believed it. Now, scientists teach that the sun is an enormous globe of fire whose flames shoot thousands of miles into its atmosphere, and almost everyone believes it. How do they know? Beelzebub says that the sun is cold and icy and that heat and light are the remorse of matter. The Sacred Aieioiuoa is the sigh of objective remorse. It is what one should feel in the presence of a being who has developed himself into a higher state of consciousness than one's own—a wish to be what one ought to be.

'Our planet, the earth, is the shame of our solar system. It is the ugly duckling, the misshapen dwarf, the beast of the fairy tales, the fairy tales in which are enshrined fragments of real teaching so that it should not be suspected of heretical propaganda. The idea is that, if men could become normal, this planet might redeem the solar system. The troubadors, too, taught this idea; they were emissaries of an esoteric school.'

'The whole of the Universe exists because of, and is maintained by, the Trogoautoegocratic system—reciprocal feeding. I, myself, eat. I feed on three foods—ordinary food, air, and impressions. We feed on each other; with some people you can say "He or she feeds me; after I have talked with them I feel nourished". Others are vampires, they will suck you dry—if you are foolish enough to let them. The food I eat is changed into substances which become the cells of my body. I am what I have eaten and digested—literally, I have eaten myself.

'The Universe is a comparable being, which eats to live. Every part of the physical universe is a product of the eating of the Great "I". "The Great I AM", which is God. This idea is to be found in myths. The early Christians thought that Jesus cut off parts of his flesh, and that his disciples ate it and drank his blood. According to Gurdjieff something like this actually happened. Many rites and ceremonies are connected with this idea (the Holy Communion, for example), and of course, distorted. In the rites of cannibalism, and in the eating of the sex organs —the source of procreation and virility—we have an example of complete distortion.

'My body eats. Where then is "I"?'

'Gurdjieff says that we must learn to distinguish between "I" and "It". What is "I"? We can offer no evidence for Individuality, Consciousness and Will, the triad or triangle of which "I" is composed. Yet we can have, in time and with work, a realization of something which is not just organism. The birth of "I" and its development has been the subject of allegorical teachings in all religions, and it was taught in the Mysteries. It plays a great part in the story of Jesus.

'If one of thine "I's" offend thee, pluck it out.

'If thine "I" be single thy whole body shall be full of light.

'Be still, and know that "I" am God.

'I Am that I Am.

' "I" is under the Law of Three.

' "It" is under the Law of Seven.

'If we have a metaphysical background it is easier to understand much of Gurdjieff's teaching. We should be able to discriminate between the potential and the actual. Read Saurat's *Three Conventions*.'

In speaking of the chapter on Art Orage said that in the time of Pythagoras artists were talked to while they worked to prevent their being emotionally caught up in their task.

He continued, 'There are two categories of art, subjective and objective—unconscious and conscious.

'Art evokes a range of emotions that nature would, but cannot, produce. The degree to which the artist is conscious in this defines his importance from our point of view. The artist must be in the spirit of

Nature, in the laws of Nature. An understanding of the mathematical principles of Nature is not an understanding of the dynamics of Nature. The artist's understanding is different from the scientist's description of its tracks. The scientist cannot anticipate Nature; the artist should be able to.

'The subjective artist pursues art for personal development. The aim of the objective artist is to produce a definite and calculated effect on people; his own personal aim may be included in this.

'Art is a means of communicating emotion. Subjective art satisfies the artist; objective art affects the recipient as the artist intended.

'Objective art is based on the understood principles of the Law of Seven in architecture, painting, and sculpture, music, writing, dancing, drama. Ruskin in his *Seven Lamps* was on the trail, but became confused. Hokusai said that when he died he hoped to join that group of Nature's artists who draw with light, and who create flowers. Blake had a vision of true creation:

> Tyger, tyger, burning bright
> In the forests of the night,
> What immortal hand, or eye
> Could frame thy fearful symmetry!

'The modern use of the word "creation" is out of place. Modern art just happens. We are speaking of the Bohemian, the typical subjective artist, expressing himself. Many artists have only aesthetic, not human emotions. We may say, "Pursue art, pursue reason". True artists are the antennae of Nature; coming Nature casts its artists before it. There is an aphorism in the Study House: "Love not art with your feelings".

'Objective art brings about a state of non-identification. The one great art, so far as this work is concerned, is that of making a complete human being of oneself.'

'In the chapter on "The Arch Absurd", Beelzebub says that we make no use of the first and third holy forces; he says: "For the coating of their own presences there are only the crystallizations of the second part of the Omnipresent Okidanohk, the Holy Denying; hence it is that the majority of them remain with presences consisting of the planetary body alone, and thus, for themselves, are destroyed for ever".

'Has it ever occurred to you that almost all of human activity is concerned, not with satisfying the legitimate *needs* of the planetary body, but with gratifying its desires and weaknesses? Take Wall Street, the Royal Exchange, the shops on Fifth Avenue and Bond Street, think of the millions who are occupied in making articles to gratify the whims and vanities of women—the millions spent on arms and explosives, on sport, on artificial fertilizers that poison the land, on the drugs devised to relieve the consequent diseases. Think of the thousands of acres of trees cut down every month to make pulp on which the vapourings of journalists and illiterate writers are printed; the energy that goes into the production of aeroplanes and cars! As the tempo of life is speeded up and life becomes more and more complicated, so man has less and less of what is his own. All of this energy and tension, useless for one's being, is taken by Nature for her own purposes.

'One of the great illusions consequent on the organ Kundabuffer is that the pursuit of happiness as an aim in itself is good. If we have a real aim, then we may obtain happiness as a by-product.'

'Although we may be familiar with theories, we cannot understand anything about the Universe until we have established a correspondence in ourselves. Gurjdieff condemns our use of the imagination because we use it chiefly in fantasy. But the book provides an opportunity for making right use of it; one of the exercises in the use of the imagination is that of the frequent shift from the personal to the universal, and vice versa.

'If we understand something of the working of the active, passive, and neutralizing forces in ourselves, we can then understand something of the Law of Three in the Universe; the same with the Law of Seven. Have you yet had some realization of the working of these two laws (whose processes are going on all the time) in yourselves? If not, it will be only knowledge; and as such, may disappear.

'Ninety-six per cent of our civilization is concerned with the instinctive-moving centre, the planetary body; three per cent with real culture, the emotions; one per cent with "WHY?", the real mind. The instinctive-moving centre, which should be the passive part, has, in our civilization, become the active, the positive. We are the inverted man, crucified upside-down.'

'Pythagoras taught this system and method, but no record of his teaching remains except some fragments from perhaps one of his subsidiary groups. The books written about him are almost all supposition. But his teaching had an enormous influence. Plato's *Timaeus* contains the cosmogony of Pythagoras. Some of Gurdjieff's dances and movements are based on the fragments of Pythagoras' teaching—"The Initiation of the Priestess; a Fragment of a Mystery", for example. When Aristotle began the sections of his book on metaphysics he meant to discuss space, time, thought, and force in the light of the teaching he had received from Pythagoras; but it seems that he never got on with it.'

'The peculiarity of beings on this planet is due to special conditions; these beings are unique, especially in the nature of their distorted reason. Why do I think that most of the people I meet are fools? Why do they think that I am a fool, and pity me? And why are we both right? Why do we in our calmer moments recognize the essential senselessness of people? Why is it that it is so easy to see the faults in others and so difficult to see them in ourselves? This has always been known; see Socrates, and the story of Sakuntala in the *Mahabharata*.

'This senselessness is taken for granted by the power-possessing beings, and is used in their dealings with what they call "the broad masses" or "the people". Why do we find it difficult to behave reasonably when confronted with a body of people? Everyone recognizes that seventy-five per cent of laws and regulations are stupid, and tries to evade them. Yet seldom does anyone protest.'

'Heat and light are the remorse of matter. When we are in a state of self-remembering, elements in our body experience remorse, not a feeling of inferiority but a kind of sorrow for what we are, combined with aspiration, and a light dawns on us; we can observe something in ourselves that had been hidden in darkness.

'It is sometimes said in modern physics that we are the products of electricity. The three forces are assembled in one—Okidanokh, electricity—positive, negative, and neutralizing. Gurdjieff says that two previous civilizations have gone down because of too much mechanical use of electricity; ours may be the third. Owing to this extreme mechanical use there is less for psychological use—hence the will-lessness, the aimlessness of people. Education is affected. In our time education leaves off where in ancient times education began, that is, between the ages of eighteen and twenty-one, the idealistic period when youth is waiting for something that will give more meaning to life than it sees manifested in the lives of those around it. At this idealistic period life is full of electricity, but there is no one to show youth what to do with it. The

146

result is that the most idealistic become cynical, become cranks, or take to drugs, or go in for an over-indulgence in sex; they fall back on their instinctive-moving centre.'

'In the chapter "Why Men are not Men" we are told that because of some "unforeseeingness" on the part of the Higher Individuums, a comet collided with the earth, and two pieces were split off. Organically, we are the product of the planet, and we reproduce the organic deficiencies of the planet. Two centres were split off—our nature became split. Sakaki came to earth to investigate and found that it was necessary that the earth and all life on it should supply the two satellites with a substance called Askokin. This could only be obtained by sweat, by effort—physical, emotional, and mental. Every organism, every atom, had to bear its share of the burden. Sakaki feared that the people on this planet, who were not perhaps sufficiently developed in reason, would revolt, and refuse to have children; so the organ Kundabuffer was made to grow in them. This had the effect of making them "see reality upside-down"; they took the ephemeral for the real; and for the first time they began to do something which was not done on any other planet—they began to destroy each other's lives, and Nature received the help she needed. As soon as it was deemed to be safe, His Endlessness had the organ removed, but the consequences remained. Man continued in his state of sleep; and from later Babylonian times, eight thousand years ago, he has slowly degenerated. We happen to be living in a period when the process of degeneration is being accelerated —even from the eighteenth century it has speeded up.

'Why this command of God "In the sweat of thy face shalt thou eat bread"? Why this curse of labour, the need to sweat? Why this apparent malevolence of God? According to Beelzebub, it is not malevolence, but a cosmic necessity. No one can escape, everyone must pay. But His Endlessness, almost from the foundation of the world, sent his Messengers to the earth, and continues to send them to teach men how to pay Nature and at the same time to work on themselves and use part of their efforts for their own being. His Messengers taught men the Method by which He Himself overcame the merciless Heropass. He gave them his only begotten Son, so that they themselves might become Sons of God and help Him in His divine purpose. This Method, in various forms, was taught by all the great teachers. We have now the possibility of paying consciously, so that even the curse itself can become a blessing. Plato, who had learnt the method from Socrates and studied the system with the priests in Egypt, said: "God's curses are our opportunities".

' "Ye are not your own, ye are bought with a price", said Paul.'

'We are dual-natured, "I" and "It", but we are only vaguely conscious of this state. As we are, the body is of no help to consciousness. When we have learnt to separate "I" from "It" then we may make use of the body. In doing Gurdjieff's movements and dances we are making use of the body—we are constrained to make an effort to be conscious. Why is the body not reflective of the mind? Why is there no correspondence between body and consciousness? Why are we like strangers in the body? Paul said: "The things I do, I would not; those I would not, I do".

'Abnormality includes not only human nature, but all nature: "The whole creation groans and travails, waiting for the manifestation of the Sons of God". Earth suffers for some cosmic purpose. If we ourselves meet misfortunes with complaining and self-pity, we suffer more and make others suffer. If we meet them consciously we can make an effort to turn them to our advantage, to our highest use. It is not enough to suffer in silence; this may result in a state of resentment. Conscious effort produces understanding. Beelzebub himself had to sweat to *understand* what he already *knew*.'

Someone voiced the perennial question: 'While I am here, in the group, listening to you, I feel with my feelings that all this is true; here I feel that I can do and that henceforth I will live according to the teaching. But I know, in my mind, that when I leave the meeting all the old weaknesses will present themselves. I shall forget and live the same old way, repeating and repeating, until I come to the group again.'

'From the tone of your voice,' Orage replied, 'it appears that you are in danger of giving way to despondency—the eighth deadly sin. In this work it is as if one were beginning again and again. Each time you make an effort you acquire a little more spiritual muscle. Like a child learning to walk you begin again and again; and this work is infinitely more difficult and complicated. But results are guaranteed. We must remember that because of the effects of the organ Kundabuffer we suffer from a kind of spinal disease which affects us as opium would; hence our difficulty in making real effort. It has made us lunatics; and although the organ is now only vestigial the results are still there. Generally speaking, we are born sane, but become insane through the influence of our elders, through the desire to do as others do, through education in the wide sense—that enemy of the human race.'

'What is the real meaning of sacrifice and sacrifices? Beelzebub speaks a great deal about it. The great teachers and heroes sacrifice themselves for humanity. In some cases they are actually put to death on earth as a sacrifice. Jesus, for example. And, according to Beelzebub, Judas (who was the nearest to Jesus and the most trusted) sacrificed himself for the good of the other disciples and for posterity.'

I said: 'It has always seemed to me that there is something wrong or something distorted in the evolutionists' theory that sacrifices and fertility rituals were the beginnings of the religious ideas of primitive peoples. It must be the other way round. The idea of a God or Hero dying for the good of humanity became distorted, became mixed with distorted religious ideas; God became incarnated in the King, and the King was sacrificed. It is said that the death of William Rufus, for example, was a ritual sacrifice to the old (not the Christian) religion. There are many examples of the sacrifice of a king or a priest, to say nothing of ordinary men, for the good of the people.'

Orage replied: 'There is much in what you say. It is possible, also, that in ancient times real priests understood that it was necessary at certain periods to have large numbers of deaths, hence the enormous number of animals sacrificed by the ancient Hindu, Semitic, and Greek peoples. In the *Mahabharata* it says that the gods are fed by sacrifices. But what sacrifices?

'From one aspect we can take the slaughter of beings in the Third Descent as slaughter of innocent instinctive desires. Again, from one of the seven aspects, the three centres of culture are three forms of Yoga, each being destructive of the unity of the whole. The third descent is to the instinctive-moving centre, where innocent desires are sacrificed by puritans, monks, ascetics of all kinds who suppress natural physical needs, instincts, and wishes.

'Objective instinctive duties are to be good father-mother, husband-wife, brother-sister, son-daughter, and citizen. Ascetic Yoga, in the wide sense, makes these virtually impossible.

'All this has a bearing on reciprocal feeding, the Trogoautoegocrat. In the Christian religion, the idea of sacrifice has degenerated into giving up things we enjoy. It reached its extreme with the Puritans, who passed laws abolishing dancing, secular singing, festivals, plays, bear-baiting, and above all, sex—because people enjoyed these. The Puritan, the most intolerant of people, believes that if a thing is unpleasant it must be good for you. In this sense we are all perverted Puritans; we will sacrifice anything but our mechanical suffering. But if we wish to progress in this work we *must* sacrifice this mechanical suffering—resentment, irritation, despondency, self-pity, sentimentality—all that represents our personality. The pangs of death of personality are the labour pains of the birth of "I". Angelus Silesius said: "I myself must become Mary and give birth to God".'

'We make an effort, by pondering and sensing, through contemplation, to understand these ideas, and when we do understand we have a sense and feeling of light. This is the true light of the Gospels which we receive through "the tender mercy of our God; whereby the day-spring from on high hath visited us, to give light to them that sit in darkness". The light of understanding: "Hail, gladdening Light, of His pure glory poured". Saints and poets have always known it. When we fail to understand, the sense of the impossibility produces an emotion. One exclaims "Why can't I understand?" We are then like the snake biting its own tail in disgust with itself. But by striving to understand we develop the real mind; for this it is necessary for all centres to work together.'

'Primordial substance is one. But one is three; affirming, denying, reconciling; or positive, negative, neutralizing. Can you differentiate these three? Briefly in an atom of hydrogen the proton is the positive, the electron the negative, the movement of the electron around the proton produces energy—the neutralizing. This is a highly metaphysical concept. We have three brains, each manifesting a form of electricity. A normal being is one in whom these three correspond. Nature has developed the brain of the planetary body almost to perfection (though we have spoilt it) but has left it to us to develop the brains of the emotional and mental centres. As such, we are abnormal. "Yes" is of the mind, "No" is of the body, the reconciling is of the emotions. Body knows the "how" of things, mind knows the "what" of things; emotion, plus mind and body, understands the "why" of things. Scientists are interested in "how", not "why". Any new invention, regardless of the harm it may do to humanity, is regarded as "sacred" by the masses—the modern superstition that knowledge is an end in itself is thus justified. An aphorism in the Study House says:

"Take the knowledge of the West and the understanding of the East, and then seek." Knowledge without understanding is the root of all kinds of evil.'

'Understanding and "I" are one. To be able to stand outside oneself— this is the original meaning of ecstasy. Eastern mystical poets used erotic love as a similitude. In the height of sexual love they experienced a sense of being outside themselves, a non-identification; not, as among most people, what Gurdjieff calls "palpitating self-oblivion". Nature will not help us to develop the second and third bodies. She has supplied us with the substances, and we, by the use of the Method, can transmute these substances into material for the higher bodies.

'In the "Second Descent", the story of engulfed Atlantis may be compared with the Objective Conscience, buried deeply within us, swallowed up in personality. Objective Conscience is the function of a normal being; it is the representative of God in the essence. What is John the Baptist? It is objective conscience crying in the wilderness of the body; beheaded by external life.'

'Beelzebub uses a superstition of the beings of this planet in order to carry out his aim. We, in this work, have to be on our guard even against teachers. The reason of ordinary man is so fantastic that teachers have to resort to tricks and even lies for a good end. Gurdjieff constantly plays tricks with us to compel us to use our reason. He has written an aphorism in the Study House, "If you have not a critical mind by nature your staying here is useless". We assume that Jesus taught the gospel of love for our good. It might have been for our good if we could have understood it; and still can be if we learn to distinguish between the three main kinds of love (though there are seven in all), and learn how to practise conscious love. And when we have disinterred the buried objective conscience we shall have an infallible guide. Jesus no doubt was aware of the ultimate effects (according to the law of the deflection of the line of force, the law of the octave), of the deleterious effects of mechanical love, which, like everything unconscious, is evil. According to the Greek texts Jesus himself used two different words when speaking of conscious and unconscious love.'

'One of the chief purposes of a man is to develop from a substance called "essence", a special kind of reason—objective reason—which will establish him as a permanent brain-cell of all life. Man, by attaining to objective reason, can help to redeem Creation. Nature, says Gurdjieff, needs these relatively liberated beings. As we develop consciousness, will and individuality, we take our place as one of the brain-cells of the Universe. The reason of ordinary man is the reason of knowledge; the reason of developed man is the reason of understanding. Instinctive reason we share with the animals, but have a higher type of it. Associative reason functions according to verbal associations. Of objective reason, at present, we know very little; again, this can be developed only by the practice of being-Parktdolg-duty. Objective reason is the opposite of mere intellectualism, mere philosophical speculation, which produce only monsters.

'Bernard Shaw once told me that when he was about the age of twenty-five he had a realization of Nature's purpose in this respect—the development of brains. But Shaw worked chiefly with his mental centre, and he became a reformer, not a teacher.

'In the Third Descent there is also a hit against the self-indulgence in sentimentality of the Hindus and modern English in their attitude to animals—the negative emotion of sentimentality masquerading as humanitarianism.'

'What is the poppy-seed that Beelzebub speaks about in the narrative of his third flight to the planet earth? What are its effects? Poppy-seed made people invent values, made it impossible for them to see reality, prevented them from taking their own instincts and experience as a guide. Take the contemporary role of advertising and connect it with the number of things we do, things we obtain, things we desire, all of which yield us no being-satisfaction; add to this the craze for publicity. In the *Mahabharata* there are many references to the endless desires of man for ephemeral things; however many he obtains there are always more clamouring to be satisfied. The useless wishes and desires of the organism are like the creeping buttercup, which, unless it is checked, will smother a mellow garden. The chewing of poppy-seed begins in infancy, when we take our parents and nurses seriously. Most children are the fore-ordained victims of the salesman. It goes on through life. If someone tells me a tonic truth which shows me something about myself, my vanity and self-love are hurt. I resent it. If he tells me something flattering, though it may be bad for me, I am his friend for life. How many people regard public celebrities as "great people", celebrities who in private are vain, conceited, and touchy. The masses worship dictators and regard as "great men" those who in reality are immersed in vanity, self-pride, self-love and egoism to the point of madness. We admire showmanship. H. G. Wells, for example, when young, read the books of C. H. Hinton, which were full of strange ideas. Hinton was a mathematician who put his ideas into the form of stories —*Scientific Romances*; but he was an indifferent writer. Wells was a good salesman, showman. He developed some of Hinton's ideas in *The Time Machine* and other books, and made a name and money for himself. Hinton remained obscure.

'Only in the form of myths and stories can people absorb truths. Gurdjieff's other book on which he is now working, *Stories of Remarkable Men* he had met, are masterpieces of the short story in narrative form—stories containing fragments of truths. Apropos, Gurdjieff when young studied Indian philosophy, and later read Madame Blavatsky's books, and in the course of his travels in India and Tibet discovered that nine out of ten of her references were not based on her personal knowledge. He said that it cost him several years of exploring to verify this. In Tibet he was not a foreign agent; he got himself appointed collector of dues from the monasteries for the Dalai Lama, and in this role was able to go into any monastery. He discovered instances of abnormal development, "high elevations", what are called "magic powers", but he says that he found little, apart from something in certain dances and ceremonies, which could be described as objective knowledge. Most of the powers developed by certain monks were diversions from the normal—interesting, but not useful for a method of self-development for people of the Western world, such as he had in mind. But the life of the Tibetan people was far less spoilt and nearer to a normal life than perhaps any on the planet at the present day. It has been less subject to the deteriorating influence of Western civilization on the one hand, and to the destructive influence of Communism on the other, than any other country. But the time is not far distant when the "sea of mud", as Gurdjieff calls it, of these two forces, will engulf the life of the Tibetans, as it is smothering the old life of the rest of the planet.

'During the journey to Tibet, Beelzebub relates how he and his companions had to make a ring of fire at night to keep away wild beasts. When we are in a state of self-remembering, we are safe from the attacks of negative emotions. When we are asleep, off our guard, "at night", they attack us. Buddha taught the method. He taught his disciples how to bear the displeasing manifestations of others; but gradually they went off the path, and eventually reached the heights of intellectualism where "life" is not possible. In the West, too, there are people who know with their minds everything about Buddhism, but understand nothing with their "being". Buddha, like Pythagoras and Jesus, was a practical workman, not merely a talker.'

'We must apply the chapter on apes to ourselves. We are a sort of ape, caricatures of normal beings. There are extreme cases—the speculative philosopher, dealing in words and concepts; the priest, dealing in symbols whose meaning he has forgotten; the financier, who has forgotten the purpose of money and deals in it only as a commodity. They work with one centre. Consider also the volumes of writings on metaphysics—the intellectual centre trying to produce by itself. Intellectualism is mere words, and produces no effect on the emotional centre.

'Beelzebub takes some apes to Mars to see if it is possible to make human beings out of them. Can we, apes, by working in the Method, become human, normal human beings?

'In the course of our existence, as we grow up, essence (in which is hidden objective conscience) becomes submerged, and there remains only personality, in which the three centres become separated. It is possible to be highly developed in one centre, rudimentary in another, and atrophied in a third. Before birth the embryo repeats physiologically the history of the species; after birth, according to Gurdjieff, we repeat the history of the planet; two centres are split off, objective conscience sinks, deserts appear, emotional deserts. The mental centre, which should be active, father, no longer seeks out the instinctive centre, which should be passive, mother; and so, instead of producing a reconciling result represented by a child—the emotional centre, the mental centre becomes, as it were, homosexual; titillation in place of breeding, words and words—mental masturbation. Apes are those whose activity is not according to objective reason.

'The Yogi is another type—self-abstracted, occupied only with the mental processes.

'Not one of us here works with three centres simultaneously; we, also, deal too much in words. In this sense we are mechanical, hence sinners, coming short of the glory of God. Gurdjieff's tremendous power and being is the result of his living and working simultaneously in three centres. This is real work. At the Institute in Fontainebleau we are shown how to work with three centres. The movements and the dances here in New York are a means to this end.'

'In Egypt, Beelzebub put himself into a certain "being-state called

Soorptakalknian contemplation", in which it was possible to read thought-forms called "Korkaptilnian thought tapes" left by previous beings who had attained objective reason. But they can be read and understood only by those who have attained the necessary degree of objective reason, like Gurdjieff, for example. Certain others, like some of the saints and mystics, may read them, but only accidentally and partially; and they are never fully understood. Certain pathological types may get a bit here and a bit there and make a mish-mash of it. This idea may throw light on phenomena like automatic writing, visions, revelations.

'When Mabel Collins produced *Light on the Path* by automatic writing, Madame Blavatsky said that it was a translation of a very rare book, unknown in the West. But the Theosophists did not have the Method; and their teaching, lacking the discipline of the Method, became thinned down to Professor Kishmehoff's famous chicken soup.

'In the "being-state called Soorptakalknian contemplation" Beelzebub learned about Belcultassi, founder of the Society of Akhaldans. One day Belcultassi had a realization of a stupid blunder he had made, and, instead of indulging in self-calming and putting it out of his mind, he began to review his past life seriously and impartially. As a result of his pondering he found this incident no more stupid than other acts in his life; but, because more vivid, it seemed worse.

'How often have you and I done things so foolish and stupid that, if they had been found out, would have ruined something precious?

'Belcultassi, reviewing his life impartially, discovered that there was no correspondence between what he had wished to do and what he had done; there was always a contradiction between his wishes and theories and his actual doing. He concluded that he must be a special kind of fool, and that it was impossible that his friends and acquaintances should be as stupid as he, for they all seemed to be so well-balanced. He then questioned his friends, confessing his folly and asking them to condemn him. His sincerity disarmed them, and they began to acknowledge that they also were leading equally senseless lives. They formed a research society for the purpose of investigating the meaning and aim of existence, and to seek a cure for the insanity of being in possession of three centres, each of which spoke a different language. They began as a small private group—not to "confess their sins" in orgies of emotion, but to be sincere in the group and to speak about their faults and weaknesses, and to try to observe them impartially. They reviewed their past lives and their current behaviour, and formulated the results for the group. Later they divided into five groups.

'Do you follow the meaning of this? Do you begin to understand how we must apply this to ourselves?

'One of these groups was concerned with mathematics in its broadest sense. Gurdjieff says that life is based on mathematics; all great art, great music has mathematics as its base. Thoughts vary in weight and rapidity, feelings in intensity, muscular movements in stress. Can you observe and tell the difference between these weights, intensities, stresses? To do this would be introducing *measure* into psychology. Modern psychology is only physiology. Who can measure and weigh in himself, and differentiate between, two thoughts? For example, Gurdjieff says, "Time is the Unique Subjective". Contrast this with the volumes of Alexander on *Space, Time, and Deity*, etc. Alexander says "Time is the Father of Space"; and in this, so much is assumed as being understood; so much is fanciful, and has nothing to do with me. Gurdjieff's phrase is so much weightier, and at once makes a greater personal impact. In Indian philosophy it is often said, "Time is 'I' ". This is similar to Gurdjieff's phrase, but of different weight.

'Emotion. Americans sometimes say "I am just crazy about it", where there is really only a small degree of interest. Those who have real emotions do not use superlative expressions for mediocre feelings. Those who have genuine emotions, even when speaking of an intense experience, will, if they can conceive of a more intense experience, continue to use the comparative.

'Can you distinguish between stresses? the difference, say, between seven and eight pounds weight?

'We must try to observe the manifestations resulting from our perceptions. We receive perceptions and manifest results.

'Another group investigated rates of vibrations. How can we, by conscious labour and voluntary suffering, raise the rate of vibrations in our own organism?

'The fourth group studied physics and chemistry. They observed, among other things, changes produced in themselves by the passage of perceptions.

'The fifth group studied phenomena occurring within themselves as a result of the working of the three centres.

'When they had made a study of the phenomena included in the five categories, they discovered that something else was necessary, and they decided to send out delegates to try to discover more advanced students than themselves. They went to Africa. Africa, in this context, is a sort of cartoon of the organism; but where is the instinctive-moving centre, the emotional, the mental centre? There is also here a description of the ancient Egyptian system and method of self-development, of self-perfectioning, and an explanation of Beelzebub's system. The one was admirably adapted to the people of that time, as Beelzebub's is to our own.

'Our emotional system is a climate—or a variety of climates. Can you chart the changing winds of your moods? Can you change from a low damp negative state to a bright breezy day? The answer, at present, is "No". While we remain as we are, we are at the mercy of every person we meet, every event, every meal we eat; we are the sport of every wind that blows.

'The ancient Egyptian priests had a conscious aim. While teaching their students how to change the negative substances in themselves to positive, they were also making changes in the exterior life of Egypt by the use of examples of objective art. The Greeks called them " Masters of Dreams "—not victims. The Sphinx, for example, is a copy of the original which existed in ancient Chaldea. In the original figure three parts were connected; a fourth was insulated by amber. The Egyptian Sphinx connoted interrogation, Why? It had no wings; for essence, which stimulated aspiration, was missing.

'The flowering of Greek culture was an indirect product of the contact of the philosophers with Egyptian schools. As a beautiful ordered garden does not happen by accident but comes about because of a kind of conscious love on the part of the gardener, so does a flowering of real culture in any civilization come about by the work of a few conscious beings. Pythagoras, Socrates, Plato, and Solon, among others, went to Egypt to study.'

'If we ponder the sayings of Beelzebub, and formulate them in our own terms, reason will have served one of its functions—to shorten the period needed for self-development; to provide us with a means shorter than arriving by trial and error through the senses.

'In the Fifth Descent Beelzebub relates that he observed from Mars that the life of man was becoming shorter. He descended to earth to investigate. In the then modern Babylon degeneration of the psyche of man had begun. Previous to this the conception of science in ancient Babylon was based on the development of the normal potentialities of man; it was taken for granted that one of the obligations of life was the development of the second and third centres, or bodies—just as ordinary education is taken for granted in our time. Life in ancient Babylon was organized for this; and art, literature, and occupation were subordinate to it. But when intuition and potentialities waned, mechanical means took their place; the objective scientist was supplanted by the "scientist of new format" who has no intuition but an amazing command of mechanical technique. Knowledge of all kinds was accumulated, and understanding waned. The new scientist became engaged, as I have said, in anatomizing the corpse of the universe; became preoccupied with "how" not "why"—seeing everything through part of the moving-instinctive centre. As it was then, so it is now, but intensified. Man, who was a sword, became twisted into a mark of interrogation.

'Can we, in this life, develop our emotional and mental potentialities, become Platos or Hypatias, which in pre-Babylonian times were normal? In this decline, from intuition and understanding, to rationalism, came the decline of religion and the invention of the maleficent idea of good and evil.

'What is our world-view? Is the cosmos the result of pure chance? Do I regard it as being governed by an all-wise and benevolent Being? Do I depend on a kindly Providence? Do I regard it as a penal settlement, or a "Vale of Tears"? Or do I regard the world as a school to which I am sent to acquire a certain understanding, a kind of gymnasium in which I can develop my potentialities?

'We should try to set down for ourselves our conception of life.'

'A first reading of parts of *Beelzebub's Tales* must be painful for some of you; it is like Egyptian hieroglyphics. Scientifically it sounds absurd. Yet constant reading lifts the dark curtain behind which nothing perceivable seems to move.

'In the Fifth Flight to the Earth Hamolinadir represents the highest form of ordinary reason admitting that it knows nothing about after-death. Incidentally, when I spoke about this chapter to Gurdjieff, he said that he was not a literary man, but that he has supplied material in Beelzebub from which poets and writers will make epics.

'It is absurd to attempt to arrive at a literal understanding of *Beelzebub*; it is a myth, and a myth is an allegorical monster to shock the mind, as an artistic symbol gives a shock to the imagination. Constant reading of the book seems sometimes to stupefy the mind, yet, paradoxically, it awakens the understanding.

'Hamolinadir read a paper on "The Instability of Human Reason".

He was a first-class scientist who had been to all the schools, including Egypt. Like others, he assumed that the mind, like the hand, had been developed naturally by evolution in response to needs; but all his learning, study, and training had not helped him to solve even one question that concerned everyone: What happens after death? He had written books on the subject, which everyone admired. He admits that, listening to the theories put forward by the other speakers, in one state of feeling he could agree that man is only a body; in another state, that he was only mind; and in another that man had an immortal soul which would go to its appointed place after death. And now he admits to his learned audience that he has had no personal experience of this question and that he understands nothing, and he invites anyone who has a method, or a means to knowledge, which he has not tried, to tell him. No one speaks. Then, completely disillusioned, he goes out of the hall sobbing, never to return. He retires to his farm to grow Choongary—a being food. That is, he goes to an esoteric school, where he may learn to work on himself.

His state is ours.'

At this point Orage told us that, as editor of the *New Age*, he had read everything in the East and West on religion, philosophy, psychology, and science; he had read the *Mahabharata* through twice; he was the friend of artists, musicians, scientists, psychologists; he had met everyone in the intellectual world and was familiar with every theory, religious, scientific, theosophical, psychological, economic, and political—and, in spite of all this, he realized that with all his knowledge he understood almost nothing about the meaning and aim of existence, or what happens at death. When he met Gurdjieff he knew at once that here was his teacher; and, at the age of fifty, disillusioned with ordinary life, he gave up everything to go and work at the Prieuré at Fontainebleau. 'Hamolinadir,' he added, 'is a cartoon of the disillusioned modern thinker, whose reason is insufficient for objective conclusions.'

'Verbal reasoning,' Orage continued, 'is based on experience of words; formal reasoning—reasoning by forms—in Gurdjieff's meaning is based on experience through the senses. A man who had read about camels, but never seen one, could enter into a long discussion about camels, but what would his opinion be worth about one kind of camel or another compared with the man who had raised camels? In our society both kinds of reason are necessary, since the existence of society depends on people keeping together, and this depends on communication by words—which, for this purpose, are symbols; they are like tokens, paper money, in relation to the gold reserve. This paper has a use but no value, or rather, a symbolic value. Verbal reasoning, like paper currency, is greatly inflated. We ought to be very clear about the merits and defects of verbal reasoning, since so much of what is called education, lecturing, preaching, and popular writing is based on this; it is not backed by actual experience.

'Verbal reasoning is the intellectual centre working alone. No one here has yet remarked that our tendency to over-verbalize is caused by inadequate action of the thinking centre in its own place. The thinking centre has energy for objective reason, and failing this proper use the energy goes into verbalizing. This energy is a form of sex energy, and our verbalization is said to be due to the misuse of sex energy which should go to the development of objective reason. Study the chapter on apes.

'We cannot understand objective reason in the light of subjective reason. Objective reason means coming to the end of subjective reason and then having a totally different experience.

'Constant study and reading of Beelzebub can bring about a changed attitude in which we begin to understand—and to reason on another plane. The end of subjective reason, as in the case of Hamolinadir, is complete despair. Fortunately, we have the Method, by the practice of which objective reason has an opportunity to develop.'

'Emotions and ideas persist as do physical objects, but objects disintegrate faster than ideas. What remains of the physical objects made, for example, by the early Jewish race? Nothing, yet their religious ideas still persist and are still vital—though we may not know how to use this vitality. The same with the ideas of the ancient Hindus, preserved in the Mahabharata. What exists of the physical objects produced by those ancient Hindus? Nothing but fragments of buried cities. Yet the ideas in the Mahabharata will revitalize our literature hundreds of years hence.

'Verbal reasoning is dangerous because words are species, entities—a humanly created phenomenon capable of giving a sort of experience. Slogans like "All power to the worker", and "Liberty", stir people's emotions, fill them with lively fantasies. When they do get their famous liberty they immediately begin to take away power and liberty from those who do not agree with them.

'Speculative reason is of no value apart from its verbal discrimination. Gurdjieff rates it lowest because it does not lead into either formal or objective reasoning.

'We ought to make constant efforts to acquire the ability to discriminate between "vegetable", "animal", and "human" ideas, which are ideas on different planes. Ideas and emotions have their place on a scale. There are emotions which expand being, and emotions which contract being. It is a question of rates of vibration. Vivifying ideas and emotions have high rates of vibration.'

Someone asked: 'What is the intellectual type? Is Hamlet an example?'

Orage: 'No, Hamlet is an introvert who can "hear" nothing. The centres are connected by a magnetic tie which, when disconnected, brings about sleep, thus giving the centres a chance to rest from sympathetic vibration. The magnetic tie between Hamlet's centres had been worn so thin that he approximated sleep most of the time. His real complaint was "Why, when my intellectual centre is so stimulated, cannot I feel the horror of this incest and murder, and why cannot I act?"

'Each time we make an effort to bring our attention back to ourselves, to what we are doing, to remember ourselves, the centres become connected.'

' "Laws of Association" have application to practical affairs. For instance, concerning weight of thought, if you follow the expression of a light thought with a heavier, the effect of the first is destroyed. A sufficient interval between them, however, would have left the first untouched. Again, you may catch a hearer in the wrong mood according to his centre of gravity. The art of psychology would consist in the understanding and use of these laws and of the laws of vibration.'

'As has been said, a man should spend half, or at least a third, of his life in pondering. Helkdonis stands in relation to the assimilation of foods as pondering stands in relation to impressions.'

One of us said: 'A man must make an effort to resolve the struggle between affirmation and denial, or else the impression goes not to essence but just to his store of information?'

Orage: 'Yes. In other words, pondering is the neutralizing force of thought. Without this, the organism is left with only positive and negative deposits. Pondering is the weighing of ideas. Pondering should include clarity.'

Question: 'How is pondering different from meditation and contemplation?'

Orage: 'There are notes in the thinking scale, of which Sol is concentration, La is meditation, Si is contemplation. But each is still a process of thought, in which the emotional may enter; and it must be present in pondering, which is motivated by the emotional centre, by the personal relation to the subject pondered. Pondering is essential thinking. If emotion were lacking, pondering would be only weighing. Pondering is establishing values by weighing; otherwise there is only clarity and logic.'

Question: 'How do you differentiate impulsive action from action due to pondering?'

Orage: 'What is weighed in pondering is inclination and disinclination as opposed to thinking, in which ideas and concepts are weighed. The contents of the emotional centre—likes and dislikes—are the units weighed in relation to the criterion of more or less being.

'Pondering is the assimilation of the third food. With the Psalmist we can say: "When I consider the heavens, the moon and the stars which thou hast ordained," I ask, "What is man that thou art mindful of him, and the son of man that thou visitest him?" This is asking, after contemplation, "What am I?"—the transfer of the note Si of the thinking octave to Doh of the pondering octave. Pondering is thinking with the emotional centre (its thinking sub-centre) which is the seat of essence. This sub-centre is said to be the most highly developed of the sub-centres.

'Suppose that our state of being depends on our serviceability to the Creator, that our future being, our life, depends upon our creation of values contributing to the Creator's purpose. Not knowing the purpose —the meaning and aim of existence—these objective values are matter for pondering. On the supposition that we exist by the will of a Being, the individual's question is whether he is producing the desired values. This question is not intellectual because my *being* depends on this understanding.

'In the book, distinction is constantly made between existence and being. Values according to likes and dislikes are infantile; calculation according to the welfare of the planetary body is existence; the welfare or ill fare of my being is contemporary with existence and at the same time is continuous. Pondering is an activity proper to being, that strain in the being which is related to continuous being. "It" can think, but "I" alone can ponder. A fine machine, or body, at the end of an existence, may find "being" shrunk to almost nothing.

'When you consider that the Creator's being depends on the growth and development of the being of his creatures, you will see that he cannot be hostile to any effort that we make towards an expansion of being. A state of being is dynamic, moving towards fulfilment of itself. The subjective attitude towards this question is determined by pondering. It asks: "What is my status, not just as a Trogoautoegocratic machine, but in relation to the cosmos?" It may be that when we come to the end of our planetary existence we shall be asked "What is your state of being now compared to what it was when you entered this spell of existence?" We might be compelled to endure another kind of planetary existence deserved by our degree of merit—perhaps one in the animal kingdom.

' "Purposive thought" is thinking with a purpose, with attention. This implies control; not thinking just by association; control of the lower thinking centre by the higher thinking centre; of the formatory apparatus by "I".

'The ordinary mind is constantly being diverted, stimulated, by incoming impressions and the contents already there.

'The parable, from the Gurdjieff point of view, is a truth for at least two, and usually three, centres, with interblended significance. Parables are the language, the speech, of mythical figures, who are conscious representations of fully developed beings. You know how we attribute more than verbal meaning to the words of relatively developed beings —"Put more into them". For instance, there is the myth of Gurdjieff, who can't ask for something at dinner without some pupils thinking his request is parabolic—that he wants something else.

'In its octave form the parable runs from allegory through the parable, with an inclusion of its meanings, until it reaches the oracle, capable of translation in seven forms. In the parable, the facts of one plane are made to correspond with the facts of another plane. In general, Gurdjieff's book is a mythological parable. When he writes of the dispersion of races he is writing of centres; though this is more a form of allegory.

'The miracles told of in the Bible obviously did not happen as they are related. Some of them may have been the manifestations of the laws of a higher cosmos in a lower one. Some stories of miracles are made so plausible that it is as if they had occurred. A genuine parable must be read for understanding; its inner significance does not show on the surface and is not on the same plane as the gross narrative. The mind that is brought to the written text is the intellect, which is not capable of understanding. But the mind that ponders can understand.

'Meanings change so much that even terms in the Gospel are meaningless to us—bread, fish, the upper room, and so on, are technical terms which we do not now recognize. Explicit meanings are of no value in the parable except in so far as they are in our current language, but the implicit meaning can always be arrived at.

'The question is, How can we find the key to a parable? What meaning would Gurdjieff's book have without the Method! It isn't that some people who had never worked in a group would not get a great deal from the book; but that, without the practical experience of the Method, the deeper meanings would not be found. What is the Bible without the keys? I suggest that the division between the Old and New Testaments has a parabolic value. The Old Testament is a triad—doh, re, mi; then there is the shock of the appearance of the Universe incarnate, after which the narrative proceeds from the history of Jesus to the history of Christ, who was born in the interval. The Old Testament, then, should be a parabolic history of the development of man through the three lower centres, and the New Testament through the three higher centres, with, of course, correspondence between them. St Paul translated some of the Old Testament stories into New Testament meaning, the story of Hagar for example. Jesus referred to the Old Adam and the New Adam. Promise means potentiality, and very few people in the Old Testament were said to have promise. The Old Testament is a historical parable; the New Testament a psychological parable. In the absence of a key interpretations of much of Gurdjieff's book—as of the Bible—can be taken as nonsense.

'It is said in the New Testament that he who practises this Method brings out of his treasury things both new and old. It increases one's inner mental resources, for one thing, and it should enable you to have greater resources of memory for use in the work.'

Question: 'Is Einstein's theory a parable?'

Orage: 'No, it is a code—not a language. In the parable common terms are used.'

Question: 'What about Blake's prophetic books?'

Orage: 'They are elaborate allegory and poetic imagery.'

Question: 'How about Wagner's *Ring*?'

Orage: 'It is an allegory. Wagner started as an amoralist and couldn't keep it up—he became a Christian, increasingly sentimental and beautiful and weak. Swinburne is an infantile atheist, like Henley, "Bloody but unbowed"; he is credible but not cosmic.

'In reading poetry, if you think what would be said or meant in prose you get a double satisfaction. Music also has this double content. But most music, like most poetry, is just bombast. If you reduce Wagner to prose you find that it is impossible platitude. Bach and Palestrina have something to say, Beethoven occasionally. Unfortunately we are, in relation to music, as most children to poetry—if it sounds good we think it is good.'

Question: 'Haven't we a right to expect an intellectual analysis of music?'

Orage: 'This is just what the poet says when he has nothing to say in his poetry.

'In exactly the way I am now asking for the reading of the content of music—apart from its sonorous form—we should be able to read parables, ignoring what they ostensibly say and getting back to the real "prose" meaning. A parable comes from an integrated statement; this is why we are not capable of writing them, or true fairy tales, which have as their content a cosmic truth.'

A question was asked about the difference between mentation and 'being-mentation'.

Orage: 'Presumably, some time, the term "being-mentation" will be as commonly known and used as "subjective" and "objective", which date no further back than Coleridge, who got them from the German, though they are Latin in origin.

'The two forms of mentation spoken about in the prologue of the book become the two dynamic rivers of the epilogue.

'Hassein says "Things are a-thinking in me". The mind is always "a-thinking", and if we take a hand in it and direct the thinking it is active being-mentation; it is the result of an experience digested and made part and parcel of our being. In "being-mentation" we are mentating with materials, which, since they are part of experience, have an emotional element. Instead of dealing with words and their associations, which makes possible verbal logic, we have to use experiences and their associations, which make possible a being-logic.

'Pondering, I associate more with the weighing of associations. Active being-mentation is used in such mantrams as "I wish to remember myself", when with each word you call up the most vivid experience connected with that word; and then you are in a state of wishing to remember yourself.

'Formal understanding—understanding by forms—is brought about by being-mentation.

'Gurdjieff frequently suggests that the value of being-mentation is in the activity of gathering up all experiences, whatever subject you touch on.

'In verbal reasoning we substitute association for real experience. We cannot yet explore the character of objective truth and the character of the technique for attaining this.

'We have reached the conclusion that we have two forms of reasoning, formal and associative, and the distinction is made without reference to objective reason. It is not possible to develop objective reason so long as our centre of gravity remains in associative reasoning; we have to go from formal to objective. The material of the language of gesture, posture, tone of voice, facial expression, and movement, is the material of formal reasoning, and the Gurdjieff method is designed to shift the centre of gravity to formal and then to objective reasoning by making use of this material.'

I said, 'A constant reading of *Beelzebub* would, in time, bring one to this state?'

Orage said: 'Yes, but if you work in the method at the same time you should attain it very much quicker. No one can impart or explain to you the experience of objective reasoning; they can show the way, but you must work for it.'

'We should try to distinguish between sensing and feeling, and feeling and thinking—the three main forms of states. People imagine they know the difference, but they constantly confuse sensing with feeling, and feeling with thinking. Begin by making a list of emotional states. How many varieties of anger, for example, indignation, spleen, vexation, irritability, rage, fury, acrimony. A person in a state of self-remembering could observe and be aware of these various states without, perhaps, being able to define them in current terms. The Babylonian scientists of "new format" instituted "word-reasoning" and put an end to the pursuit of "being"; they substituted verbal thought for trained intuition. We come into the world educable, and become corrupted by words. Knowledge is no longer the outcome of "being-experience" but of crystallized concepts.'

'There were two schools of morality in Babylon—the dualist or idealist, and the materialist or atheist. The first assumed the existence in the world of two principles—good and evil. We find in ourselves the tendency to classify things thus, not only in relation to ourselves, but absolutely. It is natural for each species to classify things in relation to its needs or wants. "This grass is good for me", says the horse; "This brandy does me good", says the man; and this implies no judgement of the object itself. If I say "This is good in itself" I am applying my personal judgement. This double use of the word "good" is the cause of most of our confusion; and this false attribution of personal values we call morality. Although Gurdjieff has said that there is "objective evil" in the Universe, nothing that we ourselves know can be said to be universally good or bad. In spite of our knowing this, none of us can refrain from using the words "good" and "evil", and feeling that we have some claim to pass judgement; this is a result of an educational system which originated in the time of Babylon. Subjective morality came in when objective morality began to decay.

'The second school, the materialist, came to the conclusion that there was no psyche, no being, no "soul". To the modern behaviourist, socialist, and intellectual, man is only a kind of animal who takes in impressions and excretes behaviour; they are preoccupied with external behaviour, with subtle psychology. The Gurdjieff system agrees that man is a machine; but this system begins where behaviourism leaves off. Man has the possibility of becoming a living soul, capable of achieving objective reason.'

'In *Beelzebub*, one of the implications is the conception of a normal human being. We cannot conceive a normal human being by taking the average of individuals. This distinction between average and human is very important. A normal man is defined in the book, but this needs to be pondered for a long time before it can be grasped. Gurdjieff often says, "What I am saying now, you will understand in a year's, or two years'—or ten years' time", although his statement is clear.

'In a normal world, a young man (or woman) at about the age of twenty-one would begin to find in himself, quite naturally, the development of that state of consciousness which we call self-consciousness, in the real meaning of the term; he would become conscious of himself, aware of his body in the sense of being psychologically in possession of it; and it would happen normally, accompanied by devotion to certain interests. At about the age of thirty another phase would occur, in which he would become conscious of the world he lives in, of this planet and other planets, and his relation to them. This would vary with individuals, but the character of the phases would be the same. He would become—not, as Gurdjieff says, "A young man in quotation marks, with a pleasing exterior and dubious interior", but a young man, conscious of himself, aware of the purpose of life and his place and function in it.

'But, on this planet, because of our abnormal life, the phases are more or less chaotic with many young people, and are accompanied by periods of frustration and despondency. Nothing goes as it ought logically to go.

'Beelzebub set himself the task of discovering why this should be so. As I have said, he reviewed the history of the planet (as it is useful for us to review the history of our individual lives), and he found that a catastrophe had befallen the earth; it had been split, and two fragments had flown off into space—the Moon and Anulios. Each of us repeats in himself the splitting; but the consequences, though serious, are not fatal, since His Endlessness gave us the possibility of turning this misfortune to our good.

'Our fallen state is due to the consequences of the results of the organ Kundabuffer. This organ is now vestigial, but the sociological tradition continues the consequences. As a condition of normal development this tradition must be seen through.

'It is impossible to attain to inner harmonious self-development through sociological ideas—through a synthesis of the knowledge we have acquired. All this is useless in the absence of the development of essence, the biological germ.

'Here is the origin of the idea of being born again—not in the current religious or occult sense, but in a return to the biological state before we were subject to sociology. This is where Gurdjieff's method comes in, a practical method for self-sensing, self-remembering, self-observation— for inner self-development.'

'Essence is truth about oneself in contrast to social and expected opinions of oneself. Essence is truth irrespective of time, place, and the feelings of anyone. It is what one would dare to avow if no consequences were to follow on a statement of the truth. It is truth before God. Personality is truth before men—before the world, conditioned by "What will people think?"

'It is necessary to know what you really wish. As you discover your real wish, external circumstances will change and become more like those you wish. Wild animals live according to essence; in this, man

168

is inferior to the animals. Domesticated animals have their essential impulses distorted.

'Sociology has distorted us; we were caught so young that it becomes almost impossible to discriminate between our native, essential state, and our sociological, personality state. No "civilized" man can arrive at objective truth; and there is no possibility of inner individual development through ordinary sociological conditions.

'Society chooses what shall be actualized of our inherited, essential, potentialities. I inherit an instrument; I, as psyche, will develop according to my ability to exploit the possibilities of the instrument. But, from early childhood, only a fraction of potentialities are actualized by the stimulus of environment; and, perhaps for my whole life I am identified with that fraction.

'At the same time, every personality is in accordance with essence, though only a part of essence. If, so to speak, I am a piano on which only jazz is played, I go through my whole life thinking I am a jazz instrument; or, if I become identified with the career of lawyer, for example, I exploit only a fraction of my potentialities. But it is possible to play one role "as if" you were identified with it, and yet not to be. Circumstances may force you to play one role throughout life, but, so long as you are not identified with it, essence develops.

'In the ancient drama the actors stood in the wings. On the stage the play was begun. Those in the wings were liable at any moment to be beckoned on to the stage, with no intimation of the role they might be called upon to play.

'A man living in essence can do seemingly contradictory things, but all are related to essence. To be able to live according to essence we must also develop reason.'

Question: 'If we acted essentially shouldn't we act inhumanly?'

Orage: 'Not necessarily. A covered-up essence is not necessarily inhuman. Essences are often better than we think. There is not one of Gurdjieff's rules of Objective Morality that essence does not instinctively obey. For most people the moon is a diabolical influence and, through the organ Kundabuffer, does something to three-centred essences. It is as if essence, arriving from the sun and planets, on reaching earth receives a chill.

'From one aspect personality is the guardian of essence. It is said that one of the Medici, trained in a Platonic school, lived in a nunnery for fifteen years and became an abbess, then went back to court; she was able to play the role as long as her reason dictated it. If we had the means and the knowledge we could trace hundreds of similar cases in Europe throughout the Middle Ages and the Renaissance.

'Gurdjieff speaks of essence "wish" and personality "want". Since I have a three-centred essence, which is a minute replica of the world, of God, in my essence I cannot but have the same wish as he has. I must discover what this essence wish is.

'There is a difference between subjective and objective conscience; and when you have experienced universal praise and have realized that it means nothing to you in relation to your objective conscience, then you will begin to understand the difference.

'Gurdjieff lives from essence according to objective reason.

'But to a person in ordinary life the behaviour of a conscious man and a charlatan is often indistinguishable. Hence the stories that arise about Gurdjieff; and the animosity from hangers-on and some of the younger pupils. With the conscious man, behaviour is related to a conscious aim; with the charlatan, behaviour is unconscious.'

'Will, consciousness, and individuality: We must not flatter ourselves that we have the slightest idea what these mean. The nearest analogy for us at present is wish (or want or desire), thought, and personality. These determine for us the value of the abstract, unrealized, unexperienced terms. The difference between an ordinary wish (or desire) and will is the difference between a passive state in which an active force operates, and an active state in which oneself operates.

'I myself do not originate the wish—it happens to me. Will is self-initiated. If, as Gurdjieff says, you take some small thing which you really wish to do and compel yourself to do it, you may then experience the beginning of a taste of real will.

'Every wish we experience can be regarded as a psychological entity, every impression a unit, playing the same role in our psyche as we individuals play in the life of the planet. Gurdjieff said that if a man could be anatomized psychologically, he would see myriads of beings— of wishes, thinking organisms. He would see his entire population.

'Personality is the sum total of our reflexes—physical, emotional, intellectual; personality is a reagent. Individuality is the ability to act— not react; it is presumed that there is a being who is capable of using the body. One of the objects of the Method is to make real the distinctions which at present we can make only intellectually.'

Question: 'Could we compare will, consciousness, and individuality to God the Father, God the Son, and God the Holy Ghost? The Holy

Ghost being the reconciling force, but now a duplex person with the Virgin Mary, which would make the Son the reconciler instead of the Holy Ghost?'

Orage: 'This is one of the disputes of the early Catholic Church.'

'Beings,' said Orage, 'only become individuals or individuums, indivisible, three in one and one in three—three centres having been developed—when active, passive and neutralizing are in their normal order: a repetition of the original state of creation. Every wish of which we are conscious derives from one of our three centres, and for the other two centres it is an apparition, an interruption. When all three centres have the same wish, this is what we call Will. Then a man can say "I wish" with his whole being. It is "I am-ness".

'When all three centres are engaged in one wish you are not aware of a wish; the whole being consents. Psychological suffering ceases, but effort continues, with often a feeling of disappointment, because of the frustration of Will. With increase of being comes increase of difficulties; at the same time comes an increase of strength.

'One of the aims of the Gurdjieff Method is the attainment of a state of self-consciousness which now we assume, without evidence, that we possess. Gurdjieff does not assume, as the mystical and occult methods do, that we are self-conscious. Man has lost his way, fallen into his present state of pathological waking consciousness, and unless he can recover the path, is doomed. This Method is devised to help him.

'All our physical and psychological manifestations are interrelations of our organism and its environment—devoid of will; that is, of the power to act on one's own initiative. So we have Gurdjieff's definition of a man: "A man is a being who can *do*". From this it would follow that in general we do not know a man, but only "men" in quotation marks. If will-lessness is of the natural order the question is, "What kind of activity is necessary to develop will?"

'It is difficult to convince ourselves, to have a realization of, the fact that all psychic and psychological phenomena are of the same order as physiological phenomena. The process of thinking that is taking place in me now as I talk, and that of you subvocally, while listening, are as devoid of will as the sense of touch in physical contact. There is no more will implied than there would be in dream figures going through these movements. We don't presume that the dream figure is initiating its own activity; neither are we the initiators of the dream figures; they are not even puppets, for this would imply a puppeteer. Our state is that we are more or less dream figures—on "the painted veil that we call life".'

A pupil: 'But suffering is real.'

'It depends upon what kind of suffering. In a dream suffering can seem very real indeed, and sometimes you can recall it for a long time afterwards. In life, although we may recall the occasion, suffering of a year ago can be forgotten. "Nothing dries sooner than a tear".

'One of the purposes of the myth in the book is to explain the influence of the moon and Kundabuffer. It is not surprising that man has no will; it is surprising that he believes he has. This persuading of man that he has will, against all the evidence, against scientific analysis, is one of the effects of Kundabuffer. One of the first results of self-remembering and self-observation would be to remove this illusion of will. At a certain stage in the practice of the Method comes the conviction of will-lessness, the conviction of one's own inner nothingness and mechanicality, of the hopelessness of the expectation of anything real in ordinary life. This, in early Christianity, was called a "conviction of sin", a realization that one had "missed the mark". This psychological experience was necessary before a being could attain will or "salvation".

'Assuming that the realization of will-lessness has been experienced, the question becomes one of whether it is possible to be born again and pass into real life, and by what means. And here, on the threshold, stands the word Will.

'The question of Will is said to be the mystery of mysteries. Real Will, the force that creates, preserves, and destroys the universe, is unintelligible to ordinary thinking. God, the Absolute, created the great universe by an act of conscious will, by overcoming inertia, inert matter. As we, in our small ways, develop real will, so shall we become like God, become Sons of God. How do we begin? Again, I repeat Gurdjieff: "Take some small thing you wish to do which you cannot now do, and compel yourself to do it".

'Whim is the beginning of will. Whim is a fly, will an elephant. St Patrick's effort to change the course of human history, to civilize Ireland, is an example of elephantine will.

'It is assumed, of course, that you have studied the Method. Every effort to remember yourself and to observe yourself impartially is an act, a small act towards the state of real will—the first step, in fact.'

At a later meeting, when good and evil were being discussed, Orage continually had to bring the pupils back to the point. He said, 'Everyone hears questions and answers them from the centre of gravity in which he is at the moment. His interpretation depends on this only; on his subjective state. Essence takes the form of the being that at the moment is occupying the centre of gravity: it is animal, child, or barbarian; and every second the psyche is changing form, and it is to such beings that doctrines are addressed. You can imagine how such a being transforms a doctrine, having heard it in one or another of the three centres. No wonder that Gurdjieff is always speaking about the strange psyche of these three-brained beings. The difficulties of a world-teacher are tremendous. No wonder that it took a Son of God—and his doctrine has apparently failed—to explain to men a few simple ethical doctrines.'

'The beings on the planet Purgatory participate in the divine plan, but suffer because they know what they ought to do, but are as yet unable to. When will, consciousness, and individuality are developed harmoniously and simultaneously, then, in the process, we are purged and may be released from Purgatory. The development of these three at once is anti-yoga. Beelzebub tells Hassein that when the rate in one centre is too high, to cease activity in it, and bring up the other two centres under order from the fourth centre. This is Iramsamkeep: I keep myself in charge of the three centres.

'The Absolute, by definition, is the whole considered as one. The Absolute to which we refer is the whole of our world. This self-contained unitary absolute presents two features—the *status quo* and movement; the static and dynamic features. These two presuppose a plan or design, necessitating the maintenance and development of the universe. This development can be called the plan of campaign, and the *status quo* is the army for carrying it out. The plan has, as its objective, the development of the potentialities of all the constituent beings of the total plan. The realization of the plan is the attainment of objective reason: the fulfilment of the "being" of each being. The plan is to be carried out by all beings, conscious or unconscious, to the extent to which they remain beings at all—and not complete Hasnamusses. A potentiality of beings is to be conscious of the plan and to develop the will to co-operate with it. The attainment of a state of conscious co-operation with the plan may be defined as good; failure to attain this state may be defined as evil. The plan is discoverable; but, in the absence of the discovery, all reports of its nature must be regarded as conventional or religious morality, subjective morality. Slavish obedience to subjective morality constitutes objective wrong-doing.

'The text of Gurdjieff's book claims that the principles of objective morality as laid down are derived from a prime source by a being who has had access to it. Each great religion, at its origin, has taught objective morality. A technique, a method is given, designed to bring into consciousness objective conscience, so that a being can understand and co-operate in the divine plan. With understanding comes the responsibility of a being for his own development.

'At present, the only objectively right thing we can do is to practise the Method, which has the effect of bringing objective conscience into consciousness.'

'The psyche is that which is not body. It is coated with the body. It is an entity, incidentally coated planetarily. Physiology is the instrument of the psyche. Within the psyche there is possible the development of the three centres. Psyche is the instrument of "I". The concept of psyche does not include the physical body. The true physical body is the etheric body. Gurdjieff refers to the other as the planetary body. The four bodies—planetary, physical, emotional, mental—signify tetarto-cosmos beings. The planetary body is formed of planetary substances, the physical body of radiations from the planet. In the emotional centre there is a duality of substances—radiation from planets and emanation from the sun, which contribute to lower and higher emotions, symbolized in the cross. Every cosmos, including the Tetarto, is a three-centred entity in which transformation of substances occurs. The Kesdjan body and the mental body are the higher bodies.'

Question: 'How do you define presence? What is the difference between presence and personality?'

Orage: 'Gurdjieff associated "presence" with what is immediately present in you. It includes potentiality in so far as potentiality has begun to give evidence of itself. Of a young tree he said: "young presence". It is both the accomplished fact and the process of accomplishment. Mass plus energy.

'Concerning chief feature, one of the characteristics is that you assume you are what you essentially wish to be.'

'A feeling of sociological guilt comes from subjective conscience, a consequence of subjective morality. Being-shame comes from objective conscience—a realization that one has failed to attain to what one should be.'

'Unless we use our energies for normal psychic development, we literally become inferior to animals.'

'The octave is the development of three primaries—the law of three. In the spectrum there are only three primaries—red, yellow, blue. If as a simile we take red as positive, blue as negative, yellow as neutralizing, in man now red and blue are reversed.'

To a question about parktdolgduty, Orage said: 'This is duty in three languages, it is conscious labour and voluntary suffering. From one aspect it is an intellectual duty to strive to understand the meaning and aim of existence, an emotional duty to feel the weight of the maintenance of everything existing, and a physical duty to make the planetary body the servant of your aim.

'I have never been able to bring home to you the feeling of the debt that each of us bears for our having been incarnated. Everything that we call "natural" is the product of beings superior to us, provided at great cost so that we could have experience. Existence—the participation in the experiences of incarnation—cost somebody something. To feel the obligation of this is to have an understanding of what is meant by paying for one's existence. Not to feel this is a sign of abnormality and an incapability of any conception of justice. We place an infinite value on life, and a long life and a happy one, but first a long one. The obligation for our life is not one that *should* be felt but that *is* felt by a normal human being.'

A pupil: 'Then we come to Hamlet's "To be or not to be".'

Orage: 'Hamlet was not normal, but mad. His was a typical case of will-lessness poisoned by German philosophy. Think! We might all be tables, or inferior animals! And, as life is shaped, the number of pleasant experiences, generally speaking, is slightly in excess of the unpleasant ones.

'Duty is defined by the Buddhists as "that which must be done without expectation of merit, but which must be done if we are to earn merit".'

'The beginning of adulthood is the wish to separate "I" from "It". An adult is one who is striving to make this separation: to separate the

Self from the self. The adult may not be fully conscious of this separation, but the presence of this wish indicates an entering into the state of spiritual adulthood.

'Without "I" no consciousness. People who have had moments of self-consciousness know the difference between these and waking-consciousness. Cosmic consciousness is still different—it is not possible to describe it, so no records of it exist. Bucke's *Cosmic Consciousness* describes only self-consciousness. Ouspensky related that he became convinced that he was not self-conscious when Gurdjieff asked him where he got the grease spots on his vest, and he could not remember.

'The difference between a thought and consciousness is that thought is a succession of images—a train or a sequence; consciousness is a simultaneous awareness of the contents of the mind—and, of course, of the feelings and sensations.'

'Presentation of a way of development is difficult because the conceptions are not familiar, axiomatic, or associative. Gurdjieff gets over this difficulty by writing parabolically. Direct exposition fails because of wrong association with psychological data.'

'Radiation disperses by its own force; emanation undergoes no diminution.'

A question was asked about organic shame, and the loss of it with special reference to women.

Orage said: 'I have heard Gurdjieff refer equally to its loss in men. In fact, in one chapter he has passages in which he acquits women in America of the state into which they have fallen; for this decline started in men, and the women only make manifest the degree to which organic shame is lost in men.

'You know that the word Jehovah or Yahveh is made up of Yod and Evoe, Adam and Eve. The Jewish religion is regarded by objective esotericism as degraded because it dropped the responsibility for evil from Yod and put it on Evoe. Those "men" who shift the responsibility, slipping from their active part to the passive, are "men of Yod".

'The Sufis say that the Jews had the truth given them—objective knowledge—but they forsook it, and, in consequence, they have been punished and dispersed.

'Organic shame is not of an organ but of the organism, which regards abnormality with fear. Only a normal organism feels this.'

To a question asked about appealing directly to objective conscience, Orage said: 'This cannot be appealed to directly. Ashiata Shiemash appealed indirectly. Curiosity for a good aim, as Gurdjieff says, is a pure motive for studying the method of self-observation, because it does not colour it. In this respect we are like Saul, who set out to find asses and attained a kingdom. The Method provides a means of discovering, and having a realization of, one's abnormality. This inspires a wish to change, which is organic shame. This is connected with the Holy Aieioiuoa—the aspiration of lower vibrations to share the experience of higher vibrations. It is that which we feel in the presence of a superior being—not a superior social item; a wish to be such; this is hero-worship, the hero being objectively superior.'

'Our mechanical reaction to people is one of the signs of our servility. One of the psychological exercises within your control is the constant striving to be aware of negative emotions. During these past months many of you have been going through an intense period of negative emotion; at the same time you had in your hands the antidote, so to say. But we are all so in love with our mechanical suffering, so lazy, so much in inertia, that we would rather suffer mechanically, passively, than make the effort to practise a little voluntary suffering.

'Regarding conscious labour, we can take Ashiata Shiemash. He began to ponder, by a whim, as it were. He pondered all preceding teachings, and eventually established a critique and a new technique. It was self-discovered. He found what his aim in life was through his own efforts; and he set to work to devise the most efficient means for putting it into effect. This was conscious labour.

'The Gurdjieff system defines an aim for every individual, which is: the attainment of self-consciousness and a measure of objective reason. The idea is ultimately to be able to relate every action to purposive conduct, which alone can give meaning to an otherwise mechanical life. Real pride begins with the work of "I". It is the "being-satisfaction" of having made effort.'

'Ashiata Shiemash began to question his own competence to formulate a method for saving the beings of the planet Earth from further degeneration. After much work on himself, after much pondering and having come to a realization that he himself had been subjectively determined, he was able to see through the coatings of his education and, having achieved a state of objectivity and impartiality, he began to formulate his mission. He left a document for a line of initiates, of whom, today, in Central Asia, a few remain.

'Remember that, in Beelzebub's tales, everything has three meanings and seven aspects.

'Ashiata Shiemash wrote "The Terror of the Situation".'

At this point Orage said that he wished we had the music with us in New York that Gurdjieff had composed to accompany the reading of this chapter, since in it the ideas are realized emotionally as in the book they are realized intellectually.

He continued: 'Ashiata Shiemash began with a prayer, that is, he put himself into a definite emotional attitude as precise as a physical attitude of posture. He consciously arranged his emotions—put himself into a state of "I-am-ness". "I" is always. "I am Father, Son, Yesterday, Tomorrow".

'With us, "I" manifests periodically; accidentally, at first.

'Ashiata Shiemash freed himself from all associations, and was able to be impartial. He surveyed the results of the religions that had been founded on Faith, Hope, and Love, and saw that beings had no longer the possibility of being affected by them; and that it was no longer possible to appeal to their ordinary reason. It is useless to preach sanity to madmen. He questioned all our emotions as well as our ideas; and reached the conclusion that there still remained, buried in essence, something that is not acquired but is our own and has not been corrupted—Objective Conscience.

'He chose thirty-six beings from monasteries, that is, individual independent thinkers, capable of thinking against current sociological trends, trends of their own organism and of the exterior world around them. (Every independent thinker lives in a "monastery".) Ashiata Shiemash taught the thirty-six the Method, so that they were able to speak from their own experience, not from books; and were able to help a number of others to do the same.

'For a long period his organization flourished, his ideas being handed on by initiates. Eventually it was destroyed by Lentrohamsanin. This name is made up, by the way, from some names well-known today. In each of us there is a Lentrohamsanin. As I have already said, in this work, too, there will come a time when certain people, with a knowledge of the Gurdjieff system, but without the necessary understanding, will use the ideas for their own subjective purposes; they will distort and change them, deluding themselves that they are on the "Path". But, always, there will remain a nucleus of those who really understand and who will keep the Method and the System as Gurdjieff has taught it.

'In our time, all appeals to Faith, Hope, and Love have a tone of sentimentality, and arouse a certain revulsion; intellectually we are on guard against them. But we are equally civilized with the Babylonians of their period and equally corrupt, demanding intellectual proof.

'With regard to the appeal to ordinary reason we have, as an example, Buddha, acknowledged among the Hindus as the world's greatest dialectician, subtle reasoner, and logician, who was so misunderstood by the second or third generations of his followers that already they began to misinterpret him.

'Ashiata Shiemash realized that teachers who had been before him who had appealed to Faith, Hope, and Love, had failed; as also those who came after him who appealed to the same would fail; and he proposed to appeal to something that we have not yet rationalized and of which few, unless in desperate circumstances, would have had an experience.'

'Why is a dog always a dog? Why does it behave like a dog? Why does it not behave, as we would say, reasonably? It behaves as it does because it is obliged to be what it is, whatever the outcome. It is indifferent to whether it is rising or falling in the scale, to whether it is multiplying or becoming extinct. It is innocent, essential.

'Mineral, vegetable, animal obey the law of their species. "All bow their head under the yoke which God in his wisdom imposes" (Attar). For them there is no evil in our meaning of the word, no need of psychological effort; their species is fixed. Man is fixed externally, but psychologically has in him every species. He can be, on occasion, a mouse, a dog, a lion; observe yourself and your friends. Man is the note "si" in the octave. This note is precarious, it is a state of responsibility, an octave in which man can go either up the scale or down. Can the effort be made by which he will ascend into the next higher octave? This is the Terror of the Situation, for if the effort is not made, man may go down, and may degenerate, like the ants and the bees.

'Ashiata Shiemash introduces the idea of God—a determinant that man should develop his potentialities in a higher direction. The species below man does not need this. Man is the first biological species to occupy this crucial point in the octave; and his cosmic function is to co-operate in the plan imposed on the Universe by the Creator: the evolution of this same Universe.

'Ashiata Shiemash taught a method, the Method, by which man could become a normal man, a Son, instead of existing, as he does now, as a mere machine for the transforming of substances. Part of the scheme required that at a certain point there should appear a number of self-conscious agents, not mere servants, who would co-operate in carrying out this arbitrary plan. Ashiata Shiemash proposed to bring consciousness into being, and to build upon it.

'The diagnosis of man and his psychic condition is that as a race he is suffering, in varying degrees, from split personality. For example, it is impossible to remind a man of his normal condition who is drunk or under the influence of a drug or that of a strong emotion such as being in love, or in hate. It is the aim and purpose of all real teachers to remind man of his normal state—a state of which the average person has, at times, at least a momentary waking realization, a moment of partial recollection of a state of real consciousness. There is the Hindu story of the child in the womb who sang "Let me remember who I am". And his first cry after birth was "Oh, I have forgotten!" This idea is familiar to followers of the Christian religion in the story of the Prodigal Son, based on the older Gnostic "Hymn of the Robe of Glory", which, like other stories, we regard as happening in "Biblical times"; we do not apply it to ourselves, or we see it in the light of subjective morality.

'Ashiata Shiemash taught his pupils a method by which they could "wake up" to the fact that they were living in the far country of the Prodigal Son, the planetary body; and by which, in time, they could cease to be identified with its innumerable wants and desires, and return to their real selves. The Method was that which we call the technique of self-sensing, self-remembering, self-observing; it is "being-parktdolgduty"; a method so simple, yet, at the same time, so difficult. Why? Because the whole of life, together with things in ourselves, is in a conspiracy to make us forget, to keep us in a state of sleep. It is dangerous, too, for a person even to attempt to use the Method from a verbal description, let alone from any kind of writing; yet you will find it recorded in every great teaching.

'If we recall the original group which founded the Knights Templars, or the Order of Chivalry, when great nobles regarded it as a privilege to be allowed to work in the kitchen; or the unknown group of men who, with simple tools and instruments, built on an island in a swamp in a remote part of England the miracle of Ely cathedral, we shall have something comparable to Ashiata Shiemash's group.

'The founders of these groups had, in a high degree, real will, real consciousness, real individuality—the triangle in the enneagram, against the flowing down the scale of the law of the octave.

'In C. H. Hinton's *Scientific Romances* a character speaks of walking down a street in Greenwich Village, New York, and seeing a plate on a door, "John Smith, Unlearner". Smith's profession was to help people unlearn the rubbish they had accumulated through education. We have to unlearn, and be re-educated.

'Ashiata Shiemash taught that a man should have a sense of obligation to discharge the service for which he was created, and that he would evolve only to the degree to which he carried out this obligation. In doing so he would have to give up all sorts of things which he had deemed necessary to a "good life"—points of view, external power, knowledge, self-love, false pride, egoism—which, besides the love of money and sex, are the real lusts of the flesh.'

'Lentrohamsanin's critique was that of a good philosopher but a pure rationalist—Objective Reason without Objective Conscience. His view was that if a man was created for service he was therefore a slave. Plausibly and craftily he proposed to repudiate this service and attain to absolute freedom. He considered it possible to attain this without making the effort entailed in conscious labour and voluntary suffering. In one sense Lentrohamsanin was the forerunner of our spiritual ancestors, the Greeks and the Romans, who are regarded by us as the beginning of civilization—anything before them being barbarous and barbaric. But Gurdjieff says that the ancient Babylonian civilization was far superior to the Greek, which latter descends, not from Ashiata Shiemash, but from Lentrohamsanin—the rationalist with no higher emotional urge.

'In each of us Lentrohamsanin tries to undo the work of Ashiata Shiemash—an unconscious force working against a conscious force.

'In this Work, the work that we are engaged in, some people in whom knowledge has outstripped understanding may not be able to endure the suffering which follows—the sense of guilt, remorse, self-

181

reproach, the despair at feeling that they are unable to do anything about themselves. This is the dark night of the soul. Some may go off at a tangent, looking for an easier way, the way of a philosophical school for example; or an Eastern cult unsuited to the Western psyche; or they may become Lentrohamsanins and, with the best of all egotistical motives, actually become opposed to the work. This work is a strong positive, and, as Gurdjieff says, "a strong positive provokes a strong negative".

'Lentrohamsanin is the personification in us of the unwillingness to bear the suffering that is necessary to obtain Objective Conscience parallel with the attaining of Objective Reason.

'God has a plan. In this plan human beings are involved, and part of the plan consists in giving to the elect the opportunity of working for themselves at the same time as for Him. It is a very high and great plan; and the degree of suffering is the degree of importance attached to the plan. Who are the elect? Everyone who is willing to pay the price of conscious labour and voluntary suffering; not the elect of John Calvin, predetermined from the foundation of the world.

'Lentrohamsanin chose to work on those simple-minded folk, of good feeling, who had not obtained Objective Reason—the dissatisfied who were beginning to think that there was no hope of attaining to Objective Reason in proportion to the suffering. In place of the great aim, he taught that the chief thing in life was the pursuit of happiness, and happiness consisted in not being obliged to make constant and unflagging effort. In certain moods we may find ourselves ready to agree. Lentrohamsanin appealed to two characteristics in man—the desire to get something for nothing, and the idea of freedom, or liberty to attain happiness in the future. He was not a monster or a conscious traitor; he only thought he knew best; he left out of account the higher emotional element. In a state of higher emotion a man cannot do evil; Objective Conscience is awake; he is in a state of self-remembering, self-re-collection. In our ordinary reason there is already enough to defeat Buddha, Jesus Christ, and Ashiata Shiemash. Lentrohamsanin's weakness was that he had no urge to understand "why" but was satisfied with the knowledge of "how".

'Gurdjieff says that "why" is for what is not known, yet at the same time exists.

'As I have said, from the two streams possible to us—Ashiata Shiemash and Lentrohamsanin—we inherited the latter, the Greek and

Roman. Yet in Greece there existed true esoteric groups, which were responsible for the flowering of her culture. Socrates was a member of one. Aristophanes was a sort of Lentrohamsanin of his time—he never understood Socrates.

'Ashiata Shiemash's followers, when his teaching became submerged in the flood of Lentrohamsanin's rationalistic philosophy, withdrew into small groups. These small groups exist in ourselves.

'All popular explanations of life are now based on the personal; the objective has been swallowed up in egoism. We cannot formulate any philosophy except from the point of view of personal interest. Nietzsche said: "I no longer ask of a philosopher, 'Is it true?' but 'What was the interest for the philosopher'?" Without the higher emotions all philosophy becomes a matter for the head, with a view to personal welfare, subjectively coloured and egotistically determined —like our degenerate reason. Without higher emotional understanding ordinary man has the idea that the Universe just happened, and that therefore life on our planet, including the human, is to be exploited; or, that God had no useful purpose in creating the world and that he has no use for us; or, that he created it just for us, that he loves human beings and only wants them to be happy—and if they will not be good and happy and do as he wants he will be angry and punish them. This is one of our more childish attitudes, that our chief purpose is to be happy and that the path to happiness is to make others happy. This is Schopenhauer's attitude. Another variation is that only individual happiness counts—the subjective error into which Nietzsche fell—that mankind exists for the purpose of producing a few supermen. Still another variation is that of the pathological Communist-Socialist: what matters my happiness now and those around me so long as there is "progress" and happiness for others in the future? And the modern scientist—inventing more and more processes for the benefit of generations to come. "The disease of tomorrow".

'Objective Reason is not attained by any subjective egotistical emotion or personal anguish: Objective Conscience is also necessary. Gurdjieff's cosmology may seem ridiculous to the ordinary mind but in comparison with the infantile concepts implicit in our general subjective point of view, it is manly and intelligent.

'Ashiata Shiemash says: "There is a method by which we can arrive now at an understanding of what *is*".

'Lentrohamsanin says: "There is a means by which we can accommodate ourselves to what is, without understanding it". The Greeks were responsible for the corruption of human reason, the Romans for the corruption of organic conscience.'

'Beelzebub, during his sixth and last descent to the planet Earth, sets out to investigate the causes of the shortening of man's existence. Recent statistics in the West show a lengthening of people's physical existence. In this parable Beelzebub is concerned with making us wake up to the fact that man's *three-centred* existence is becoming shorter. If we study the modes of existence in the Western world it is fairly obvious that the essential life of man has suffered a considerable and rapid diminution during the last two or three hundred years, and this is still going on. One of the causes is that, after the age of twenty-five or thirty, people cease to think originally; they think mechanically, in the same old way; and at forty most people cease to have any originality of feeling but continue as vegetating animals, repeating and repeating, two-thirds dead.

'What is the cause of this premature death? It lies partly in education —in the failure to develop Objective Conscience, and to the absence of Objective Morality.

'In a normal society, possessing a normal education, its members would find themselves arriving at a development of the two higher bodies in the direction of Objective Reason. For Objective Conscience, Will, Consciousness and Individuality, we substitute philosophy, psycho-analysis, science, art, literature, religious sects, sport, health, and so on. We are like Amundsen in his airship over the North Pole, whose compass pointed in all directions and nowhere in particular. None of us has any clear interior sense of the direction of life. We are in space, yet compelled to move; and the only direction we can move in is that agreed upon by those around us: hence the confidence in sociological conventions, morals, and ideals—a pragmatic agreement. The subjective criterion is either idiosyncratic and rebellious, or conventional; objectively there is not a pin to choose between them; both are subjective. So we fall into various sophistries. For example, the criterion of value is "adaptation", evolution. Jung's school is based on "Are we adapted?; if so, we must be right". This is the posture of maximum comfort—the armchair in the water-closet that Beelzebub writes about; substituting means for ends. If one does not have a conscious aim, a conscious end in view, one will over-value the means. For example, the end of philosophy is truth; but the end is lost sight

184

of, and we succumb to brilliance of process, epigram, rhetoric, subtle reasoning. We worship the means.

'The same with the idea of justice. The true idea of justice is impartiality according to rules which apply to all. But we have become legalists, pursuing legal forms and legality instead of psyche logica.

'And sex. From an objective point of view the purpose of sex is twofold, procreation and self-creation—the procreation of planetary bodies, and the creation in ourselves of the body Kesdjan and the mental body. Thanks to the Romans we find ourselves using sex objectlessly, substituting the pursuit of pleasure derived from the sexual process for the real satisfaction derived from its use as an end. Or, under the influence of organized puritan religion, we deny sex, regard it as an evil, as the great sin; people then indulge in sexual phantasies. Why the enormous amount of thought in the West directed to the study of the results of the misuse or non-use or mis-direction of sex energy? Sex problems do not arise in the East except where people have been influenced by Western puritanism. With the rest of organic life we have a right to the pleasure derived from sexual union, but as human beings we must use the force, or part of it, for a conscious aim. And when sex energy is not so used it becomes diverted to purposes much more harmful than what we call "abnormalities".'

'Our objective inheritance is that we should know why we are born, know it early in life and be trained to carry out our functions. Animals and vegetables in their natural state do this. Plants produce seeds and, although there may be frustrations which delay, they do not divert the function. The vegetable world has great powers of adaptability for overcoming obstacles. Three-centred beings have three brains for the development of the germ of Objective Conscience, but education and environment from birth press down and bury this germ. Like Esau, we gave up our birthright for the mess of pottage of ordinary life; this is the meaning of the story.

'We have no inherent natural criterion, so we perforce accept the criterion of those around us. The difficulty is increased by the fact that we have no accurate knowledge of the planet, of its geology and races. We have only speculations by scientists, geologists, archaeologists, ethnologists; and one generation, or one school, will dispute or dis-prove to their own satisfaction the findings of another.

'Can anyone recall preceding civilizations, their rise and fall, their culture, art, and philosophy, and call himself their heir? There are only rumours about them, there is no continuity of knowledge.

'Gurdjieff says that there has existed from Atlantean times a chain of esoteric schools, custodians of secret knowledge, which, from time to time, is interpreted and taught by teachers who are sent out from these schools. All the great Messengers from Above have spoken of this —Krishna, Moses, Buddha, Jesus, Muhammad. There have also been many lesser messengers and teachers.'

'The chapter on Art is a description of the means devised by a small group of conscious men for the handing on of objective knowledge; not for a generation or two, but for a thousand years or more. What we call "art"—ordinary subjective art—is as natural to man as building nests is to birds. An artist should not be a special kind of man, but every man should be a special kind of artist; and he was, comparatively, even within living memory. Consider the peasant art of Europe, including Russia, and that which existed even in England until the coming of industrialism and the spread of education. The English countryside with its villages, cottages, and gardens, its farmhouses, was considered to be the most beautiful in Europe, a fruit of the inherent sense of beauty and proportion of the English yeomen, craftsmen, and labourers. With the fall of man into the "Age of Progress" this began to disappear under the rash of red-brick of the speculative builders and manufacturers. In Russia, peasant art, folk customs and dances, religious ceremonies—the organic life of Russia—have been killed by communism. The old capitalism, the destroyer of the organic life of the West, and the new communism, the destroyer of the organic life of the East, are symptoms of the inner degeneration of the psyche of man.

'Gurdjieff says that degeneration, deterioration, and decay of civilization on a world-scale has happened more than once; and the degeneration and decay of individual races and nations is too obvious even for us to be unaware of it. In the *Mahabharata* there are references to this gradual degeneration, of which we are in the last stages—the Kali Yuga.'

'Beelzebub relates that the adherents of Legominism used the principles of cosmic laws which they understood; and they introduced innovations, "lawful inexactitudes", into various forms of art. They rejected literature, not only because of the perishability of papyrus or paper, but because literature is the most subjective of all the arts; it depends on languages, which change and die. Everyone can appreciate the ancient works of art in Britain, like the Burghead Bull, Stonehenge, certain of the White Horses on the Downs, Celtic ornaments and pottery—"prehistoric"—but what do we know about the people who produced them? Nothing. And because these ancient people committed nothing to writing, popular educators in England are convinced that civilization began in Britain with the Romans. How many people can even read Anglo-Saxon, our language of yesterday? Another thing, literature is the shape of shadows. Novels are the daydreams of writers.

'Minor art is concerned with self-expression. Major art is an effort at conveying certain ideas for the benefit of the beholder; not necessarily for the advantage of the artist. In speaking of ordinary subjective art, we say that a perfect work of art completely satisfies our sense of harmony—every part of our sensory, emotional, and intellectual being. From Gurdjieff's point of view, from the point of view of one aspect of his aim—to wake us out of sleep, the said satisfaction of harmony (which is not real tranquillity but a form of higher sleep) is the last thing to be desired. Aesthetic contemplation is sublime sleep; consciousness is in abeyance.

'The object of the Adherents of Legominism was to cause people to "remember". They introduced lawful inexactitudes into works of art of all kinds so that people would ask "Why is it so?". This idea was found in the ancient Zen Buddhist schools, which were responsible for the flowering of great Japanese art; among the traditions which grew out of it was that in a perfect work of art something should be left unfinished.

'Gurdjieff relates that during his travels in Central Asia he and his companions came across a figure, an enormous image, in the desert. At first they thought it was no more than a relic. They camped beside it. Something about it raised their curiosity, and they began to study it. As time went on it seemed to be teaching them something—not through their minds, but their feelings and senses. It was an objective work of art.

'No one says of Greek art "This is strange; what does it mean?" It satisfies completely. It evokes no inner curiosity. But when we look at certain Egyptian frescoes we have a feeling of something strange and wonderful; and the Egyptian artist had the technique of the Greek, and was not inferior as a craftsman. The strangeness of the work results from the artist's wish to disturb the beholders, not just to please. Even in Greek art, at one period, there were, it seems, objective works of art; there is the legend of the statue of Zeus at Olympia which produced upon everyone a definite and identical impression. Leonardo da Vinci, studying ancient works of art, pre-Greek, asked "Why, with such mastery, did these ancient artists make such and such juxtapositions?" And he, according to Gurdjieff, came near to finding out.

'The same principles, based on cosmic laws, were used in music. Some of Gurdjieff's dances are examples of objective art, the music also. Those who understand the laws of vibrations can compose music in which there are three separate sets of vibrations, having different effects upon the respective centres, consciously composed to induce in the hearers a striving, a wish *to be*. It is as if one were reduced to a state in which one is compelled to remember oneself in order to free oneself from the pangs of aesthetic misery.

'They also introduced lawful inexactitudes into the religious and social ceremonies; and these were understood by the founders (not necessarily the "fathers") of the early Christian Church. Gurdjieff says that the Christian religion in its early days was perhaps the best of all forms of organized religion so far invented; that the founders of what became the Catholic Church, who introduced the ritual and liturgy, understood the principles of the effect on the senses and the emotions, of colours through stained glass, of the music, of the pressure of the volume of air, of the lines and form of the architecture: they understood and used all this for the good of the worshippers. The effects were consciously and mathematically calculated. The shrill ringing of the bell in the Mass, for example, was introduced from a ceremony in ancient Babylonian times to break a ritual which otherwise might become soporific, and to arouse the question "Why?" The tolling of the Angelus, making the sign of the cross, were reminders to the monks to "remember" themselves; the tolling of the passing bell, a reminder that we are all mortal. Echoes of similar effects were to be found in religious processions, and even in the coronation of kings and queens.

'In architecture we have examples of objective art in Chartres and Notre Dame, and the Taj Mahal, which is a product of a Sufi esoteric school.

'Examples of objective painting may be found in some fourteenth-

and fifteenth-century Persian paintings. There is an agreeable disharmony caused by using contiguous colours in a non-natural way. When the eye perceives a colour, the complementary colour following the law of the spectrum is naturally expected by the eye, and is formed on the retina. The Babylonians, understanding the "expectation of the eye", put in an unexpected colour which, though disturbing, was pleasing; but it required a conscious adjustment. When this is done unconsciously, or for effect, the result is often anything but pleasing. Quite simple people feel this: they say, "Those colours don't blend".

'The dances, movements and rhythms of the adherents of Legominism were of two kinds, religious and social. They introduced certain movements, non-natural, which affected the dancers in a certain way, so that the dance, or movement, became an invocation to a higher centre in the dancer himself. The movements, if performed correctly, produced a certain psychological state. Disturbing, contrary states were aroused. In addition, the dances were scripts, a kind of book, in which the spectator could be reminded of certain things. The dances were designed also to produce in the spectator a wish to remember himself, a state of remorse of conscience. In this connexion many of Gurdjieff's dances are objective works of art. He did not invent all the movements, he saw many of them and studied the principles in temples in Central Asia; but, understanding the laws of three and seven, discovering the ancient objective art of dancing, he based his movements and dances on this conscious art, and adapted them to the Western world. Incidentally, his school of dancing will be a source of inspiration for generations to come.

'Gurdjieff says: "You may judge a country by its dances". Countries everywhere are giving up their old good folk dances for empty American jazz. Moronic crooning is taking the place of folk song. It is an example of the corrupting influence of bad customs. Because it is new, it must, to the illiterate and semi-educated, be good. No discrimination.

'In America, a form of religious dancing exists among the Hopi Indians; the Snake Dance is an invocation. But of what? They have forgotten. In Central Africa the rhythm of the drums has an extraordinary effect on the instinctive and emotional centres, and so in India; but whereas the rhythms of the Negroes are involving rhythms, the Hindu rhythms are not. The rhythms of the Negro race, like its art, are not the beginnings of a culture of a primitive people, but the faint remains of a once-great civilization. Among the Hindus and the Sufis are to be found evolving rhythms; Gurdjieff's dances are in this category.

'The adherents of Legominism, understanding that dancing is an instinctive need of people and would always exist, introduced into popular dances and folk dances certain bits of objective art. So we find among "primitive" people, in Central Europe for example, folk dances which make a strong appeal even to English and Americans. Among the fertility dances, which grew out of religious dances, may be found fragments of real knowledge. The same with fairy tales. Again, the Saturnalia, in its original form, was a religious ceremony, consisting of dances and ritual. The ancients understood that at certain times of the year sacrifices of animals on an enormous scale were necessary. At other times, release of human energy, instinctive, emotional, and sexual, on a large scale, was necessary. Nature demanded it. The ceremonies were consciously organized and controlled, and the customs were found all over the world. Captain Cook discovered that in islands of the South Seas, at certain times of the year, dances were held which ended in mass copulation; the reason for it was forgotten. In England up to the time of the reign of the Puritans, every year an Abbot of Misrule was appointed, and in London a Lord of Misrule was elected from the apprentices and a whole day was given to jollification and dancing in the streets, and masters acted as servants. When the ancient customs degenerated, Nature was compelled to find other ways: hence the waves of mass hysteria, mass psychosis, crime, bigger wars and revolutions.

'Dancing played an important part in early Christian religion. Jesus is said to have led his disciples in a ritual dance.

'The adherents of Legominism based their sculpture on the Law of Seven, on mathematics. Lawful inexactitudes were introduced so that he who looked at the sculpture would ponder, would wonder why. The Sphinx and the Assyrian bull with five legs are examples.

'The section on drama presupposes a knowledge of and control of the body. I have a body composed of instincts, feelings, wandering thoughts. I wish to learn to use it; I *wish* not always to let it do as *It wants*. Before we can control the body we must have an "I". The Method provides a technique for the achieving of the "I", then I can manipulate the body with its three centres for my aim; this includes my relations with other people; but this, again, presupposes a knowledge of types of people, of which there are twenty-seven. Esoteric schools—not "occult" or schools of magic—used the drama as exercises for behaviour in life, and for putting plays on the stage of life, as we now put plays on the stage of the theatre; the mystery and miracle plays, at one time performed in cathedrals and churches, are echoes of these.

'Those who understand the principles and laws of Objective Art understand also the nature of man, his psyche, how his three centres almost never work together harmoniously and simultaneously, but vary according to the degree of experience in each. In general we classify people into three types—physical, emotional, intellectual. We say "over-emotional", "too intellectual", when we ought to say "under" in one or another centre. The knowledge of types can be expressed mathematically. A conscious man, understanding types, can produce the reaction he wishes from a person; he knows how that person will react.

'In old civilizations types tend to become fixed. In our own small way we can make a list of exterior types—Falstaff, Hamlet, Micawber, Sam Weller, Don Juan, Becky Sharp; or, the lawyer, the petty official, the soldier, janitor, priest, and so on. Behind these exterior types is the, so to say, essential type; and the divination of these is true sociology.

'Experiences are physiological processes taking place in us of which, at the time, we are usually unaware—we remember them afterwards. The changes of direction or divisions of the blood-stream have psychic counterparts, which are ordinarily known as consciousness.

'When a being is going through experiences, his manifestations are the only form of communication. My subjective never becomes the spectator's objective; he can only see my manifestations and understand just as much as I manifest myself.

'In ancient drama the pupil was taught to "act" consciously; that is, not to give way to an unconscious manifestation of his feelings, thoughts, and desires, but to convey the impression he wished. You may say that if we do this in life it is a technique of insincerity; it is, if what you mean by sincerity is an inability to control your manifestations.

'The actors in the school of objective drama had to learn to act consciously in one, two, or three centres. St. Paul spoke about being all things to all men; but this is for a conscious person. If we try to do it we shall find ourselves becoming identified with all the other men. We can begin by trying to put ourselves in one other person's place.

Remember the aphorism in the Study House: "Judge others by yourself and you will rarely be mistaken".

Conscious drama has to do with playing roles.'

'Included in the real education of children would be, among other things, allowing them to develop their faculty of mimicry, which, as with all animal life, is part of their natural play. Guessing, also; the green blade of a power which, if trained, would develop intuition with certainty; which, again, is true judgement. But children are discouraged from guessing and using controlled imagination—it is dubbed "telling lies", one of the results being that children learn to lie like adults.

'Gurdjieff says that certain of the early Greek plays were improvised, as described in *Beelzebub*. Plato, also, speaks about improvised plays. With such plays a critical audience was necessary. In the ancient schools of drama in India, epics like the *Mahabharata*, and later in Greece the *Iliad* and *Odyssey*, long before they were written down, were recited on a stage, and the reciter had to act the various parts. When several people took part, the older pupils played the higher roles, of gods—not gods as celestial beings but men possessed of objective reason and understanding, men in a state of ecstasy ("ek-stasis") outside and above the mechanicality of ordinary life.

'The dramatic school was originally a training ground for life, universal life: a real university, not as now, as half the young people complain, a monastery out of touch with life. The school of Pythagoras was such a training ground. The Pythagoreans were "myster" creators. In mystery is the extraordinary, the not-ordinary. The spectators had to keep their attention on the actor in order to discern the unexpected, from which they could learn something.

'In the higher forms of conscious drama the pupil was expected to take a situation and play a conscious part, but with unconscious actors, and so that he could be understood.

'The Christian Mystery, the birth, life, and death of Jesus Christ, was first rehearsed in an esoteric school of the Essenes, with whom Jesus worked. At the appropriate time it was played historically so as to affect the thought, feeling, and conduct of people for generations. It may be that the Christian Mystery was the outcome of the school of the adherents of Legominism. In *Fragments of a Faith Forgotten*, collected and translated by G. R. S. Mead, there are hints of how Jesus trained his pupils, his disciples, to play special roles, to dance special dances.

Judas, the most conscious and devoted of the disciples, had the most difficult role to play, certain to be misunderstood and like that of the villain on the stage, to be hissed by naïve audiences through the centuries.

'The life of Christ was not the life of Jesus. Christ existed before Jesus and after him. The divine mission was chiefly Christ. Jesus, pursuing his aim and mission, was perfecting himself, as Paul says, through suffering—not ordinary mechanical suffering, but voluntary suffering and conscious labour.

'Gurdjieff plays roles which few would or could play. I, myself, am often baffled; and even Stjoernval, Hartmann, and Salzmann, and especially Ouspensky, are sometimes deceived, let alone the younger pupils.

'What is left of the Pythagorean school of drama? A few echoes in the old mystery plays. The modern theatre has two purposes: amusement and propaganda. Mystery is no longer possible; there are no conscious actors. Our actors imitate, not from within but without; they merely provoke an illusion in the spectator, who is never challenged, but stimulated to recall previously recorded experiences. Drama, today, is not a new experience but a re-experience; it is titillation. It is not an influx of new material, but a stimulus that sets old material in motion. It is evocative, not representative—procreative, not creative; and its effect is an intensification of the mechanicality of both actor and spectator.'

'There is, in *Beelzebub's Tales*, in the book as a whole, a parallel with the Bible, in that it opens with a cosmology and a cosmogony, an account of how and why the world was created, and of the fall of man.

'The Bible proceeds through a series of semi-historical episodes interwoven with myths, into which eventually come clear the major and minor prophets. The reader of the Bible is expected to become aware of his state and his duty to God. When Objective Conscience has been awakened, there comes the New Testament, the Method, taught by individuals. Then comes Objective Reason, which proceeds to grow according to the Method. It culminates in the elevation of the personal nature of the pupils who diligently apply the discipline of the Method. Thus the Bible may be considered as a drama, an objective work of art of the highest kind.

'The Old Testament is mechanical man, waking up; the New

Testament, conscious man. The Old Testament represents actualities; the New Testament, potentialities.

'The Bible is symbolical and historical; it is doubtful if anyone (at least anyone that we can be in touch with) has the key to all the mysteries of the Bible. Gurdjieff may have. *Beelzebub's Tales* is a sort of Bible; the anomalies that seem to us incongruous and absurd may be a text within a text, which, when rooted out, may comprise an alphabet of the doctrine.

'According to Gurdjieff, the key to the Legominism and the key of the inexactitudes are both in our hands, the latter to be discovered by intuition. The key to the Legominism is the Method. Our understanding of this book can be said to be a test of our understanding and realization of the Method. The book is the only exemplification of a coded work of art accessible to us in our time; there is no use in going to far places to find other examples. Gurdjieff claims that a proper reading of the book would make unnecessary the decoding of all the works of art produced at the time of Aksharpanziar. Gurdjieff's book, perhaps, is a kind of bible for the future.

'Each of us is a cosmos with unknown parts spatially distant; ships are necessary to visit places and to find forgotten things. Cosmology is concrete psychology. Gurdjieff's system is complete. It has literature, drama, dancing and music—and a method with exercises which can only be taught in groups by teachers who have studied and worked for years.

'The theme of Gurdjieff's book is that we, as human beings, must accept suffering and labour; we cannot escape it, it is obligatory; and although the suffering is so distributed that at times some seem to escape their share, "Time grinds every grain". The total tax is the same. More than two thousand million people pay this tax. The purpose of genuine teachers is to show how this tax of suffering, in addition to being paid, can be turned to the use of the individual. There is no idea that it can be lifted. Everything in the Universe suffers—though not as we ordinarily understand suffering. One of the ideas in the book is that we should be of help to "His Unique Burden-Bearing Endlessness" by striving to understand the Method, and that by working correctly, we help to lighten the sorrow of our "Maker-Creator".

'Man exists for a purpose not his own. This includes all beings—animals, birds, insects, and bacteria. Each species is designed for a certain cosmic use. The norm of man is the discharge of the design for which he was created—like a machine designed to do a certain bit of work. But because of certain circumstances, unforeseen by the Higher Individuums, this planet (and men with it) has become an abnormal machine and no longer fulfils its design; it has even become a menace to the Universe. Hence, life here now exists only by Grace; and Nature has to "puff and blow", to adapt and adapt, so that the machine shall work.

'Existing as we do, we men are no longer capable of real happiness, that is, capable of the happiness which accompanies the fulfilment of a design.

'Renan, in his *Philosophical Dialogues*, said that Nature is hostile to the development of man and desires man's imperfections. Gurdjieff says that while this is true, it is not irremediable, and that Nature now has need of relatively liberated beings. The small chances of man's salvation are strengthened by two things; one, the wish of the Creator that this machine should function normally—hence the Messengers that have been sent from time to time to point the way; and two, the continued existence in all men, except the Hasnamuss, of Objective Conscience—an inner unrest at our awareness that we are not as we should be.

'In the Hasnamuss the germ of Objective Conscience remains unawakened, perhaps dead; he is incapable of organic shame.

'All the Messengers from Above are agreed on the terror of the situation; on man's being diverted from his true purpose, turning aside to false gods, being absorbed in the physical, practical side of life, or in current ideals, in social values instead of personal values, of substituting vague aims for common sense, of developing and complicating the outer life at the expense of the inner.'

'*Beelzebub's Tales to His Grandson* is like an onion with an almost infinite number of skins. You peel off a few, and then you realize that underneath there remains skin after skin, meaning after meaning.'

'In every mind there is a certain grammar of association. There are two categories; association of words—verbal reasoning, and association of forms—mentation by form, reasoning by ideas. This has nothing to do with what we are accustomed to speak of as "formality" or the ordinary "formal" mind. Nine-tenths of what we call thought is mechanical association of words. If you say "agony" to a superficial writer, he will answer "sweat", "anguish", "dark night of the soul" as readily as a parrot, with no personal realization of the fact of being in a state of agony. Association by form, or "mentation by form", is dependent on personal experience; it is still an association, but different from mere words. It is the form in which peasants and animals—or those we call "understanding persons" often think. It has strict reference to experience—a grammar of people in whom experiences exist. Verbal association is developed by words; formal, by being in the company of men of understanding and by being with "simple" people. Men who have spent a long time in the company of Arabs and Gypsies, for example, have returned with increased understanding. Why is it that all unspoilt children love to associate with craftsmen and farm-workers?'

'A true function of the formatory apparatus is to formulate. Formulate your feelings as well as your thoughts; the effort to do this will result in a clear crystallization, things will become clearer to yourself, hence to others. Almost all our communication with each other in life is by verbal association—no inner content. One of the things that strikes people in meeting Gurdjieff is the way he communicates by form; a platitude comes to life, full of meaning.

'All beings can be classified according to their reason. Every one of them is on a step of a ladder, evolving or involving—Jacob's ladder. The reason of a being is the co-ordinated sum of his functions, and is expressed in his manifestations. Man is higher than the animals only because the elements entering into his reason are more complex. Since the majority of human functions are abnormal, his reason is abnormal. Man by definition is superior to the animals, but, in fact, his reason is abnormal.

'Normal man is a being who feels; who is designed to encounter, create, and overcome difficulties—a contrast to ordinary man, who believes that man exists for his own happiness and peace. What counts is "overcoming", "effort"; a man may create difficulties within the field of his own choice, and must have an aim which requires effort to attain. But, as the aphorism states, we must use work as a means, not an end.

'In ordinary life we have respect for the person who encounters difficulties and makes effort to overcome them; if he succeeds we admire him, if he fails we feel sorry for him and we condemn the man who shirks his life responsibilities.'

'Gurdjieff passes on to us the counsel of his Grandmother; "Eldest of my Grandsons, listen, and always remember my strict injunction to you; in life, never do as others do . . . Either do nothing—just go to school—or do something no-one else does".

'This does not mean that we should cultivate eccentricity or mannerisms, or deliberately go against convention. He says, in fact; "In Rome do as the Romans do". He also tells us that we should consider outwardly more than we do now—be more thoughtful of other people.'

Orage said that when he was editing the *New Age* and saw the current of opinion flowing mechanically in a certain direction, he would initiate a current in the opposite direction.

He continued: 'One of the ways of gaining understanding is through pondering, which is an effort to think about abstract subjects, like metaphysics or cosmology, in order to try to get at the meaning. There are very many ideas in the book which we never shall be able to understand, in this life at least; but there are also many which we can understand if we make the effort to ponder them. Ordinarily, we assume that if the truth is stated clearly, we shall understand it. This is an illusion; understanding is developed not only by pondering, but by handling situations practically, as a good gardener manages his garden. Understanding is developed by "suffering perceptions of truth"— about ourselves and the cosmos.

'When we speak of psychology we speak of the kind of desires that animate a psychic being. A normal man is the cutting edge of the Universe. When we diverge from the norm we are abnormal; this explains the accumulated criticism in the book of those artists, writers, actors, scientists, politicians, and business men who substitute for normal aims some temporal form, such as the pursuit of beauty, the material conquest of the planet, the greed for power or the acquiring of riches. And since, for example, the subjective artist and subjective writer influence other men, Beelzebub regards them as evil influences that tend to divert man's interest and energy from a normal aim to one that is hostile to the great scheme.

'In the essence of a normal man is a Biblical hunger and thirst after righteousness—a thirst for Objective Reason.'

'One of the current views of life is that there is no cosmic purpose, no conscious aim, that protoplasm was formed accidentally and that everything just happens; another is that man was created for the State, whose object is to provide him with an increasing standard of living

197

—in the future. Another view is that God is omnipotent and all-loving; he created the world out of sheer benevolence and presides over the Universe with no other idea than that his children should be happy; that we have no duty except to each other, that man was given power over the earth and the animals and is authorized to exploit them; this is the attitude of the ordinary spoilt, selfish, over-indulged child towards its parents, who is not old enough to realize that nothing comes which did not cost Nature or someone something. This last is a widespread attitude, and it is the doctrine of the organized Christian Church.

'As an exercise, try to set down in your own words the idea of life as seen by one of your friends, or by yourself. What is your idea of the world? Is it merely chance, or is there a design? Is there a conscious purpose, an aim, an objective?

'In the first chapters of the book, there is an adumbration of the view that the world is knowable, that the Universe is a work of conscious creation, and consciously maintained for a conscious purpose—an enormous machine. God created it, not for our delight, but in pursuit of a conscious aim; and the onus of the reason is on God. This, perhaps, is an anthropomorphic view; it is also theomorphic; if it makes God in the form of man, it also makes man in the image of God.

'Animals can neither make nor understand machines. Man has reason, with the possibility of understanding a machine vaster than any he himself could construct. Man's purpose is to do this, but because of the catastrophe which occurred almost at the beginning of his existence on earth, his reason became distorted; and since then he has been in a state of hypnosis, as if under the influence of a drug. While the fumes of the drug remain we cannot pull ourselves together and reason normally. At the same time, there stirs in our conscience a dim reminder that we are not acting reasonably—like the Prodigal Son we are vaguely aware of it in the far country of the body, but we cannot remember our father's country. The problem is, how to wake up. There is no short cut, no magical means to this. The only sure way to a state of being permanently awake is by voluntary suffering and conscious labour; and we can begin by making a daily attempt to ponder and sense the meaning of life, and to try to deal with situations not only without complaining, but spiritedly. Here we shall have a taste of normal activity, activity according to Objective Morality.'

'Ask yourselves what you really wish. But before you can do this
198

you must learn to distinguish between ephemeral wants and desires on the one hand, and an essence wish on the other. Professor Denis Saurat says that wishes and ideas are entities. If you have a wish you will have harboured a being; if it is an ephemeral wish or a want, not gratified it will soon die. If it is a real, higher wish, it will live as long as its energy permits. If you have a rich nature you may have wishes which will last your whole life. From Saurat's point of view our immortality depends on our having wishes which will outlast the body. From our point of view a wish for understanding and being might outlast the planetary body.

'Gurdjieff says that "A real wish is the highest thing; but I must *be*, in order to *do*, in order to *wish*. If I *am* I can; if I *can*, I can wish; if I *am* and *can*, only then have I the objective right to wish".'

'As opposed to the present orthodox physicist's conception of the Universe as a machine whose energy is running down, the book takes the view that the Universe is expanding, growing. Though each part is subject to decay, it is replaced. This vast machine needs constant attention. For this His Endlessness has helpers. When man appeared he decided to make use of him also as a helper, but, because of the catastrophe, man has become a kind of zombie, he goes about his work in a dream-state, a drugged slave.

'Yet we are within reach of normality; it is as if only a thin wall separates us.'

'God is a three-centred being; his mental body is the Sun Absolute, his emotional body all suns, his planetary body the planets. We are made in the image of God, with three centres, but two of ours are undeveloped; our function is to aid their development. The normal life of the Kesdjan body is a passion for understanding; of the mental body, the power to understand. By pursuing the Method we gratify the need and develop the bodies. The pursuit of a minor aim, of a short cut to development and understanding by means of magic or Yoga or by the various systems imported from Asia and Indonesia, will result in distortion of growth of the emotions and the mind. All attempts to get rich quickly in the sense of development and understanding come within the realm of black magic. It is characteristic of the principle of Lentrohamsanin in man that no sooner does a real teaching begin to be given out, than someone or some group, afraid of the terrific efforts that may have to be made, begins to try to find a short cut and so distort the teaching. It has always been so.

'How can we become aware of genuine being-duty? We, as beings, incarnate this duty. Start by asking what you think is wrong with the human race, then try to formulate what you regard as the characteristics of a normal human being. Since you are Western-trained, use pencil and paper. Man questions with his reason, he wishes with his feelings.

'We are constantly engaged in avoiding difficulties, in trying to reach a point where effort is no longer necessary. Man is in a boat, rowing in one direction while looking in another.'

'One of the results of the consequences of the organ Kundabuffer is that reading, the cinema, radio, television, have become the modern opium. The communists said that religion was the opium of the people; so, for religious processions, with their colour, richness, and ancient music, they have substituted military processions and brass bands.

'Kundabuffer is vestigial but its consequences remain, so that people judge by what others say, and not from their own inner experience. We have been told as children that to be rich is a happier state than to be poor; that people are superior or inferior according to their station in life, or their possessions or charm, education or gifts—such as a gift for writing, which is comparable to a wart or mole. We are taught to believe that natural greatness is a condition of individual happiness, that amusements amuse, that distinguished company is brilliant, that other people's praise is necessary and that their disapproval is debilitating, that books, pictures, and music are stimulating, that leisure without work is desirable, that it is possible to do nothing, that fame, the possession of power, titles, success, have real value.

'We accept all this without pondering or reflection. We do not wish to ponder because it might disturb our self-calm, which is peace of mind with no wish to understand the meaning of existence; because of egoism which, for objective morality substitutes "I like" and "I don't like"—the expressions of children. We are victims of suggestibility, which is the mechanism of our psychology. We depend on reward and punishment, which are a necessary part of a young child's training— but we never grow up. We seldom acquire understanding through experiences; always we look outside for understanding. Paradoxically, we can understand only by experiencing. Understanding is inside us.

"If you know yourselves you shall be aware that you are the Sons of the Father".'

'Planets are enormous beings, and have relations between themselves as people do. They are reactions, tensions. They vary in shape and form, but their revolving in space causes them to appear as spheres. They communicate by emanations—a pure force which does not operate through and by means of matter; and by radiations—which operate through and by means of matter. Our earth is a planet which communicates with other planets through its organic system, which is like a skin, thinner than a coat of varnish on the great stone globe at Swanage. Tensions between planets are felt on our earth and occur at special times; then happens what Gurdjieff calls Solioonensious.

'In very ancient times, priests, who were then men of understanding, knew how to organize religious ceremonies on a vast scale so as to use the forces of the tension. But the organ Kundabuffer caused them to forget, and war was invented. We ourselves as individuals are subject to these tensions, we get out of sorts, irritable, rash, and find ourselves doing and saying things that we afterwards regret. How often a person pursues a certain course under the influence of one of his I's, completely identified, oblivious of everything else; and then, with a start, as it were, he comes to himself, wakes up, and is horrified with the realization of what he has been doing. Examples of this, from the comic and merely irritating to the tragic, are to be seen every day. Ovid's *Metamorphoses* has many examples. This is the result of the influence of the planets, and especially the moon, working on us through the results of the organ Kundabuffer when we are not in a state of self-remembering, that is, when we are unconscious; with the result that evil manifests itself. But "the fault, dear Brutus, is not in our stars, but in ourselves, that we are underlings", that we are slaves at the mercy of every planetary tension, the sport of every emotive wind that blows.

'We, as a group, have the Method—we are beginning to see what we ought to do. We ought to begin to be able to use the energy stirred up by tensions between ourselves and others; we ought to be able to use some of this energy instead of letting it all go out to the moon. Nothing is lost in the cosmic scheme—the energy we waste in negative emotion is used by the moon. And negative emotions are not only those of a violent and depressing kind, such as resentment, anger, and despondency—the various kinds of sentimentality are equally negative—like the emotion manifested at a religious revivalist meeting, or at a meeting for raising money for the support of stray dogs or cats, or the feeling of pity—which is really self-pity—aroused on reading in the newspaper about some mischance to someone you are totally unacquainted with—all this is negative emotion.

'Friction, which is a result of a tension, can be of great use if only we can remember ourselves at the moment. At the Prieuré Gurdjieff frequently organizes friction between pupils when they appear to be going through a period of sleep. For example, a pupil, a former army officer, whose way of giving orders was rather peremptory was in charge of the physical work. He understood much of Gurdjieff's teaching. Another pupil, a young man, not very intelligent, who understood very little, resented being told what to do by the older pupil. There was a clash of vibrations, and he refused to obey. The older one told Gurdjieff, who said, "Next time he refuses, insult him". Gurdjieff foresaw the result. It happened, and so much friction, so much negative emotion, was stirred up that we all had enough stimulus for self-remembering for several days. The young man should have learnt something from the shock. He may have done—but we at least were able to. Gurdjieff said that when we had a row with someone we should at once use the energy, so generated, in useful work.

'It is said that Wagner accidentally hit on the idea. When he got into the doldrums he would stage a row and use the resulting energy to go on with his writing and composing. In ordinary life, in a mechanical way, it is beneficial to be able to use this release of energy in doing something that one has put off doing, even tidying up a room, otherwise it turns to hatred and resentment, or sulking and brooding.'

'Certain vibrations are needed for the maintenance of the relations between Earth, Moon, and Anulios and for their harmonious relations. The same with our three centres. A being's reason is the sum of his total functions; if some are missing or abnormal, reason is abnormal, and he is unable to provide the necessary quality of vibrations, Askokin. There are two kinds of effort; Voluntary conscious effort, and involuntary, mechanical effort. Involuntary effort is determined by external circumstances and conditions—it is the effort of slaves, soldiers, servants, useful for the moon. Periodically the tension on certain parts of the planet becomes such that people go mad, the accumulated energy explodes, and they begin to destroy each other's existence, sometimes in millions. Conscious effort, conscious labour, produces that which helps us, helps God and his purpose.'

' "Love all that breathes", says Gurdjieff; this has to do with conscious love. We know chiefly self-love, egoism. "Sincerity" is a faculty for being unjust to others, to those we love and those we hate. Self-love is preferring to be in a pleasant state of dream about ourselves rather than that the false something within us should be hurt. What Gurdjieff calls "Mr Self-pride" and "Madame Vanity" refer to the ignorant presumption that the qualities of the organism and our station in life are due to merit; that we already "know" and do not need to be "taught". Both gifts and defects are due to biology and sociology. If I pride myself on my gifts I am ignorantly impertinent, equally so if I apologize for the lack of them. To understand this we must have had some realization of "being-shame". Continued reading of *Beelzebub's Tales* and pondering them will bring this. But, when realization of something weak and ineffective in yourself comes, don't fall into a state of despondency, we are all in the same ship, though perhaps in different parts. Every bit of real effort you make to work on yourself has permanent results, though the process may take years and even lives.'

'In the Arch-Absurd, Beelzebub shakes his head over the beings of this planet. "Our Sun neither lights nor heats". When we are presented with high ideas such as are in the book and make an effort to understand, the result is light in the true sense. "In the beginning was the Word, and the Word was God. In Him was Life, and the Life was the light of men". By pondering the ideas in the book, understanding comes—light; and with the light comes life—a vivifying something.

'Okidanokh is the substance of life. When scientists understand the third force of electricity they may make organic life. In the way things are going it is perhaps to be hoped that they never will discover it, since, in addition to producing explosives powerful enough to destroy a city at one blow, they may create monsters who will bring death to the human race. And it will all be "in the interest of science" and, therefore, according to the semi-educated, "legitimate".'

'The Universe, as a whole, exists for the sake of the Sun Absolute. The Sun Absolute is the soul body of God. Our body exists for the sake of "I"; "I" is the God of our organism.

'Prana is the substance of essence (Shaw came near to it with his "life force"). The life of the planetary body is the blood, and the life of the Kesdjan body is Prana. If Prana is crystallized in a being consciously or accidentally, the being must work on himself to perfect this germ of a soul, or he will recur perpetually with various exterior coatings, and meanwhile suffer and languish, until perfection is attained. "Blessed is he that hath a soul, blessed also is he that hath none, but grief and sorrow are to him that hath in himself its conception". Perhaps this is the reason why some of us are here, why we meet in groups to work on ourselves for self-perfectioning. This is where the love and compassion of His Endlessness is manifested—His wish to help these relatively few in their difficult state. At death the essence of beings is thrown into the melting pot (Peer Gynt and the Button Moulder) from which new beings emerge, but not with the same essence. They recur like the leaves of a tree, with the same tendencies for growth, in the same way, with perhaps minor variations —fulfilling a cosmic purpose.

'Every teacher has shown a way in which the germs of souls may develop and release themselves from suffering. As Attar says: "Each teacher shows it in his own way, and then he disappears". Buddha, for example, showed them the eightfold path of right thinking.

'What is Akhaldan? Khaldan means "moon", "A" means "not" or "against". He is a seeker, a ponderer, one who struggles against the current of ordinary life, which flows down the scale to supply the needs of the moon.

'Why is it that at certain times, certain parts of the planet become intensive war areas—parts of Europe, for example? Why do other parts become centres of enormous population—London, New York, Paris? It is because Nature demands certain vibrations from these areas, which can be obtained only by the death of beings and the tension occasioned by masses in close proximity.'

Questions about reincarnation were constantly coming up in the groups. All that can be said openly has been said by Gurdjieff as Ouspensky has reported in *Fragments of an Unknown Teaching*. In *Beelzebub's Tales* much more can be discovered; and by those who will seek, almost all that we can understand about recurrence and reincarnation is to be found there. But everyone must discover this for himself, otherwise, as Gurdjieff says, it will lead to misinterpretation and distortion and deeper sleep.

Orage gave an analogy of recurrence. He used the round stick of Brighton Rock, a kind of sweet which we ate as children. The words 'Brighton Rock', in red, ran down through the stick, so that wherever you cut you found the words. Our past and our future exist in this kind of solid tube. But we have the possibility of changing the tube —or getting into another tube. He said: 'In addition to the static pulsation of the tube there is a dynamic movement. The tube itself moves. Every cross-section is complete, revealing the time tube. In the static-dynamic aspects all that has been and will be is implicit.

'Theosophical teaching, based upon its interpretation of some passages in the *Mahabharata*, assumes that everyone reincarnates. Gurdjieff teaches that this happens to very few, and only those of high development. They choose. The essence of the mass of people recurs in other forms. And then there are those in whom something has been crystallized, in whom there is an urge for perfection, who begin to look for a teacher and perhaps find one. We have no personal experience of what happens after death. It is explained in *Beelzebub* in some detail, but you have to search for it. There are those who come into life again and search for the Method, and recognize it when they see it—they "remember". Let us take the analogy of the tree again. There is a difference between the seed and the leaf. The aim of the tree is to produce seed. In the autumn the leaf surrenders its life to the tree. But with the seed, part of the life of the tree goes with it. At death we surrender our life back to Nature, but we have the possibility of acquiring part of this life for our own use; with work, effort of the right kind, this life becomes for us imperishable being. In Norse mythology, the tree of life, Ygdrasil (whose origin is in Hindu mythology) from time to time produces seeds—gods and heroes who sacrifice themselves for the good of the world. They incarnate, having crystallized and perfected Prana in themselves.

'We can say that first dimension is identical recurrence; second dimension spiral recurrence; third dimension, a cross-section of all aspects.

'In speaking about coming into being, Gurdjieff ruled out "embodiment" and "materialization" because of spiritualistic implications; the psyche does not take on a body. It is the same with the expression "taking on flesh". Trees, rocks, and all sensible objects from his point of view are "incarnated", come into being. How can we express the idea of the psyche manifesting its potentiality of manifestation? Gurdjieff suggested some word from electrology—dipping something imperceptible into an electric bath whereby it becomes perceptible. So we used "coating" to mean the superimposition on a real but imperceptible object of something that made it sensible.'

'To sum up, we begin by asking, "What is the meaning and aim of existence?" Ashiata Shiemash defines it in the Five Strivings of Objective Morality. As Beelzebub relates: "All the beings of this planet then began to work on themselves in order to have in their consciousness this divine function of genuine conscience, and for this purpose, as everywhere in the Universe, they transubstantiated in themselves what are called "the being-obligolnian strivings".

'What must *we* do in order to have in our consciousness the Divine function of genuine conscience? We must transubstantiate in ourselves the five being-obligolnian strivings.

' "*The first striving is to have in our ordinary being existence everything satisfying and really necessary for our planetary body.*"

' "Satisfying" here has nothing to do with gratification. We have an obligation to strive to keep the body in health, to satisfy its needs as far as we can in order that it shall be a good instrument for our use. That is, to maintain in a state of readiness this body which we have inherited. I have a body. This includes not only health, but a kind of elasticity, so that the body is ready for the use of the intelligence. While it is necessary to be completely competent in some special field, a special skill obtained at the expense of elasticity is against Objective Morality. Gurdjieff said that in addition to his own special field, in which he was a master, he had worked at forty different crafts. In none of these was he a specialist, but he had two purposes —one, to give his instinctive-moving centre the feel; the other, to be ready for potential needs in pursuit of his aim. Most people have a feeling of criticism towards the extreme specialist—a vague feeling that the ideal development should be in the direction of wholeness.

' "*The second striving is to have a constant and unflagging instinctive need for self-perfection in the sense of being.*"

'This is not to be defined by what we ordinarily know or do, it is a state based on real KNOWING in order to Do. Individual growth consists in the growth of essence, in the achieving of "being"—not exterior personality. What sort of a being am I? We know when we have made "being-effort". To be in a state of constant activity is not necessarily "being-effort". A form of being-effort is compelling ourselves to do simple exercises morning and evening; not the usual physical exercises, but those given in groups. Or we can make being-effort by compelling ourselves to overcome physical or emotional inertia and doing a job that the body resents. Being is achieved through conscious effort, by doing small things voluntarily. In this sense life is a gymnasium—or as St Paul says, "running in the great race". Gurdjieff says that we must always be a little ahead of inclination, but not to excess, then we become in Gurdjieff's sense "spiritualized", by which he means "spirited"—not spiritual, but endued with life, spirit.

' "*The third is the conscious striving to know ever more and more concerning the laws of World-Creation and World-Maintenance.*"

'The aim of true philosophy is the understanding of life, and this is not a privilege of the few, it is the function of a normal human being to ask "Why?". We may not be able to give the right answers, but the dignity of man consists in his concern with the questions. In every situation there is material for questioning; with one faculty one is enquiring, while with others one is behaving ordinarily. There is no need to be aloof from life or to be idiosyncratic. The effort made in pondering the working of the laws of World-Creation and World-Maintenance inevitably stretches the faculties of the mind; the attention, memory, concentration, real imagination increase, not by direct but by indirect exercise. After half an hour's pondering you may have not a word to say; worse, there may be merely an increased realization of ignorance, but, according to Socrates, "The realization of ignorance is the beginning of wisdom". Gurdjieff says: "You will find that the more you realize you don't know, the more you will understand".

' "*The fourth is the striving from the beginning of our existence to pay for our arising and our individuality as quickly as possible, in order afterwards to be free to lighten as much as possible the SORROW OF OUR COMMON FATHER.*"

'Generally speaking, all of us are parasites. Gurdjieff constantly uses this expression at the Prieuré. Not one of us has discharged his debt to Nature. To be alive is a unique miracle—to have the possibility of Being in place of Non-Being. Think of what it has cost Nature in the preparation of planetary conditions, the long periods of experiment perhaps, so that, in addition to serving her, we might become Sons of the Father. And in return, what do we do? We behave in the family of Nature like self-indulgent children whose only object is to enjoy ourselves. If you will only ponder seriously for half an hour on the way we exploit natural resources, land, forests, and animals, for the gratification of abnormal desires, you cannot help but be appalled.

'Emerson said "Earn your living"—earn the right to live.

'It is sometimes astonishing that Nature permits the members of the human race to continue their existence, and does not render them harmless or discontinue the human species as she has done with other species.

' *"The fifth striving is always to assist the most rapid perfectioning of other beings, both those similar to oneself and those of other forms, up to the degree of the sacred Martfotai, that is, up to the degree of self-individuality."*

'We must discriminate between gratifying the weaknesses of others in order to obtain their good opinion of ourselves, and helping them to become what they really wish to be. But we can only become "hard" on others when we have learnt to be "doubly hard" on ourselves. The one real service we can render to others is a service that will help them to discharge their functions as human beings.

'There is a key here to what is sometimes called Gurdjieff's ruthless behaviour to others. He is completely indifferent to what others think of him. When he has humiliated you before others, called you offensive names, treated you "abominably", then, a week after, or perhaps a month or a year, there will come to you a feeling of gratitude to him and an awareness of increased inner strength.

'The Five Strivings of Objective Morality contain the essence of the Gurdjieff Method. But before we are able to strive in the right way, we must understand the meaning of conscious labour and voluntary suffering, for on these two basic principles—Being Parktdolgduty and the Strivings—hang all the law and prophesyings of the Gurdjieff system. They form a basic octave, and nothing can be added to or taken away from them.'

'One of the things we have to do is to anticipate—and not become identified with—the inevitable state of pessimism which comes with the breakdown of modern science, religion, and ethics. The ideas in Gurdjieff's system are at present premature for most people. To speak about them is like recommending a doctor to a man who imagines he is in good health. But it is desirable and necessary that there should be a growing nucleus of people working according to these ideas. Pessimism affects the finest minds; not all will escape as easily as Bertrand Russell, who is "terribly at ease in Hell", who once said, "I build my house on the rock of unyielding despair." '

'Beelzebub gives seven factors which make the organism what it is.

These go far beyond anything the modern Behaviourists have contributed. He says: "You remember that when I explained to you how these favourites of yours define 'the flow-of-time' I said that when the organ Kundabuffer with all its properties was removed from their presences, and they began to have the same duration of existence as all normal three-brained beings arising everywhere in our Universe, that is, according to what is called the Foolasnitamnian principle, they should then have existed without fail until their second-being-body-Kesdjan had been completely coated in them and finally perfected by Reason up to the sacred 'Ishmesh'. But later, when they began existing in a manner increasingly unbecoming for three-brained beings and entirely ceased actualizing in their presences their being-parktdolg-duty, foreseen by Great Nature, by means of which alone it is possible for three-brained beings to acquire in their presences the data for coating the said higher-parts; and when, in consequence of all this, the quality of their radiations failed to respond to all the demands of the Most Great Common-Cosmic Trogoautoegocratic process—then Great Nature was compelled, for the purpose of 'equalizing-vibrations', gradually to actualize the duration of their existence according to the principle Itoklanoz, that is, the principle upon which, in general, is actualized the duration of one-brained and two-brained beings, who have not the same possibilities as three-brained beings, and who are therefore unable to actualize in their presences the said, foreseen by Nature, 'parktdolgduty'. According to this principle, the duration of being-existence, and the whole of the content of their common presences, are in general acquired from the results arising from the following seven actualizations surrounding them:

1. Heredity in general.
2. Conditions and environment at the moment of conception.
3. The combination of the radiations of all the planets of the solar system during the formation in the womb of their producer.
4. The degree of being-manifestation of their producers during the period in which they are attaining the age of a responsible being.
5. The quality of being-existence of beings similar to themselves around them.
6. The quality of what are called the 'Teleokrimalnichnian' thought waves formed in the atmosphere surrounding them during the period of their attaining the age of majority—that is, the sincerely manifested good wishes and actions on the part of what are called the 'beings-of-the-same-blood'.
7. The quality of what are called the being-egoplastikoori of the given being

himself; that is, his being-efforts for the transubstantiation in himself of all the data for obtaining Objective Reason."

'These, simply and succinctly stated, are the seven factors whose results constitute the organism. While we can examine them briefly it must be recognized that, like all other statements in *Beelzebub*, they can only be understood when taken together with the rest of the book. Keys to the doors of understanding will be found in other chapters. As in everything else in the book, there are three main streams of understanding.

'Well then, with this in mind, let us take the seven aspects.

'(1) "Heredity in general." This is not only one's immediate parentage but the whole of both families, and behind them, the race—and there are five main races, each with its peculiar history, experiences, and psyche. Behind the race, again, is a biological history—mineral, vegetable, and animal. The body is the result of a complicated biological process going back to the appearance of organic life on this planet.

'(2) "Conditions at the moment of conception." At the moment of conception we start life as a unicellular being. This moment includes factors of the physical and psychical state of the parents and their recent history; also the geographical position, air, soil, magnetic forces, and so on. It is all too complex for us to analyse. Our ability to experience is determined by the foregoing factors. We are born a machine with a series of windings. As we are, we can no more diminish or increase our experience than we can control the length of the kind of dream that happens to us.

'(3) "The combination of the radiations of all the planets, etc." Radiations of planets—planetary influences, are operative on us through our mother during the period of gestation. This has always been accepted by the ancients, though it cannot be proved. But there is plenty of circumstantial evidence in favour of it.

'(4) "The degree of the being-manifestation of their producers, etc." Being-manifestations are from essence, genuine, and therefore, rare. An act of real sincerity has an enormous effect on a child—on its character. One reason why children grow up without character is not because the parents do not love them but because they conceal their love in their behaviour.

'(5) "The quality of 'being-existence of beings', etc." The nature of being-existence of people with whom children are brought in contact. Modern civilization brings about all kinds of artificial behaviour on

the part of people, and this affects children—also, the young are fed
on de-naturized food, hence a host of drugs supposedly to correct the
bad results, as we grow up, of wrong food, wrong clothing, bad sleep,
wrong posture, and so on. And, usually, we exercise only one centre
at a time, and become a sedentary type, for example, or an unnaturally
active type such as a professional sport-addict. Few of us breathe
naturally; we spare ourselves fatigue and have never been compelled
to take long breaths as a labourer does. We have almost no need to
think; this is spared us by education, newspapers, books, radio. Everything is prepared for us; we are told what and how to do everything,
about everything that happens on the earth; and all is told us by those
who are devoid of real understanding, whose knowledge is partial and
whose conclusions are therefore false. Real teaching is replaced by a
mechanical exercise of memory, so that the bright boy or girl is one
who, endowed with a photographic memory, can win prizes by passing examinations and intelligence tests, which, as everyone will admit
in private, have almost no real value. Food, air, and impressions—the
three basic foods, already spoilt. Town children begin with the disadvantage of not being able to copy the behaviour of normal beings;
life in the country comes nearer to the normal, so that so-called
"uneducated" children from farms often outstrip the city children; this
is especially so in Europe, because they have to use their faculties.

'(6) "The quality of 'Teleokrimalnichnian' thought waves, etc." We
do not yet understand enough even to discuss this. We can only hint.
For example, if the two parents are hostile to one another, even
though their outward behaviour may be polite, the children will sense
the hostility and suffer accordingly. In modern civilization the "only"
child is usually neurotic, and becomes a "problem" child. Almost all
child-psychologists are parents of a problem child and, like most
psychiatrists, are neurotic. Child delinquents, rich and poor, come from
homes where their natural instincts and possibilities have been diverted,
distorted, or suppressed.

'(7) "The quality of the being-egoplastikoori of the being himself, etc."
"The exertion to understand", which children up to the age of
adolescence have been encouraged to make. We presume that they
have curiosity; and we gratify this at once, thus sparing the child its
own effort to gratify its curiosity. An appetite for this would exert
itself; but fuel heaped on the fire puts it out.

'Curiosity is so valuable a manifestation in life that its gratification
should be delayed. The teacher, instead of being anxious to teach,

should encourage real curiosity, that is, to know about life. Gurdjieff says that in the East there are no teachers, only learners. Now, with the break-up of the old ways of life in the East and the spread of education —with the so-called "backward" peoples becoming "civilized", that is, industrialized, the ancient wisdom will disappear, to be preserved only in esoteric schools. The saving grace is that underneath the changing surface of life there continues to flow the deep stream of the human unconscious or subconscious. Life is vitally curious; yet we must beware of becoming identified with curiosity. Read Prince Lubovedski in the Second Series.

'Life, from the period of adolescence, is the unconscious unrolling of a film which has been wound up in us. After adolescence it begins to unwind in the form of experiences we meet. For example, you take up a profession (it cannot be said that you decide, it just happens because of a combination of something in you and something outside you). Your fate is not determined by what you will do in it, but what you will do in it is already determined by these preceding factors. We are not really living; we are watching unfold that of which we are the un-conscious victims—our little spool. As it unwinds, we, as we say, "live". Actually, we exist. This is behaviourism with a vengeance. Gurdjieff says that the Behaviourists do not even begin to realize to what extent they are determined.

'True, accidents occur—the wound-up spool may be dropped. We may have a premature unwinding of the spool as the result of an accident, or the influence of people around us; this latter is one of the perils of civilization as opposed to accident. We cannot speculate about what an "accident" is, but we can about the other. What is it, apart from accident, that causes a premature unwinding? It is suggestion. For example, each of us has a fixed capacity for thought; if we act, not from a native wish, but from the suggestions of others, we may find our-selves reading a great deal that does not really interest us, and attending "learned" lectures in order to acquire information which we can pass on to others and so appear in their eyes as "a somebody", as Gurdjieff says, "and not just a nobody".

'This passive titillation exhausts our potentiality without any active thinking on our part.

'The same with emotions. By associating with pathological artists of whatever branch of art, we become victims of "beauty", without genuine human emotions. To follow an aesthetic career, not actively but appreciatively, is a short cut to the loss of innate taste and power. Pursue art, pursue reason. And again, "Love not art with your feelings".

'Similarly in the physical world, the world of sport; there can be a premature ageing of the organs from exercise taken not because it was needed, but from pseudo reasons of rivalry and publicity.

'Our specific against a premature running down of any one spool is the Method, the aspect called "Iramsamkeep"—I keep myself; never to abandon oneself to the activities of one centre; never to become an extreme specialist aiming at intellectual, emotional, or physical greatness, but to strive to keep a balance of the three.

'Society creates monsters because it is difficult to resist the inducement society offers. Leonardo da Vinci, one of the really greatest Europeans, refused to become a specialist in spite of the financial rewards offered him. When he found himself in a rut and thereby becoming unbalanced, he would throw up whatever he was doing. This is a working rule for everyone, and the best modern educational systems understand it. But when the pupil leaves, he is expected to specialize.

'At the same time, one should strive to excel in anything that one takes up. By working in the Gurdjieff Method, whose aim is the harmonious development of the three centres, directed towards the increasing of consciousness, being, and understanding, it is possible to excel without becoming identified with the pursuit. The difference between being identified with something and not being identified with it is not a question of efficiency, but of putting or not putting one's whole strength and attention into the job.

'This brings us back to the definition of the final goal. At the outset we stated that the normal in man is a passion for understanding the meaning and aim of existence. This is the master magnetic current. The positive magnetic pole is the cerebral part; the negative, the instinctive-moving part. When the current is flowing normally, all functions begin to fall into their proper places. But we are negatively polarized; and when, as in us, the current is passing from the spinal to the cerebral, we are disharmonized. Then we are Peter—crucified head downward.

'The psychological human being is a human being with a passion for understanding. Those in whom the current passes normally find their function in life becoming increasingly normal. The prime need is the presence of that active passion for understanding. Why? Because man was created for the purpose of producing a Soul; and a soul may be defined as a being capable of producing Objective Reason.

'*Beelzebub's Tales* are not wholly allegorical; some parts are historical, some contemporary. We must be able to read parabolically the thought between and over the lines.

'During Beelzebub's sixth and last descent, three Messengers from above appeared on the planet—Jesus, Muhammad, and Lama. Why three in this short time?

'Each left a doctrine, but the doctrines became so transformed that their authors would not have recognized them. First the followers split into sects, then they introduced ideas which had nothing to do with the original doctrine and were often contrary. Apropos, we can see from our own personal experience that owing to our strange psyche, ideas, even when clearly stated, are certain to be differently interpreted, split up, and changed. This has always happened, and must continue to happen so long as our psyche remains abnormal.

'Beelzebub's description of the Last Supper and the Sacrament is what has always been known by a few people in certain esoteric groups. Before his crucifixion Jesus shed his blood into a vessel, perhaps the disciples partook of it; and a link was formed between the Kesdjan body of the teacher and his immediate followers. After his death they were able, by putting themselves into a certain state of consciousness, to communicate with him through the blood. Communication was not by speech. This gave rise to the report that Jesus had been seen. Communication was possible only for a certain period; after it ceased came the Ascension.

'Events moved too quickly for Jesus and his disciples; and Judas, the most trusted, undertook to gain time and so entered into intrigue with the Romans. He offered to arrange for them to take Jesus quietly and so with the consent and knowledge of Jesus, gained the time necessary for the ritual to be carried through. Judas emerges as the most conscious of the disciples, and the one who rendered the greatest service. This is the true Judas. The conventional one is the traitor, cursed by Christians for two thousand years. But both the curses and the applause of this world are of equal value—which, in the objective sense, is none.

'In each of us there is a conventional Judas. At the Prieuré Gurdjieff often refers to pupils in this sense when they are asleep and going off the track.'

'One of the titles suggested for Chapter 47 was "The Mountain Pass of Impartial Mentation". From this point of view the book represents a climb through the various stages of reason. Beelzebub has reached this pass and has attained to the state of Impartial Objective Reason. A new order of life is now possible. What does it mean, the surrendering of part of their development by the others for the sake of one of their kind? We can make an analogy. If our "I" is to grow and develop, then the other "I's" must give up something of their possibility of satisfying their own needs and wants. The time comes when, instead of struggling against this, they will wish to do so.

'At the end Hassein voices the question which concerns us all. Is it still possible by some means or other to save the three-brained beings arising on the planet Earth, and to direct them into the becoming path? Beelzebub answers: "The sole means now for saving the beings of the planet earth would be to implant a new organ in their presences, an organ like Kundabuffer—but this time of such properties that everyone of these unfortunates should, during the process of his existence, constantly sense, and be cognizant of, the inevitability of his own death as well as the death of everyone on whom his eyes and attention rests. Only such a sensation and such a cognizance can now destroy the egoism completely crystallized in them that has swallowed up the whole of their Essence, and also that tendency to hate others which flows from it—that tendency which engenders all those mutual relationships existing there, and which serve as the chief cause of all their abnormalities, unbecoming to three-brained beings and maleficent for themselves and for the whole of the Universe." '

IV

FONTAINEBLEAU 1928

DURING THIS WINTER I became aware of a growing wish to go to the Prieuré and do some real work with Gurdjieff. I could not formulate clearly what I wanted to do there; but as time went on the wish to go grew so intense that I could no longer resist it. It was not a desire to escape from life and its responsibilities, for never had Fortune treated me so well. I had everything that ordinary life, the world, has to offer—interesting friends and acquaintances, a place in the country, and a flat in New York, cars, satisfying work that brought in money; above all, Orage and the group: but all this weighed light in the balance against going to Gurdjieff.

This longing to 'be what one ought to be', 'to have being', to be able to 'do', to 'understand', has been expressed by poets and mystics—Hindu, Sufi, and Christian—in terms of an exile longing for home, or more often the lover longing for the beloved. The ache in the solar plexus that accompanies this longing for perfection is similar to that felt by the exile or the lover.

Eventually, after a good deal of inner struggle, we gave up our life in New York and sailed for France. Before we left I said to Orage: 'I trust that it will not be too long before we meet again?' He said: 'We are the kind who will always meet. I shall not go to the Prieuré this year. As a matter of fact, I'm beginning to feel that my work here is coming to an end; another two or three years, perhaps, and then we may meet in England.'

We arrived at Fontainebleau-Avon early in June. In the fiacre from the station my feelings were stirred, as always, by the familiar sights and sounds and smells—the train passing under the bridge, the jangling of the tramcar, the smell of sawn pine, arriving at the gate and pulling the bell marked 'Sonnez fort', and the plashing of the fountain in the courtyard. I had no idea of what was going to happen, but I felt that it was something very big for me.

Gurdjieff made us very welcome, as did everyone. I did not explain why I had come—in fact, as I say, I could not clearly formulate it; but, as events showed, he understood.

For the first weeks we worked as usual, in the house or the gardens, and went about with Gurdjieff in his car. In July he took Mme de Hartmann and myself on a trip to Biarritz and Lourdes. On the way I began to think about what my 'idiot' represented in me, for so far I had not a clue. I made up my mind that I would ask him as soon as I saw an opportunity. I knew that if I could discover its meaning I would have a key to my state and my behaviour—to that something so plain to others but hidden from myself. So far, each time I had questioned him about my 'idiot' he had turned it off or had not even replied.

One day we stopped at a wayside restaurant and ate in the shade of a pleasant bosky garden. It was very hot, the food and armagnac were particularly good, and the perspiration streamed down our faces. When, during the ritual of toasting the idiots, we came to my category, I asked him to tell me what it meant. At first he would not. But I pressed him and almost begged him to give me at least a hint. Soon he began to speak, and then in a sentence of five words told me. I was astonished at the clarity and simplicity of his words, and under the influence of his presence and the clairvoyant effect of the armagnac I saw my chief feature, something I had never even suspected. When we left, and were driving along, I thought about it, and I saw how this something had been my worst enemy even from a child. It was the chief thing perhaps among the causes that formed the pattern of my life and had brought so many difficulties and spoilt so much for me in my relations with other people. I realized also that had it not been for Gurdjieff and his method I might have remained always the same, repeating and behaving in the same way. I cannot remember the name of the place where we had lunch, but I have a vivid picture of our sitting in the bower on that very hot day, wiping the perspiration from our faces.

It is astonishing and even terrifying that one can go on for years living with a false picture of oneself; and even with a wish to know, to have no real picture of how one manifests oneself. How can the 'dead' know, when even those who are beginning to wake from sleep find it so difficult?

From that day something began to change in me.

At Biarritz Gurdjieff began to make difficulties. We met his brother Dmitri and his wife, and they, with one of the children, all joined us in the car. He put his brother in the front seat with him, and myself between them—those two big men. It was a small car, with just room for four people. What with the luggage in the back and the six of us crowded in, we were all most uncomfortable, and as the day went on it became real torture, but I made up my mind not to give way. At last Dmitry Ivanitch and his wife Astra Gregorievna could stand it no longer, and they returned to Fontainebleau by train; Gurdjieff, Mme de Hartmann and myself went on our way, I still sitting with him in front. At Lourdes we went to the place where the halt, the maimed, and the diseased lay, rows and rows of poor creatures waiting to be healed, some of them almost monsters. A little later we met a long funeral procession, a dead bishop being taken to his grave. It was impressive, with the tolling of the bells, the incense, the chanting of the priests and monks as they passed along the road lined with people— the pageantry and circumstance of organized religion.

Often, as he drove along, Gurdjieff thought out passages for *Beelzebub's Tales,* and dictated them in Russian to Mme de Hartmann, who sat in the back ready with notebook and pencil. When we were becoming soporific, beginning to day-dream, or if he himself needed a shock to keep awake while driving, he would stage a scene, and sometimes shout at us with what appeared to be rage. We were soon awake. Then there would come a halt at a café, or armagnac and sandwiches by the roadside, when he would talk. In passing through the country Gurdjieff seemed to be able, almost literally, to smell out the best food, the best local produce, so that every day we ate something new and tasty.

Sometimes he would draw me out, make me say things, and then with a look of pity shake his head at me; and I would realize that I had exposed some weakness, an imperfection, in myself. These incidents, these constant shocks which exposed one and then another of my seemingly innumerable enemies within, remained in my memory.

A day or so after we got back to the Prieuré from the trip, he put me to work with two other men, digging a trench in the forest. It was pleasant working in the shade, and when we stopped for spells still pleasanter to sit and talk about 'high ideas'. A few days passed in this congenial toil. Then first one man was sent to another job, then the other, and I found myself working alone. Gurdjieff told me to dig and find a spring which was said to be somewhere close by, the spring that he had spoken about five years before. As the days passed and no one came near me and no sign of water appeared, a resistance began to grow in me, a revolt against doing what my mind knew ought to be done. It was not the difficulty of the hard physical work. In British Columbia I had been a well digger, blasting every foot with gelignite— a difficult and dangerous job. What I had to overcome now was a revolt—a tremendous resistance of the body and the feelings to continuing this dull, monotonous, apparently purposeless task in the sweltering heat. After working for some days I had dug a long deep trench and a deep pit through the heavy clay. No one came near me, and I was no longer asked to the meals in the English dining room. Then Gurdjieff took my wife and some others on a car trip, which added to my emotional difficulties, since I enjoyed nothing so much as going about with him.

When he returned some days later and came and looked at my work —his first appearance for two weeks, I said: 'There is no water here; it is useless to go on.' He merely remarked, 'Must be water here. Must find it. Now dig here.' He pointed to another spot and went away. So I began again. But a nagging thought tormented me. I wondered why I had given up my comfortable interesting life in America to come here and work like a navvy and be humiliated. Was this just a whim of Gurdjieff's to keep me occupied? I fell into a state of discouragement and despondency. At the same time there was an inner feeling that the task must be fulfilled, and that this, perhaps, was the first real effort I had ever made.

A day or so later, after tea, I went to my room to rest. The physical posture of lying on my back may have increased the feeling of despondency; the fact is I was on the point of giving up, when I reached out and opened the *Pilgrim's Progress* and read:

'Then I saw that they went on all, save that *Christian* kept before, who had no more talk but with himself, and that sometimes sighingly, and sometimes comfortably; also he would be often reading in the Roll that one of the shining ones gave him, by which he was refreshed.

'I beheld then that they all went on till they came to the foot of an Hill, at the bottom of which was a Spring. There was also in the same place two other ways besides that which came straight from the Gate; one turned to the left hand, the other to the right, at the bottom of the Hill; but the narrow way lay right up the Hill (and the name of the going up the side of the Hill is called *Difficulty*). *Christian* now went to the Spring and drank thereof to refresh himself, and then began to go up the Hill; saying,

> This Hill, though high, I covet to ascend:
> The difficulty will not me offend;
> For I perceive the way to life lies here;
> Come, pluck up, Heart; let's neither faint nor fear;
> Better, tho' difficult, th' right way to go.
> Then wrong, though easie, where the end is wo.

'The other two also came to the foot of the Hill. But when they saw that the Hill was steep and high, and that there was two other ways to go; and supposing that these two ways might meet again, with that up which *Christian* went, on the other side of the Hill: Therefore they were resolved to go in those ways (now the name of one of those ways was *Danger* and the name of the other *Destruction*). So the one took the way which is called *Danger* which led him into a great Wood; and the other took the way directly up to *Destruction*, which led him into a wide field full of dark Mountains, where he stumbled and fell, and rose no more.

'I looked then after *Christian*, to see him go up the Hill, where I perceived he fell from running to going, and from going to clambering on his knees, because of the steepness of the place. Now about the midway to the top of the Hill, was a pleasant *Arbour*, made by the Lord of the Hill, for the refreshment of weary Travailers. Thither therefore *Christian* got, where also he sat down to rest him. Then he pulled his Roll out of his bosom and read therein to his comfort; he also now began afresh to take a review of the Coat or Garment that was given him as he stood by the Cross. Thus pleasing himself awhile, he at last fell into a slumber, and thence into a fast sleep, which detained him in that place until it was almost night, and in his sleep his Roll fell out of his hand. Now as he was sleeping, there came to him one and awaked him, saying, *Go to the Ant, thou sluggard, consider her ways and be wise*: and with that Christian suddenly started up, and sped him on his way, and went a pace till he came to the top of the Hill.'

Then I remembered Orage's similar experience here. He had felt as I did, perhaps in this very room. And now something constrained me to make more effort. I went back to my task, took up my shovel and pick, and began again; to remember myself and keep my restless mind from wandering into daydreams, pleasant or resentful, I worked sometimes faster than usual, or slower, did counting exercises, repeated lists of words in sequence. But the days still passed slowly and monotonously.

One day, when I had given up all hope of finding water, results came. As I struck my pick into the clay a spot of water showed. I dug deeper, and as I dug a trickle appeared, then a larger trickle. With a stirring excitement I dug again, and suddenly a spring of water was bubbling round my feet. I stared in astonishment, scarcely believing my eyes, for the water was welling up to my ankles. As I stood gazing it was as if a veil within was being lifted, a cloud disappearing, a light breaking through.

I climbed out of the pit, out of the miry clay, and went to the house to tell Gurdjieff, but he was away. Gladness and joy bubbled up in me like the spring. I went to my room and sat down and picked up my Bible. At random, it seemed, I read: 'Blessed is the man that endureth temptation, for when he is tried he shall receive the crown of life.' Turning the pages, I came to Revelation: 'He that overcometh shall inherit all things. I shall be his God and he shall be My Son.' 'He that overcometh will I make a pillar in the temple of my God, and he shall go no more out, and I will write upon him the name of my God, and I will write upon him my new name . . .' 'And he showed me a pure river of water of life, clear as crystal, proceeding out of the throne of God and of the Lamb . . . and they shall see his face, and his name shall be in their forehead.'

These words, which from childhood I had heard and read hundreds of times, and which formerly had stirred up pleasant religious feelings, now became free of associations. It was as if I had seen them for the first time, and their meaning was clear. They have to do with not some far-off past or some far-distant future, but with *now*. They are connected with *doing*, with overcoming one's weaknesses, with not giving up just at the moment when greater effort is needed. They have to do with psychological processes of inner development, which in turn are the result of conscious labour, of a sort of super-effort.

The state of ecstasy, the glimpse through 'the doors of perception', the presence of God, or as we now say, the 'state of higher consciousness', lasted throughout the day. When the intensity died down something remained—not just a memory but a crystallization, so to speak. When Gurdjieff returned next day he came to the well, looked at it, and said, 'Now, I think, finish. This no longer necessary. I have other plans. We look for water in another place.' The task had served its purpose.

This was Saturday morning. The same evening, in the Turkish bath, during the few minutes' quiet before we went into the hot room, he began to speak to me, seriously, but with light radiating from his eyes:

'You have done good task in Prieuré. Now you shall no longer be just Nott but Patriarch Nott, and you shall have a new name in Prieuré which shall be yours for evermore.' We were silent for a time, then he beckoned me. We got up and filed into the hot room. When we went into the steam room he made me sit by him, and himself flicked me with branches after the ordeal of steam. At dinner, I was put next to Dr Stjoernval, on Gurdjieff's right. During the toasting, when 'round' was proposed, he said to me, 'Now you no longer round idiot, what kind idiot I not know yet, but some other kind. As the blind man said, "We shall see". Now, tomorrow, I give you three bottles of armagnac. Doctor shall make you special Prieuré salad, and you take all the men and have party at your spring. Only men, no women. Understand?' I nodded.

That night I began to ponder about a 'new name', and I found in Revelation: 'To him that overcometh will I give to eat of the hidden manna, and I will give him a white stone, and in the stone a new name written, which no one knoweth save him that receiveth it.'

This is one of the mysteries of esoteric Christianity.

The next day, Sunday, in the evening, the men met at the water-hole with provisions for the picnic. After eating, and talking, someone, warmed by the armagnac, began to sing a Russian folk-song, one of those 'soul-tearing' songs from the depths of the Russian heart, about nothing in particular. Others then sang Greek, Armenian, and German folk-songs. I myself sang 'Through bushes and through briars'. Then Stjoernval, a big man with a beard, stood up, in his Russian blouse and trousers tucked in his boots, and sang in a fine deep voice which made the forest resound. This, I believe, was the only time he was heard to sing at the Prieuré. Gurdjieff purposely did not come; it was my party, but he smiled with approval next day when he heard about it.

Later, about the end of September, when the evenings were chilly, Gurdjieff came back from Paris, and just before supper-time sent word for Stjoernval, Hartmann, Salzmann, and myself to join him at the small round swimming pool which lay hidden from the windows at the far end of the sweep of lawn. He said, 'Now we undress.' We stripped. He went and sat on one of the steps that led into the pool, his legs in the water, and motioned for me to sit by him, the others sitting behind us. He joked a little, then moved down another step. He began to speak about the need for certain efforts to be made when a man has reached a stage in work on himself, a stage in an octave, and how necessary it is for him to make the effort. If he does so, he moves up to another octave, taking with him all that he has acquired. If the effort is not made he may slip back and what he has worked for may be lost. At first, this effort has to be made under the direction of a teacher; later, a man can himself know when effort has to be made, and can know how to make it. He said also that I had had a taste of super-effort. In this work the ordinary effort we make is by the way. Everyone, willy-nilly, has to make effort; Nature constrains us, as she constrains the salmon to leap the falls. A man must be able to *do*. Magic, real magic, is rooted in *doing*. We must make super-efforts. As we go on, the work becomes more difficult, but more strength comes. If you make conscious effort, Nature must pay, perhaps at once. It is a law.

'Next step,' he said, and we moved lower into the water. He now began to speak in Russian and talked for some time; of this I understood very little. And so, still lower, from one step to another, still talking until he and I were sitting up to our necks. It was cold. We began to shiver. At last Gurdjieff plunged in and swam round, we following. We dressed and went to his room and ate before a big log fire.

The next day Stjoernval asked me if I knew about Zen. 'A little,' I replied. 'Well,' he said, 'in the real schools of Zen the teacher often uses strange methods with his pupils to fix some teaching in them. Mr Gurdjieff's reason for yesterday evening was to impress on you what you had learnt about "doing".'

It had been a process of initiation, self-initiation. Gurdjieff had planned the steps in the task. And thanks to him I had accomplished it. He, like the gods in the mysteries, but with his own peculiar and effective ritual, had confirmed it. And I had been able to move to another octave of being and understanding.

From this time my relations with him and others were on another level.

POSTSCRIPT

AS FOR ORAGE'S RETURN to London and my association with him there; my subsequent association with Ouspensky in England, and in America during the war, and the renewal of my contact with Gurdjieff after the war—all this is another story. I will only add a few words about the question that is often asked, 'What was Gurdjieff's aim? What did he come to do?'

Possibly only Gurdjieff himself understood his great aim and foresaw the consequences of his work; and only two or three of those who worked with him from the first and never left him, understood some part of it.

Concerning the question 'What did he come to do?', I will quote a summary of talks with an old friend, F. S. Pinder, a man who was very near to Gurdjieff.

He said that Gurdjieff came to strike a big Doh, to help the upflow of the Law of Seven against the current of mechanical life. Always, with any teacher, in the process of his work a few earnest strivers are netted. But in any case the Law of Seven flows on, if only from the friction arising from the inevitably ensuing squabbles and differences—which needs must come, but woe to him, etc.

Gurdjieff came to give us a New World, a new idea of God, of the purpose of life, of sex, of war. But who are 'Us'? 'Us' are those who accept him and his teaching and help to carry out this work. This world of ours cannot be saved in our measure of time. Had it been possible it would have been 'saved' long ago by the prophets and teachers who have been sent. Those who look for the world to be saved by a single teacher in a given time are shirking their own responsibility. They wait in hope of a 'second coming' with no effort on their part—indulging in the disease of tomorrow.

'If take, then take,' says Gurdjieff. By working on ourselves we can 'take the ableness' to become Sons of God, the Christos, the Anointed or Messiah, where the anointing is by token of the higher body. But, having slid down so far, the way back is long and difficult, we have forgotten. 'The ox knoweth his owner, and the ass his master's crib. But my people do not consider. They have forsaken the living waters, and hewn themselves out broken cisterns.

We are what we are through our failure to do our own prison chores, so we have to tread the mill again and again. The treadmill is a good analogy, since it symbolizes the difficulties—the backslidings, the sighings, forgetfulness, self-reproachings, settlings-up, tomorrowings; but we can take heart, since we are not called upon to do anything that every particle of the Absolute—and Gurdjieff himself—has not had to do.

Although Gurdjieff tempered the wind to his shorn lambs—to each a chance according to his state of being and understanding—his shocks annoyed some. People think that a man can be taught in a real school as at a university; universities being now no more than re-formatory apparatuses for conventional science, art, and literature, whereas their original function was to teach the universals.

'The torn-off mask,' says Lucretius, 'lays bare the thing that is.' *Persona* means mask, and the idea comes from objective schools. Gurdjieff said: Kill our personality, the false personality, the false thing which we think is us. It has to die so that individuality may grow. To achieve his aim Gurdjieff, like all real teachers, had to play a role, playing at the same time several ancillary or sub-roles, working on himself for his own development. While spreading his teaching he had to adapt it to people of different levels of development. In a group at meal-times, for example, he used hyperbole, exaggeration, joking, seeming contradiction, saying something to one person while meaning it for another; which was bewildering to some, who often took him literally and made strange statements on what they had misunderstood.

Every man would like to have a 'better world', but according to his own ideas. The gangster's is that of more and better plunder; the communist wishes for the ant-like state, himself on top. The farther from reality the school of the world-betterer, or reformer, the more people will he attract, since he would leave everything to God, or the State, himself taking no responsibility. This is the opposite to 'accepting things' in Gurdjieff's sense, that is, in not fretting and worrying about what we cannot change. 'What can't be cured must be endured'.

The hymn says, 'When wilt Thou save the people, O God of Mercy, when?' As if it depended on God's whim. Only man can save himself; and God has given him every possible means and opportunity. We might as well ask a power-station to give us light and heat while withholding the fuel. The organized Church says that salvation is full and free, that man, to be saved, has only to 'believe and be good'.

When the waggoner appealed to Jupiter to get his waggon out of the mud, Jupiter said, 'First put your own shoulder to the wheel'.

Men cannot see that it is necessary first of all to do something about themselves; for thousands of years they have been trying to re-form each other. If a man would set about working on himself instead of praying to his far-off God to save the people, he would find that the kingdom of heaven is not indifferent to those who try. To see ourselves as we are—the old man—and to create the new man is the Way of the Cross, esoteric religion. The Way of the Cross was the way of all objective teachers. All have to go down to Egypt and all have to be crucified. As Sakra, lord of Gods, says to King Yudhisthira at the end of his life on earth, 'All kings must behold Hell'. They have to experience life in all its aspects, play the devil with the devil—that old adversary Shaitan. And the successful doing of this is Holy Firm, in contradistinction to being identified with the Negative force, which is Shaitan. Mechanical life, with its education, is very positive in this negative role. This chewing up is Trogoautoegocrat—I feed on myself, eat myself up, and so acquire 'I-Kracy', I-headship, power. Tria-Mazi-Kamno, with three together I do. Mazi or mazy, deriving from metaxy. Kamno, 'do', as against *kamno* in classical Greek meaning to 'toil and moil', to work and drudge laboriously, and only secondarily to 'do' in Gurdjieff's sense for which *poiein* and *prassein* had to be used. The mechanical stream of life was contrived and adapted by Dame Rhea Persephone Nature under necessity, who has left us in goloshes, not caring two hoots about any single one of us, concerned only with producing mass vibrations and so on. She, although on a higher level than we, took no pains to foresee. We are among her experiments. But the Everlasting has left us a remnant of which she could not deprive us. As Isaiah (1. 9) says, 'Except the Lord of hosts [that is, of heaven] had left us a very small remnant, we had been as Sodom and Gomorrah'. This has to do with Gurdjieff's particle in *Beelzebub's Tales*; but this particle, or remnant, is powerless to evolve by specific gravity when the proper being-effort is not directed towards it. Here, Dame Nature has to make an apologetic re-entry. She has been compelled by higher powers to keep

226

and make available to us certain organs otherwise than exclusively for her own use; she has had to bestow this possibility upon us as part of her payment to the powers above her. If she is not concerned with the individuals but only with the mass, it is the same with us, who show little care for the individual cells in our tissues, though we care very much about the health of the organism in general, sometimes losing parts of it for the good of the whole. As to the remnant, Perdita in *The Winter's Tale*, says: 'For I have heard it said that there is an art which in their piedness shares with great creating Nature'. Polixenes: 'Say there be, yet Nature is made better by no mean but Nature makes that mean; so, over that art which you say adds to Nature, is an art that Nature makes . . . We marry a gentler scion to the wildest stock and made conceive a bark of baser kind by bud of nobler race; this is an art which does mend Nature, change it rather, but the art itself is Nature.'

We have to do all the preliminary chores, however irksome and wearisome and time-absorbing; yet 'what we sow in tears we shall reap in joy'.

But we cannot begin to grow until we have formed the growing point, the moon, in ourselves. Our centre of gravity, along with that of the earth, is in the astronomical moon, and so we lack the counterpart in ourselves—since we must 'contain of everything one representing world'. The forming of the moon in us comes from the balancing of centres, from Being-Parktdolgduty, conscious labour and voluntary suffering; and the Five Strivings of Objective Morality.

The word 'lunatic' comes from objective schools; though it was long ago plain that men were moonstruck; and the word 'lunatic' is now used facetiously or for the obviously mad whose state is also ours, though in a less acute form. In the Greek myth, Selene the moon, who kissed Endymion to sleep, related to this. Endymion is derived from Endyma, a garment-wrapping, a body, a mere body-man, a being wrapped in a body.

'Moreover', says Isaiah (30. 26), 'the light of the moon shall be as the light of the sun, and the light of the sun shall be sevenfold, as the light of seven days, in the day that the Lord bindeth up the breach of his people, and healeth the stroke of their wound'. And again (60. 20): 'Thy sun shall no more go down, neither shall thy moon withdraw itself'. And Revelation (12. 1): 'A woman clothed with the sun, and the moon under her feet'. Ouspensky's pupils took this all too literally, or too poetically, or from one aspect—that the earth must become a sun and the moon an earth. The moon is an inductive coil, setting up induced

227

currents, sweeping up all wasted energy, lost, for us, by our mechanicality. Objective schools have known this, and about magnetism and electricity, from very ancient times; it has been left to the moderns—in the fever of industrialism brought about by teeming myrmidons, ants—to exploit them.

Gurdjieff spoke and wrote in a picture-form of speech, symbolical language, which is necessary for understanding, because words, being counters or characters of account, result in definitions, and definitions eventually freeze language, for when all is defined and determined it is lost, or leaves only a shallow impression on him who hears or uses the definitions.

'The Tao which can be expressed in words is not the Eternal Tao.'

Allegory forces one to ponder to get at the meaning. This is a principle in all objective methods and techniques.

There is no short cut to inner development. All teachers have spoken of this. Those who, having once taken up the work, leave it for a seemingly easier way, will, sooner or later, have to begin again.

Each of us has a duty. Each has a path to follow. Each has a task and must do it. Do I know what mine is?

Again, it comes back to man himself, the study of himself. Among the turmoil, the comings and goings of ordinary life, we cannot escape the constant wish, conscious or unconscious, to know, to be, to understand. 'If I ascend up into Heaven, Thou art there; if I make my bed in Sheol, Thou art there; If I take the wings of the morning, and dwell in the uttermost parts of the sea, Thy hand shall hold me.' 'I am fearfully and wonderfully made. My frame was not hidden from Thee when I was made in secret, and in Thy book were all my members written.' *Psalms.*

'The book in which all mysteries lie is man himself; for he himself is the book of the being of all beings, seeing that he is the similitude of God.' Jacob Boehme.

'I tell you, whosoever you be that wish to explore the depths of Nature, if what you seek is not found inside yourself you will never find it outside. O man, know thyself, for in thee is hidden the treasure of treasures.' *Isis Unveiled.*

'The Kingdom of God is within you. Seek therefore to know yourselves, and you shall know that you are in the city and that you are the city.' Jesus.

INDEX